Jung at Heart

Tools for Psychological Hygiene

Tess Harper-Molloy

Christine and John,
Wish best wishes,
Tess Harper-Molloy.

Cover Image
Photograph by Tess Harper-Molloy
of a woodblock carving from Nepal

Cover design by Aisling Publications
Typesetting, layout and design by Aisling Publications

Printed by KPW Print Management, Ballinasloe, Co. Galway.
The paper used in this book is 'carbon balanced', certified by the World
Land Trust, which contributes to the protection of critically endangered
tropical forests.

ISBN Paperback: 0-9534792-3-4

Published by Aisling Publications
a project of Aisling Árann
Mainistir, Inis Mór, Aran Islands,
County Galway, Ireland.
www.aislingpublications.com
www.aislingarann.ie
aismag@iol.ie

Aisling Publications

This book is dedicated to

Dara
earth to my sky

Our children
Tuán, Macha, Surnaí and Anú
my joy and delight

Clare
friend of many, many lifetimes

and to my parents
Clare and Robbie Harper
for loving me, no matter what.

We are alive when we feel alive,
and what makes us feel alive is the contact with that flow
of the unconscious psyche.
That's why dreams are so important.

Marie-Louise von Franz
The Way of the Dream

CONTENTS

Acknowledgements

Thirty-odd years ago Barbara Ó Flaherty of Dundalk bought and gifted me with the *COLLECTED WORKS of C.G. Jung*. The books (all twenty volumes) came from America to Aran in cardboard boxes and it was like opening a treasure chest. This treasure has sustained me for many years and continues to be my most prided possession. I am and always will be very grateful, Barbara. In 2008 I was awarded an MA from the Higher Education and Training Awards Council, Ireland, when I submitted a version of this book and other material. My thanks to Bernadette Flanagan and Pauline Logue for their generosity of time and skills which helped to make that happen. My thanks to Jerry Wright for reading the text and for his encouragement. And to Lisa Flynn for proofreading that version. Helmut and Irmtraud very kindly invested in printing some hard-covered A4 versions of the earlier text and gave me my first feel of the work in print. Thank you both.

And this time around:

I have been blessed by great friendship. I am forever grateful for Clare Donnelly who has saved me a fortune in the therapy that I never have had to take because of years of weekly, hour-long phone-calls. Darina O'Rourke also has faithfully companioned me in the twists and turns of life and Lisa Flynn has always been there when I needed her.

I am blessed by my children: Tuán, Macha, Surnaí and Anú. Their companionship, unique personalities, gifts and ever-increasing skills make me constantly proud. They have enriched my life immeasurably. I want to thank Surnaí for reading the text and for her encouragement.

And Dara. You have been my constant companion for so many years. I am eternally grateful for you. Thank you for reading this book, for your faith in it and in me, for your support and for your continued love.

Copyright Acknowledgements

Why Yet Another Book on Jung?

The Ninth Wave

I shall dream
a currach
of oak frame,
covered with stretched hides
of wolf and bear,
a wren at the helm.
And I shall set sail
for the ninth wave.
To wait
for the wild magic.
To endure the waiting, –
a life unfolding.

This book emerged organically. In 1986, when I came to live on Aran, I received a gift of *THE COLLECTED WORKS* of C.G.Jung. It was a life saver. For some years I lived in a very open house that invited people to experience a way of living that was increasingly self-sufficient and that was rooted in a spiritual ethos. From 1992 I worked with young people from all over the world as they explored self-sufficiency. In all these years I relied heavily on Jung's theories to make sense of the many living situations I was experiencing and of my own psyche in relation to them. By 2000 I had three young children under the age of three and when I managed to get a child minder for three hours, twice a week, Tuesday and Thursday mornings found me systematically revisiting *THE COLLECTED WORKS* of Jung and taking notes. As I took the notes this book took form.

I wanted to totally immerse myself in these concepts of Jung and the more I did, the more I confirmed what I had already experienced for years in a practical way – they were brilliant. Not only are they as relevant today as they were when he came up with them but they are also a set of practical tools that greatly enhance day to day life. Jung developed ideas that have become commonplace in our language: extraversion, introversion, projection, complexes, archetypes, shadow, animus, anima. Many of us are familiar with the terms but are not exactly clear what they mean and even less clear on how we could use them in our lives. A better understanding could only be helpful in exploring who we are and what our place in the world might be.

In 2008 I submitted a version of this book with some other material to HETAC (Higher Education and Awards Training, Ireland) and was granted an MA. At the Viva Voce interview I made it clear that I did not come at these ideas from a therapeutic point of view. I had no training whatsoever in therapy or counselling and in no way felt that this work, if ever published, could replace counselling or therapy where called for and did not carry the weight of a trained therapist. It was simply created by someone with a passion for the work of Jung, someone who uses these concepts and tools daily.

Now twelve years later my youngest and fourth child is sixteen and it feels right to take this out and offer it to anyone who might be interested.

I propose that Jung's way of naming various elements in the human psyche offers us valuable ways of perceiving our personal psychological hygiene and growth. Each concept I outline in this book can be used as a psychological tool, as a way of looking at, and the possibility of taking responsibility for, one's own psychological health and hygiene. *Jung at Heart* can be used as a manual, a workbook that elucidates key ideas of Jung and attempts to make them work for us. With this information people can have a better idea of what is going on in their lives, in themselves and in the people around them.

Psychological hygiene is a term that came to me as I worked with the ideas of Carl Jung. It is perhaps one of the predominant areas where this book can be useful.

Physical hygiene is about having clean hands while eating, having a shower or a bath regularly, changing one's clothes when they are dirty, brushing one's teeth. This is what we have all been taught since we were children. When physical hygiene is lacking it is more difficult for people to live and work together. But how many of us were taught psychological hygiene?

Psychological hygiene is when we know that it is better not to contaminate the atmosphere with our bad humour but rather to focus on what is wrong, to name it and to deal with it. The *Course in Miracles*[1] says that we are never upset for the reason we think. If I come home to my family and I find myself furious that the house is a mess, that the dishes have not been done and that everyone is off doing 'their own thing' I can behave like an antichrist and let off steam at everyone who is foolish enough to stay around or I can back off, leave the mess, find a quiet place and pay attention to what I am really feeling. There is a very good chance that I have unconsciously fallen into the 'poor me, I'm the only one who does anything around here' way of thinking, or 'I'm the only one who never gets to do my own thing'. If I can name this, the dishes become a simple, practical thing that can be addressed and the excess emotion can find its right level by finding its right cause.

Or, rather than hating someone or being irritated by them or even blaming them for making us feel bad, it is so much better if we look at what exactly they might be stirring up in ourselves and claiming it as our own and dealing consciously with it. This can happen often in our day-to-day experience. We find ourselves overreacting to a person who, in fact, we know little about. If we take a step back and observe our reactions we can find that they actually remind us of a sibling whom we have had issues with, or of a friend who has hurt us in the past. They can even remind us of an aspect of ourselves that we are not proud of or even consciously aware of.

In Jungian terms contaminating the atmosphere with our own ill humour, is called being caught in a negative complex. Disliking someone for the characteristics we ourselves have but are unaware of, is projection. I have spent years working on my psychological hygiene and have no illusions about the amount of work required and the amount of energy involved. Or even about how psychologically hygienic I am now. Yet it is a constant challenge for me to try to

---

1 *A Course in Miracles.* Page 83. Published by the Foundation for Inner Peace. (2007)

understand what is going on around me and in me and to determine what can be done about it. In that attempt to understand I have used Jung as my guide and offer this book as a guide for you.

We can be aware of psychological hygiene. We can work on it. It is better that we do as it does not necessarily happen automatically. Psychological growth, as opposed to psychological hygiene, on the other hand, does happen naturally, much as a child's body grows naturally. It is a given unless it becomes blocked and psychological growth can become blocked. When it is blocked one can become physically ill and sometimes mentally vulnerable. The blockage needs to be located. Jung offers us a map of the psyche that can help us to understand what may be happening. He speaks of a failure to adapt to the day-to-day demands of life and that this failure of adaptation causes psychic energy to dam up rather than flow outwards. It then begins to flow backwards/downwards into the unconscious and it stirs up or activates dormant complexes.[2] When psychological growth becomes blocked it is often important to access professional therapeutic help in order to address it. No information in any book can replace the safe container that a skilled therapist, in whatever therapy is appropriate for the case in hand, can provide.

This book does not attempt to address serious blockages in the psyche. Rather, it comes into play when all is well or reasonably well and we are, therefore, in a position to actually accelerate our psychological growth. We can do this by working on dreams, becoming conscious of habitual thinking patterns, of behavioural patterns, by naming one's shadow and holding it in consciousness, by understanding the energies that flow in us and through us.

---

2 See *COLLECTED WORKS*, Volume 4, paragraph 378-383. (*C.W.* Vol. 4, par 378-383). Jung speaks of the mountain climber who, rather than adapting to a situation, becomes infantile. See also page 29 of this work (*Jung at Heart*) where a woman shares a flat with friends and fails to acknowledge the complexes activated.

So it is in the area of psychological hygiene and of accelerating our psychological growth that the information in this book can be useful. Understanding the ideas that Jung developed gives us maps, tools and an understanding of how to go about these things.

This work consists of nine chapters. It starts by looking at the structure of the psyche. Complexes are the basic engines of the psyche. At the heart of every complex there is an archetype. Chapter One outlines the structure of the psyche as proposed by Jung and explores what complexes are and what an archetype is. It is by looking at complexes and archetypes that we can appreciate the different forces that flow through our lives. Only then can we hope to find a conscious way of relating to them. Chapter Two describes how psychic energy works. According to Jung psychic energy flows between various opposites. We can learn to understand the nature of psychic energy and thereby become more empowered in dealing with the ebb and flow of our own psychic energy.

Dreams are the messengers of the unconscious. It is by working with dreams that we can see our blind spots. For dreams show us our backs. Dreams show us where energy lies, where energy is blocked and where energy needs to go. Chapter Three looks at different types of dreams. Dreams have a language of their own and it is only by understanding this language that we can maximise their value to us. Chapters Four and Five deal with Jung's psychology of types: the attitude types and the function types. The attitude types consist of an introvert type and an extravert type. The function types are: thinking, feeling, sensation and intuition. Chapter Four looks at the introvert and extravert attitude types and at the role the inferior function plays in accessing the deep unconscious. Chapter Five looks at each of the functions.

Chapter Six takes a look at the pattern of psychic growth or what Jung calls the *process of individuation*. Jung often spoke of there being a natural gradient towards wholeness in the psyche. He tracked this developmental path and discovered that a person experiences various archetypes along the way. Often when one has grappled with a particular archetype in one's life the psyche can then present the next archetype. Chapters Seven, Eight and Nine explore one by one the first three major archetypes that we encounter on this path of individuation. These are Shadow, Animus and Anima. These are the archetypes that can bring us along our own path of individuation. They also are the archetypes that we need to embrace consciously in society today. By splitting off from our shadow we leave ourselves vulnerable to that shadow. It is only by facing the darkness that we can live fully and consciously. In these chapters we will see that animus can be understood as the archetype of meaning and anima as the archetype of life. These archetypes have enormous significance for us both personally in our individual psychological growth and collectively as a society. No book on Jung can finish without mentioning Self. Self is the orchestrating principle that has no opposite. I offer merely the briefest glimpse of Self in Chapter Ten. Its study involves a whole other enterprise.

Archetypes are morally neutral energies. They can be used for good or evil. It is our relationship with them that decides how they manifest in the world. Therefore, it is important to begin to understand how these archetypes affect our psyches. To understand archetypes we must first understand complexes, the engines of the psyche.

CHAPTER ONE

Complexes

The Engines of the Psyche

Árainn

The deepest truth I've found so far
is in the soil
and in the people who have memory
of hands caressing earth's curves,
challenging its rhythms to provide a living –
even if that memory is but a haunting dream.

On this island, storm battered, sky wrapped,
the stone walls stand in solitary worship,
silhouetted
against the winds,
as if to defy the doubters –
to cry that if the heart is real
the land is won.

No land of easy living and mild winters this,
not easily taken from rock, is food to feed the poor,
those poor who lost themselves to a wilderness –
whether born or travelled new – no matter.
It takes love to remain,
and love is in the very soil.

Complexes

The word complex is often used in conversation. We might say, 'watch out, she has a complex about that' or 'he has an enormous mother complex'. It is usually understood to mean 'an issue' – someone has an issue or a sore spot or a sensitivity around something. The consequences of the said issue being addressed are usually negative and to be avoided. Complexes, however, are neither positive or negative and we all have them. They are the basic nuts and bolts of the psyche. They are what make us tick.

Complexes are emotionally charged sets of ideas associated around a nucleus idea. The nucleus idea acts as a magnet to other ideas and when something happens or is said that triggers these ideas, the complex is triggered. This is a normal occurrence. It is how the psyche works.

Marie-Louise von Franz, who worked closely with Carl G. Jung, said that if one's complexes were not being activated one would be bored. If one did not have any complexes one would be dead! She also said that complexes are like a set of engines that whirl away all the time, keeping the psyche alive. She described them as the motors of the psyche giving it movement.[1]

In trying to grapple with what a complex is it is useful to look at what stirs us. Each human being is uniquely different and each will be stirred by something different. Similarly, we are bored by different things. We find ourselves stirred when one of our complexes has been touched upon. We find things dull when no complex in our psyche is activated. This might bring to mind hours in school trying to stay attentive in classes that you had no interest in and perhaps because of

---

1   Dr. Marie-Louise von Franz in conversation with Fraser Boa. Chapter 2, page 26, von Franz speaks of complexes. (1988) *The Way of the Dream.* Windrose Films Ltd., Toronto, Canada.

this, no aptitude in. If a subject does not awaken some complex in you it will awaken no interest and therefore no aptitude or motivation. However, on the positive side, it might also call to mind time when you avidly followed a lecture, a conversation or a person. Where you were held spell-bound and felt elated and excited. Whatever the activity, the degree of one's engagement shows just how much a complex is or is not activated.

If complexes are emotionally charged sets of ideas associated around a nucleus idea, what is the nucleus idea? It must be powerful if it can act as a magnet for the orbiting ideas in the complex. Without it these ideas would not come together. It is, therefore, not surprising that the nucleus idea at the heart of every complex is an archetype. I will speak of archetypes presently in more detail. For the moment it is enough to understand that archetypes are recurring motifs or dominant ideas in our experience as humans and therefore are powerful energetic entities in our psyches. It is the energy of the archetype that makes a complex cohesive.

We all have archetypes in common simply by being human. We have each been born of a mother and regardless of our relationship to our actual mother, we have a mother complex. Similarly, we have a father and thus a father complex. We have all been children and have a child complex and so forth. These and more archetypal energies are present in each and every human being's psyche. However, how the complex is constellated around each nucleus archetype is unique to every individual. The archetype acts as a magnet to associated ideas and these ideas are defined by strong emotional experience in the individual's life. The centre, or archetype becomes activated by an emotionally charged experience that attracts associated ideas that are emotionally charged and it holds these ideas in orbit around itself.

Imagine that a man has a nucleus idea that says 'nobody really loves me'. It is the archetype of the child in its abandoned state. This core idea has been activated in the man by a traumatic childhood experience of being rejected emotionally by his mother. Because of this complex, the man has a particular sensitivity in this area. Any situation where he is criticized or ignored, however mildly or unintentionally, can stir these original feelings of abandonment. The new feelings reinforce the old idea of 'nobody really loves me'. Over time a negative complex is established. This complex can become activated again and again by a whole range of triggers. Depending on the amount of energy in the complex; for example, if it is a complex that has tremendous energy then something small, a certain word, a dismissive hand movement, a particular tone can all trigger the person into the most awful mood. If the complex has less energy then it would take a more serious situation to trigger it – for example a person's partner leaving them or a fight with a close friend.

The common perception of a complex is that it is a negative phenomenon. This is not necessarily so. It is more accurate to say that most complexes are neutral and that if they are functioning without too much or too little energy in our lives they are simply doing what they do – keeping us engaged and alive. However, it is the complexes that are overactive, the ones that skew our lives slightly, these are the ones that draw our attention. These are the ones that tend to define us. Take, for example, a woman who loves her husband and children dearly, who is successful at her work – this woman has many complexes that are smoothly at play in a day. However, it may be her anxiety about her weight that defines her for herself. It is the haunting taunts she hears whenever anyone innocently mentions a weight-related issue. It is the constant searching for diets that preoccupies her. This complex is a key complex and it drains her energy and has her struggling daily. This is a food complex that all humans have but for this particular woman it has become negative and over-active.

It is interesting to note that a 'too-positive' complex can disrupt our lives as much as a 'too-negative' one. A man might have a complex where he wants to do good for other people. This complex can be healthy and can function well for the man. However, if he becomes obsessed with doing good for others it can become a negative complex. The excess energy he puts into doing good for others can have him neglect his own needs. It can lead to other destructive patterns in his life, for instance it can give rise to an unconscious resentment towards the people he is helping. Then, his 'too-positive' complex has become destructive.

It is worth looking closely at von Franz's analogy of complexes being like a set of engines whirling away all the time, keeping the psyche alive and giving it movement. Imagine that a group of engines are working away evenly and smoothly. They are all run off the same fuel source. If they each run evenly the fuel source is not overly challenged and they are not compromising each other. However, if one engine goes on overload, it firstly sucks a huge amount of energy to keep itself going and secondly, it can affect the work of the other engines. This is how one experiences an overactive complex.

How exactly is a complex formed? I have said that at the heart of every complex is an archetype and that every person will experience the archetypal energies within themselves differently. How they experience these energies will depend partly on their disposition and partly on their environment. A person's disposition is the result of their psychic past. Jung says, "Our present mental state depends upon our history".[2] He goes on to say:

---

2   *C. W.* Vol. 4, par 67.

> The events (in each person's past) which do not awaken any strong emotions have little influence on our thoughts or actions, whereas those which provoke strong emotional reactions are of great importance for our subsequent psychological development. These memories with a strong feeling-tone form complexes of associations which are not only long enduring but are very powerful and closely interlinked … Every emotion produces a more or less extensive complex of associations which I have called the "feeling-toned complex of ideas."[3]

Jung says that the nuclear element of a complex has two components: environmental and dispositional: "…first, a factor determined by experience and causally related to the environment; second, a factor innate in the individual's character and determined by his disposition".[4] An experience in one's life, and how one responds to that experience, combine to activate a nucleus idea which in turn has energy and attracts emotionally charged associated ideas. If as a child one was sent to live with relations for a period of time because of circumstances at home, for a temperamentally versatile personality this could be an exciting novel experience. For a different temperament this could be a traumatic experience of abandonment which could then give rise to a nucleus idea, which, according to the emotional intensity of the trauma, could then attract to itself all associated experiences in the same vein from then on. An abandonment complex has been established.

It is not the experience itself that creates a complex but rather the experience combined with the disposition of the person. Once the

---

3   ibid.
4   *C.W.* Vol. 8, par 18.

nucleus is activated, each ensuing experience will be attracted to that nucleus. That complex can then build upon itself and will in fact influence how the person will experience the world.

The same process applies on the positive side of things. If as a child one has had an emotionally charged experience of being profoundly loved, then a nucleus of being loved and being lovable will become activated. From then on all similar experiences will gravitate around this nucleus. It is so much easier to spot the negative complexes: victim complex, abandoned child complex, scapegoat complex, little princess/prince complex. It is more difficult to name the positive ones: leader complex, self-reliant complex, life is worth living complex, I'm loved complex. In reality the negative ones are the flip side of the positive ones and we can have a complex around any significant and emotionally charged experience, positive or negative. So everyone's collection of complexes is unique. The combination is unique and the energetic value of each one is unique.

Structure of the Psyche

Some complexes belong more to the *personal unconscious* and some to the *collective unconscious*, while some belong to both, for example Mother or Father complexes. In order to put complexes into some context I want to look at what consciousness is and what the unconscious is, what the personal is and what the collective is. The *ego* is the centre of *consciousness*. Consciousness is "the relation of psychic contents to the ego".[5] The things we experience immediately are the contents of consciousness. We experience them through the ego. The ego, in Jungian terms, "is a complex of ideas which constitutes the centre of my field of consciousness and appears to possess a high degree of continuity and identity".[6] The ego is one complex among

---

5   *C.W.* Vol. 6, par 700.
6   ibid., par 706.

the many complexes in the psyche and even though it is the centre of consciousness it is not the centre of the entire psyche. For there are many complexes that we are not conscious of at any given moment and some, perhaps, we never will be conscious of. The centre or the subject of the entire psyche is the Self.

According to Jung:

> 1. Consciousness possesses a threshold intensity which its contents must have attained, so that all elements that are too weak remain in the unconscious.
>
> 2. Consciousness, because of its directed functions, exercises an inhibition (which Freud calls censorship) on all incompatible material, with the result that it sinks into the unconscious.
>
> 3. Consciousness constitutes the momentary process of adaptation, whereas the unconscious contains not only all the forgotten material of the individual's own past, but all the inherited behaviour traces constituting the structure of the mind.[7]

Jung says elsewhere that: "The activity of consciousness represents, biologically speaking, the individual's struggle for psychological adaptation. Consciousness tries to adjust itself to the necessities of the moment … there are tasks ahead which the individual must overcome".[8] The 'definiteness' and 'directedness' of the conscious mind is something that has developed over time. Very early in humanity primitive peoples lived largely in the unconscious.[9]

---

7   *C.W.* Vol. 8, par 132.
8   *C.W.* Vol. 4, par 553.
9   'The original situation which is represented mythologically as the uroboros corresponds to the psychological stage in man's prehistory when the individual and the group, ego and unconscious, man and the world, were so indissolubly bound up with one another that the law of *participation mystique*, of unconscious identity,

Consciousness, therefore, is extremely important. It comes, however, with a particular disadvantage, if it is fair to even call it that. Consciousness by its very nature demands one-sidedness. It chooses a position and can only maintain that position by keeping all other possibilities out (or in the unconscious). The judgement that the consciousness makes is based on what is already experienced and known. It is these acts of judgement that determine one's conscious attitude and these same acts of judgement that determine what will remain in the unconscious because it is incompatible with that conscious attitude. What happens, once this one-sided conscious stance is established, is that a counter-position establishes itself in the unconscious. The counter-position in the unconscious compensates for the one-sidedness in consciousness. This is harmless once the conscious stance is not too one-sided. When the conscious stance is too one-sided then the energy level of the unconscious counter-position increases proportionately and can then break into consciousness. This often happens when it is of the utmost importance for the person to maintain that conscious position. So a young man, who has over-worked himself in his job trying to get to management level, gets a fit of the giggles at the crucial interview which will determine his position in the company.

Modern western society demands a high level of concentrated, directed conscious functioning. This involves a drastic split-off from the unconscious contents. No matter how effective this conscious position may be in the material world, it is only one-dimensional and cuts us off from the wealth of possibilities in the unconscious. It is perhaps the cause of the crisis in meaning that many people experience. The richness of the unconscious storehouse is not available to us and we dry up psychically. The danger in this is that an equally

---

prevailed between them.' Page 266. *The Origins and History of Consciousness*, Erich Neumann. (1970) Princeton University Press.

intense counter-position to the conscious one-sidedness is present in the unconscious, which will eventually break through. Because it is repressed, cut-off from consciousness, it will appear in negative form and may have a traumatic impact. Even though, in reality, it is like rain falling in a desert after a drought, it will be experienced as a disastrous flood.

Archetypes

The psyche is therefore made up of two parts. We have the *ego,* which is the subject of *consciousness* and we also have the *unconscious,* which is all that does not relate to the ego. Jung made a further distinction and differentiated between the personal unconscious and the collective unconscious. The *personal unconscious* contains four different categories:

> 1. Lost memories - "all those psychic contents which have been forgotten during the course of the individual's life. Traces of them are still preserved in the unconscious even if all conscious memory of them has been lost".[10]
>
> 2. Repressed ideas - "all psychic contents that are incompatible with the conscious attitude".[11]
>
> 3. Weak sense perceptions - "all subliminal impressions or perceptions which have too little energy to reach consciousness.[12]
>
> 4. Contents not yet ripe for consciousness - "To these we must add unconscious combinations of ideas that are still too feeble and too indistinct to cross over the threshold".[13]

---

10 *C.W.* Vol. 8, par 588.
11 ibid.
12 ibid
13 ibid.

The personal unconscious is personal to each individual, created out of our experience of the world and who we are in the world.

One of Jung's most outstanding discoveries was the naming of the *collective unconscious*. These are psychic contents that do not merely belong to one individual but to all of humankind. "[They] are not acquired during the individual's lifetime but are products of innate forms and instincts".[14] Jung speaks of these products as "inherited possibilities" rather than inherited ideas. These possibilities are inherited from our ancestors and are basically the "deposit of the psychic functioning of the whole human race".[15]

Jung looked to mythology to explore the collective unconscious. "The collective unconscious so far as we can say anything about it at all – appears to consist of mythological motifs or primordial images, for which reason the myths of all nations are its real exponents. In fact, the whole of mythology could be taken as a sort of projection of the collective unconscious".[16]

What creates a myth? In many myths we find a psychic parallel to daily physical occurrences. A beautiful example of this is that great myth where every single morning a divine hero is born from the sea and he climbs onto the chariot of the sun. In the West a Great Mother waits for him and she devours him in the evening. In the belly of this beast he travels the depths of the night sea and after a tremendous battle with this dragon/serpent he arises again victorious in the morning. The myth found in many cultures deals with the experience of the sun rising and setting every day and night. A psychic parallel for something experienced every day. Yet why not simply describe the sun rising and setting in actual terms, why the imagery? The cultures

---

14 *C.W.* Vol. 8, par 589.
15 ibid.
16 *C.W.* Vol. 8, par 325.

that produced this myth experienced the world very differently to how we experience the world. Where we see a definite and clear division between subject and object, these peoples experienced what has been termed by Levy-Bruhl *'participation mystique'*.[17] What is inner is outer and what is outer is inner. There was no hard and fast difference between the person and the world they were living in. Therefore, when the sun rose every morning the person experienced relief and felt delivered from the night and the fears and dangers therein. The experience of the Divine hero rescuing them from the Beast of the night was emotionally charged and deeply personal.

We have come so far from that today where, for most, the sun's rising and setting is a matter of no concern or comment. Yet, as the institutional churches are losing influence, more and more people are returning to the natural environment for symbols to nourish their souls. The symbol of hope that the sun signifies in its rising and setting and rising again every morning becomes something to draw on. The yearly cycle of the sun through the heavens, marked by the solstices and the equinoxes, are once again being celebrated by people. The shortest day in winter and longest night, which heralds the birth of the hero (Jesus in Christian terms), when the sun will once again rise in the sky and bring warmth and growth to the earth is something to celebrate. And so, having reduced everything to the rational, we are now ready and hungry once more for symbol and myth. Myth is the exponent of the collective unconscious; it is also that which nourishes us in our day-to-day living in the world, for without it our conscious mind becomes dry as dust.

Myth for the 'primitive mind', as Jung would term it,[18] was these people's way of explaining and grappling with the world they found

17 Jung refers to this in *C.W.* Vol. 8, par 329.
18 Jung speaks of his visit to East Africa to the Elgonyi tribe. He refers to 'the primitive mind' in *C.W.* Vol. 8, par 329.

themselves part of. It does not explain our world today for we now have science to do that. We cannot hope to return to that naiveté. Mythology does, however, reflect the psychological dynamics that take place in a person's life. We can still speak of the dark night of the soul, battling with our inner demons or rising victorious to battle again another day. Mythological language enables us to be lifted out of our small, personal world of suffering or happiness and be part of something bigger and truly enriching.

We can begin to understand how myth is created if we realise that when physical conditions are experienced such as hurricanes or storms, even the rising and setting of the sun, it is not the physical reality that leaves an image behind in our psyche. A fantasy is left behind that has been caused by the effects, or emotions, that the conditions experienced have aroused. Physiological conditions, hormones, glandular secretions and so forth, can also arouse images and fantasies, which are charged with emotion or affect. So, sexuality and hunger have created many gods and goddesses. Psychological conditions of the environment, for example dangerous situations, either dangerous to the mind or the soul, leave similar emotionally charged images behind them. These three sets of conditions, physical conditions in the environment, physiological conditions and psychological conditions, leave mythical traces behind them. When the situations repeat themselves over and over they give rise to archetypes, which are, what Jung has called, myth-motifs in general.[19]

The ordinary everyday events of life are eternally repeated. These therefore gave rise to the mightiest archetypes of all. Realities like mother, father, child, family and so forth all have mythological associations and are present, even with our scientific and rationalistic mentality, in the major religious motifs of our time. In the Christian

---

19 *C.W.* Vol. 8, par 334.

tradition, Father, Son and Holy Spirit are a family grouping, especially when we realise that the Holy Spirit in early Christian times was seen as Sophia which was thought of as feminine. Mother Mary later replaced the Holy Spirit as the feminine counterpart of the Sacred Family.

A complex needs a nucleus idea in order to exist. The archetypes are the providers of the nucleus ideas for they are the repeated daily experiences of all humanity. The nucleus of every complex is an archetypal image. The archetypes are a given in the psyche or a potential given. They are the universal patterns within the psyche.

A universal pattern, say fatherhood, becomes, over aeons, a motif in the collective unconscious. This motif has life and is an archetype. An archetype has a life of its own. This universal pattern of fatherhood is the god archetype. The Judaic and Christian father god is Yahweh. Every archetype has two sides, light and dark. (The only exception to this is the archetype of the Self.) The dark side of this god is his arch-enemy, Satan. The universal pattern of motherhood manifests as the archetype of the goddess, the dark side being the Bad Witch. "…The archetypes or dominants have crystallized out of the course of time. They are the ruling powers, the gods, the images of the dominant laws and principles and of typical, regularly occurring events in the soul's cycle of experience".[20] Jung adds as a footnote: "The archetypes may be regarded as the effect and deposit of experiences that have already taken place, but equally they appear as the factors which cause such experiences".[21]

In trying to understand the nature of an archetype it is helpful to think of the layers of an onion. At the core lies "the deposits of the constantly

---

20 *C.W.* Vol. 7, par 151.
21 *C.W.* Vol. 7, page 95, footnote 3.

repeated experiences of humanity".[22] Because this centre has been created over centuries it holds tremendous energy. It becomes the experience par excellence, in purified form, crystallized and zapped into life. It is indeed a god or goddess whom one cannot look in the face. Layered around this archetype are the ideas and associated contents of endless generations of humanity. Finally layered over all this is our own personal set of ideas sprung from our own experience of life and our own dispositions. The line between these last two is the line between the collective unconscious and the personal unconscious.

As with complexes, there are an immeasurable number of archetypes. An archetype is an inherited potentiality in the psyche of every human. It is like an empty air bag. It needs energy in order to be activated. Certain archetypes take centre stage according to the energy they receive from the collective – thus the Patriarchal Father God has in the Western world been very active at a societal level and at an individual level.

It is important to look at the relationship of the ego to the complexes in the psyche. The ego is itself a complex, but one which has a high degree of continuity. Its function is to allow us to be in the world in a consistent fashion. It is our interface with the world and is our centre of consciousness. It is how we consciously see ourselves. The ego consists of personae, which are masks that we put on, in order to function in different situations and roles. These personae are essential for a healthy functioning in the world though we can tend to become identified with them. This happens when we experience ourselves as nothing more than our role – mother, businessperson, priest, politician, or doctor. It also happens when we get caught into a way of being; always pleasant, always appearing serious, intelligent, or helpful. We then become one-dimensional. We need many personae in order to

---

22 *C.W.* Vol. 7, par 109.

deal with the many situations we experience in our lives. The ideal is that we use these personae but do not become identified with any one of them.

In a similar way we need to be careful not to become exclusively identified with the ego, since, even though it is the centre of consciousness, it is not the centre of the entire psyche. If the ego is subtle and strong then it can enable us to relate to the inner world of the unconscious to our great benefit. If it becomes rigid then the inner world will work to right the imbalance and this will be devastating for our rigid conscious ego. "For it is the function of consciousness not only to recognise and assimilate the external world through the gateway of the senses, but to translate into visible reality the world within us".[23]

The ego is the tool with which we consciously get to know the unconscious world. It safeguards our sanity. Its role is to keep us anchored and functioning in the outer world and, if it is strong, it will protect us from getting sucked into the unconscious world, though it will keep us in touch with it. Some people believe that one must be rid of the ego before one can experience enlightenment. However, rather than getting rid of the ego, it is perhaps preferable to allow the ego to be a strong container, to healthily interface both the inner and the outer worlds while realizing that it is not the centre of the psyche but merely the centre of consciousness. The role of the ego is central for sanity. Without a strong ego one becomes victim to the unconscious energies which can so easily inflate the ego and take over. If the ego knows its place in the bigger picture of the psyche it plays the role it is meant to play and does not need to be transcended for it claims no false centrality.

---

23 *C.W.* Vol. 8, par 342.

The ego is the centre of consciousness. In the unconscious there are many complexes which, if activated, will disturb our consciousness. This is how Jung discovered complexes in the first place. Complexes are not self-evident; they are for the most part unconscious. Sometimes they are unconscious because the conscious mind cannot integrate or deal with them; they are at odds with one's conscious attitude. Sometimes they do not have enough energy to cross the threshold into consciousness. Other times they have too much energy and can actually attract energy to themselves and therefore take energy from consciousness and leave a person lethargic. A complex may have a lot of energy in the unconscious and yet a person may remain unaware of it. They can feel the effect of the complex in the events of their life and not know why these things are happening to them. Finally, a complex may be so strong that it takes over consciousness and the person cannot see beyond it and does not realize that one is in it.

When a complex is unconscious it is difficult, for the above reasons, to become aware of it and to discover what it is about. In attempting to discover a complex what appears in consciousness are associations with words or with dream images that can seem to be random and irrelevant. Yet in pursuing these associations, one can discover a chain of associations which leads to the complex. This is how we track a complex. The associations are, in fact, far from random. Each is a mini sign or even a symbol of the complex.[24] To establish this Jung carried out what he called *association tests*. "Here we discover the remarkable fact that associations relating to feeling-toned complexes are much less easily remembered and are very frequently forgotten".[25]

These tests presented a person with a series of words to which they were to respond with the first thing that came into their minds.

---

24 *C.W.* Vol. 4, par 43.
25 ibid., par 211.

The responses were studied. On close inspection it was noted that the responses were not random. An unusual reaction indicated a constellated complex. For instance, a young man answers:

> TO DANCE with *NOT*
> ILL with *NOT*,
> DETEST with *RASCALS*
> and
> PITY with *NOT AT ALL.*"

Jung claims that more objective or ordinary connections would be:

> "TO DANCE : *music, dance-hall.*
> ILL : *disease, doctor.*
> DETEST : *respect, contempt.*
> PITY : *for the poor, compassion.*

The unusualness of this man's responses indicates that there were complexes at work here. The young man in question cannot dance and is extremely embarrassed by it. He also failed to win the heart of a young woman who is Jewish. The episode almost made him ill but he did not become seriously ill. He now detested the 'rascals' or the Jews because the woman was Jewish.[26]

In association tests the time of response was measured. Some responses were instant, others were quite delayed. The delayed responses were often in quite definite places. It was these responses which also pointed to the complexes. The complex was activated by the word and thus disturbed the train of consciousness. The instant responses were not the ones which revealed a complex since they presented ideas which were not at all disturbing to the consciousness of the person. Jung

---

26 ibid., par 741.

gives us the following example: A young man was given the following series of words, on the left column. His responses were recorded (the right column of words) and the time of his response:

head	hair	1.4 secs.
green	lawn	1.6
water	*deep*	5.0
to stab	knife	1.6
long	table	1.2
ship	*sinking*	3.4
to ask	to reply	1.6
wool	to knit	1.6
sulky	friendly	1.4
lake	*water*	4.0
ill	healthy	1.8
ink	black	1.2
to swim	*to be able to*	3.8[27]

It is clear that some words elicit a longer response. These are *water, ship, lake* and *to swim*. They have stimulated a complex. When the subject was asked about his hesitation in responding to these words it was learned that he had seriously thought of committing suicide by drowning in a moment of despair. In this case the subject could explain his hesitation but it is also possible to piece together the contents of a complex from these association tests without the cooperation of the subject (though in order to verify it one must have it confirmed by the subject).

Generally, one is not aware of one's complexes. Jung says of the complex that it "...behaves like an animated foreign body in the

---

27   *C.W.* Vol. 2, par 743.

sphere of consciousness"[28]. He goes on to describe their behaviour … "complexes behave like Descartes' devils and seem to delight in playing impish tricks. They slip just the wrong word into one's mouth, they make one forget the name of the person one is about to introduce, they cause a tickle in the throat just when the softest passage is being played on the piano at a concert, they make the tiptoeing latecomer trip over a chair with a resounding crash. They bid us congratulate the mourners at a burial instead of condoling with them … They are the actors in our dreams, whom we confront so powerlessly…".[29]

We all have experienced times when we have exclaimed: "I don't know what came over me". Or "I don't know why I said that". A complex has hijacked our conscious mind. If it is merely a slip of the tongue it is not too serious. If, however, it is a pattern of behaviour that becomes established every time there is a stimulus word or action, then it is more of a problem. This can be a pattern of positive or negative behavior. For example, every time a certain young woman sees a child crying she rushes over and does anything she can to help. She feels she simply must help the child. Another person may respond to a child crying simply because the child is crying. However, in this woman's case this, albeit helpful behavior, is in response to her own needs, it is not about the child. It is prompted by a complex, perhaps around her own neglect as a child and not by the actual child in the situation. She is being driven to behave in a certain way whether or not it is appropriate for her. On the surface it seems a noble action, yet it is driven by the person's own inner agenda and is therefore unrelated to the real situation. Perhaps this is what T.S. Eliot meant when he had Beckett in *Murder in the Cathedral* say: "To do the right thing for the wrong reason", that is the greatest treason.[30]

---

28 *C.W.* Vol. 8, par 201.
29 ibid., par 202.
30 In the first act of T.S.Eliot's *Murder in the Cathedral* Thomas à Becket returns to England from exile to confront his childhood friend, the king. As he is thinking of what

I have listened to a man become very angry and indignant when he heard that a couple was pregnant with another baby after their first child was only four months old. When challenged that the couple were happy about it and further that it was none of his business he admitted that there was just a year between himself and his younger brother and that his brother's birth had been very traumatic for him as a very young child. He was responding to his own history and not to these people's actual situation.

It is a common experience for someone to make what one might think was a harmless comment and to have a listener respond by exploding into tears or anger. A mother is changing her baby's nappy when the child resists and accidentally bangs his head. The father of the child jokingly teases saying "your mother is so cruel". The mother gets immediately upset and shouts at the father that that is such a hurtful thing to say. What the husband's teasing has triggered is a complex which nags at the woman telling her that she is a bad mother, that she is not good enough and that she secretly wants to harm her child. The woman feels depressed and deflated after this encounter. She has, in fact, tripped into the dark side of the Mother complex. This archetype is lying at the heart of her own complex around mothering, which had built up over the years from her ideas and associations. The woman feels unsure of herself as a mother as she did not have a good relationship with her own mother. She is vulnerable to the negative side of the Mother complex which can manifest in the unconscious as the Bad Witch archetype or even the Devouring Mother.[31] She needs to

---

he is to say to the king he is visited by three tempters. The first temptation was to be loyal to the king for the sake of their friendship. The second was to be loyal because of the temporal power he would gain. The third was to oppose the king and win sainthood. Becket's response is this: "The last temptation is the greatest treason/ To do the right thing for the wrong reason".

31 Marion Woodman throughout her books *The Pregnant Virgin*, (1985) Inner City Books, Toronto, Canada and *The Ravaged Bridegroom*, (1990) Inner City Books, Toronto, Canada, refers to the witch archetype. Marie-Louise von Franz also speaks of it in *Shadow and Evil in Fairytales*, (1974) Spring Publications Inc., Dallas, Texas.

steadily build up a strong positive ego picture of herself as a mother so that she can withstand the influence of the negative side of the archetype.

Much of our conscious behaviour is influenced by our unconscious complexes. Jung writes about when a complex interferes with a discussion: "The discussion loses its objective character and it's real purpose, since the constellated complexes frustrate the intentions of the speakers and may even put answers into their mouths which they no longer remember afterwards".[32] Some of our behaviour is actually driven by our complexes. Jung explains: "The complex must therefore be a psychic factor which, in terms of energy, possesses a value, that sometimes exceeds that of our conscious intentions … An active complex puts us momentarily under a state of duress, of compulsive thinking and acting…"[33]

A woman was sharing a flat with two other people, a man and a woman. Initially they were all getting along fine. The others, however, had busy lives and were occupied with their work most of the time. The woman had more free time and had certain high expectations of friendship. She became disillusioned with the arrangement but did not address it consciously. The woman became ill and had to go to hospital. Her flat mates made phone calls to the hospital but did not visit, partly because of their workload but also because the hospital was very far from their home and the illness was not serious. They did, however, stay in touch with their friend. Once out of the hospital the woman went on holidays, not returning to the flat. When the holiday was over she returned to the flat, careful to choose a time when the others were not there and she removed all her things from the flat. She left no note. The others returned to find her room empty and

---

32 *C.W.* Vol. 8, par 199.
33 ibid., par 200.

everything belonging to her gone. When they contacted the woman, she said she could not speak to them, that she had no concrete reason for doing what she did other than that they had hurt her deeply. She could not say how they had hurt her. The other people in the flat were left feeling confused and angry.

The woman was driven to act by a complex, which over time was becoming more and more stimulated. She did not address her feelings consciously. In Jungian terms, she did not adapt well to the situation and the energy that should have gone into addressing the situation went underground. It then fed her complex, which had to do with an infantile dependency on others (her expectations of friendship). She had, in fact, unconsciously projected her parents onto the two people and once she was in this complex she was a child expecting that they should mind her. These were unreasonable demands to put on her friends yet she was unconscious of them. When they did not fulfill her unconscious demands she was driven to cut her friends off. Still within her complex she felt wronged, self-righteous and hurt.

If a complex remains in the unconscious it takes on a compulsive character. The further it is from consciousness the more compulsive it is. Jung says that complexes "… assume by self-amplification, an archaic and mythological character and hence a certain numinosity… Numinosity, however, is wholly outside conscious volition, for it transports the subject into a state of rapture, which is a state of will-less surrender".[34]

In the case of the woman, she was in a state of "will-less surrender", her rational conscious judgment was suspended and she felt certain that reality was as she perceived it. Yet she was seeing things from the perspective of a complex. She was in the complex. The certainty

---

34 ibid., par 383.

one feels from within a complex is overwhelming. People have done amazing deeds from the centre of their complexes, both good and bad. The selflessness of some people, doctors, for instance, can be fueled by a complex, which, if deeply unconscious, has at its centre the archetype of The Healer, or The Shaman. Their work can feel numinous and their actions can take on mythological proportions. The potential danger for them is that their ego gets cast aside. They lose their individuality and become inflated by the archetype. They can burn out and/or can become physically ill. The illness is an attempt by their bodies to call them home to themselves. They are humans who are trying to live as gods/goddesses. A mere human cannot survive being inflated by an archetype for any length of time without damage to the ego. There is a right relationship that can be reached between the ego and the archetypes and this is what must be attempted.

The complex, if made conscious, can be corrected and transformed. Jung says, "They slough off their mythological envelope, and, by entering into the adaptive process going forward in consciousness, they personalise and rationalise themselves to the point where a dialectical discussion becomes possible".[35] This way we can benefit from the potent energy at the heart of our complex without being driven by it or burnt alive by it.

Making a complex conscious is no easy task. It is an heroic task, which requires huge amounts of energy and a very strong ego. To make a complex conscious one must, as it were, walk around the Walls of Jericho. This is a wonderful image.[36] The idea is to walk around the

---

35 ibid., par 384.
36 The Walls of Jericho refers to the story in the Old Testament (Joshua 6: 16) when the Israelites, on the way to Canaan, have to travel through the city of Jericho. The people of Jericho hated the Israelites and when they saw them coming they closed the city gates against them. Joshua, who was leading the Israelites was told by God to order the priests to carry the Ark of the Covenant, a wooden chest, around the outside of the city walls. They were to be followed by Joshua and the Israelite

walls of the complex for as much time as it takes, until the effect of the complex on a person is weakened. If a complex has taken over consciousness then the ego has lost its centrality – the complex has you. Something from the unconscious is in the driving seat. The strength of the complex, that is, how much energy it has, will determine how serious the take-over will be. The task at hand is to discover the parameters of the complex and to walk around it until it disengages. Then the steering wheel is back in the hands of the ego and you can become conscious of the complex. This is walking around the Walls of Jericho.

The most important thing is to recognise when we are actually in an activated complex. In doing this we are working against the energy of the complex. This is not easy. It is, in fact, very difficult to acknowledge a complex when we are in it. We feel that it is reality, that how we are seeing and experiencing things is exactly right and that we are working against ourselves if we try to see another perspective. We are not working against ourselves we are working against the complex, which has at its centre an archetype, with which we have become identified.

If we wish to succeed in separating out from a complex that has us in its grip we have to become aware of what triggers it and what is our pattern of behaviour once we have become triggered. We must become observant of our behaviour and especially of repeated patterns of behaviour. When caught in that pattern of behaviour we must try to resist playing it out. We must battle the inclination to think a certain way and to act a certain way. Finally, we must hold this tension in the blind faith that something will shift. And something usually does. The

---

army. This procession marched round and round the walls of Jericho in silence for six days. On the seventh day the priests alone marched around seven more times. They blew sacred trumpets and as they blew the walls of Jericho crumbled and fell down. This image was brought to my attention by Cully Ó Muirí.

ego re-establishes itself and has a new perspective on the complex that has been activated. Every time we manage to do this the ego is strengthened, every time we fail, the ego is damaged.

A woman wants her partner to do something. Rather than saying it to him directly she drops vague hints and gets more and more angry that he is not picking up on it. She goes into a black humour and her inner voices start up – "he doesn't care about me". These voices are joined by another chorus that say "he doesn't love me". Driven by these voices she attacks her partner saying he does not love her. She now needs him not only to do the thing she has not overtly asked him to do but now she also needs him to reassert his love for her. She is frantic. Unless her partner is remarkably mature and can withstand her assault, which is driven by her unconscious complexes, his unconscious material gets activated in response. Shadow will call to shadow without fail. They have a blazing row. The pattern has run its course. Both are left feeling deflated and damaged.

What has happened is that the woman has avoided directly asking her partner for something. This could be because of an idealized notion that if her partner really loved her he should know her every need. Therefore she could be working out of a complex about romantic love. Or it could spring from a complex around feeling guilty about having needs at all and deflecting the responsibility for her needs onto her partner. It could, in fact, be because of any number of complexes activated. The relevant point is that the energy that should have gone into dealing with the situation is blocked and it goes into the unconscious where it activates these complexes and lends them tremendous power. They then become the driving forces of her thoughts and behaviour. If her partner, when attacked, could adapt to the situation ideally, he would keep his own energy conscious and challenge her position calmly. However, this is very difficult to do, and like most of us, when attacked, our energy goes into the unconscious and our own complexes get constellated.

If the woman can get her head above water for even an instant she can see that a complex has her. Then she can acknowledge that this is a pattern that happens each time she wants her partner to do something for her. If she can hold back from acting out of the negative voices, if she can hold that tension between her ego and the voices, then she is walking around the walls of Jericho. Around and around she walks, plodding on, marking the limit of the complex. She has moved from inside the complex to outside. And in doing so she has re-established her ego-position and has de-powered the complex. She would be wise to stay well clear of her partner while doing this. This is not about him at all. Holding this new position takes tremendous discipline. The battle to withstand an activated complex is not to be underestimated. If the complex is a serious one then all the energy it holds is working against the ego-position.

When a person disengages the complex from interfering with consciousness there is a surplus of energy available to him or her. The energy that was draining the consciousness is now freed up. This surplus of energy will find its own level in the unconscious. It will find the archetype at the centre of the complex and the positive side of the archetype becomes available to the conscious mind. Therefore, the value of doing the work of walking around the walls of Jericho is two-fold. The ego is strengthened and the positive energy of the archetype at the heart of the complex is available to the conscious mind.

It is an interesting consideration – are we ever upset about what we think we are upset about? When we are disturbed it is always valuable to reflect on what has disturbed us. Has an actual incident upset us or has the incident triggered some complex in our unconscious? If it has it is our responsibility, in the name of psychological hygiene, to track that complex and to walk around it enough times to disengage it and to make it conscious.

How Deep Do You Go?

Jung opens up the possibility of a new paradigm concerning the relationship of the conscious mind to the unconscious. In the past, mystics and mad people were seen to enter the world of the unconscious. They experienced a type of ecstasy, a free-fall into the unknown. They upped their anchors and set sail into the vast ocean. Those that came back to the real world and related their experiences of dark nights of the soul or their ecstasies were called saints, those that got lost in that world were considered mad. It was an 'all-or-nothing' paradigm. When people came under the influences of the archetypes they tended to lose their hold on their ego-reality. They were lost and when they returned, if they returned, they brought back countless riches from this otherworld.

Mythology all over the world is rife with images of this journey. Jesus was forty days in the desert where he battled the devil. Francis of Assisi fell ill on his way to battle and experienced a kind of madness that was to change his life entirely.[37] In Celtic mythology the fairy world was the land of the Tuatha de Danann, a magical early race in Ireland.[38] When the Milesians came to Ireland and fought the Tuatha de Danann, the struggle became locked in a stalemate. To resolve the issue the Tuatha de Danann used their great magic to create a world below the known world. There they lived, and still live, in great palaces in a magical land full of wonder where time moves slowly and people

---

[37] For a beautiful telling of the story of Saint Francis go to: *Francis, The Journey and the Dream* by Murray Bodo, (1972) St. Anthony Messenger Press, Cincinnati, Ohio, U.S.A.

[38] One version of this story is told in Charles Squire, (2001) *Celtic Myths and Legends*, Parragon, Bath, England. Chapter 10, page 119.

do not age. This, in Celtic lore, is known as the Otherworld. There are thresholds to the Otherworld all over the landscape – fairy rings and fairy forts. There are certain threshold times as well as threshold places. The threshold times are liminal times, in-between times. They include the mystical time just before the dawn, and the time of dusk. Halloween is a liminal time where the people of the Otherworld can come into this world and we can cross over there also.

This Otherworld mythology indicated the unconscious world. There are many stories where people experienced the Otherworld but always at the expense of their lives in this world. In other words, at the expense of their ego-consciousness. Cú Chulainn follows the fairy woman Fand into the Otherworld and when he returns his wife Emer asks a druid to give him a drink to erase his memory of the place as he keeps getting pulled back there. Óisín lands in Tír na nÓg and hundreds of years go by until when he finally returns home everyone he once knew was long dead.

In these myths and in the stories of various religious traditions, the emphasis is on the experience in the unconscious where the person loses connection to this world. However, when we look at Jung's work, we can see that he points to a new paradigm which allows for the possibility of the ego being flexible enough to withstand the unconscious by not becoming identified with it and on the ego having the ability to stay conscious as this experience takes place. This is something we can practice in the smaller events in our daily lives. By becoming aware of our complexes and the archetypes at the heart of these complexes we can get a sense of when we are, literally, 'getting carried away' by the unconscious complex. Once we are aware of what is happening and why, we are then in a position to address what may be driving us. We make it conscious.

Consciousness, as we know it, is a relatively recent development in the evolution of humankind.[39] Early humans had a blurred sense of what separated them from their environment and from their unconscious visions. The consciousness that we now have is highly individuated. It is refined and capable of tremendous differentiation. We are still collective creatures, however the freedom to act, think and exist independently of the collective is evident. Also, as a species we have developed and refined consciousness by advancements in science, physics, psychology, technology and in all the various intellectual fields. The vulnerability of our sophisticated consciousness lies, however, in its one sidedness. We have gained it at a terrible cost. The cost is the dramatic split that exists in our modern Western culture between consciousness and the unconscious world. The one-sidedness of consciousness becomes dangerous for two reasons. Firstly, the conscious mind can dry up and become a shell, cut off from the compensatory balancing mechanism and therefore the richness of the unconscious. Secondly, the unconscious can constellate monstrous energies which are the exact counter-balance of the conscious mind and these energies may appear as monsters, which could devour the consciousness gained.

The outer reflects the inner. The one-sidedness of consciousness has led to a driven and frenetic achievement-orientated culture and in this one-sidedness we have become cut-off from the earth, from our bodies, from nature and from the unconscious. We are experiencing a sense of disconnectedness and meaninglessness. The planet also is responding with climatic changes and global warming.

Whatever the cost of achieving this differentiated consciousness the point is, we now have it at our disposal. If we can learn to use it to its

---

39 Cf. *The Origins and History of Consciousness*, Erich Neumann. (1970) Princeton University Press.

fullest, we may save the day. The image is this - how deep do you go? How flexible can the ego be?

The idea that one needs to be rid of the ego before one can experience the Divine, or the Other, is not appropriate here. The ego, much like the physical body if it is to be fully functional and fit, needs to know its limits and know its strengths. The first thing is an attitude of humility in the face of otherness. If the ego can accept that it is not the centre of everything then it is in a healthy state. It is the centre of what is known. There is, however, a whole realm that is not known to the ego, the centre of which is the Self. The Self is the centre of the entire psyche, including the ego. If the ego can allow for the centrality of the Self it will not become inflated and can be what it is meant to be – a strong and flexible container for consciousness. It is the role of the ego, on the one hand, to function in the known world. On the other, it is its role to hold its ground while the unknown communicates with it without becoming inflated or dismissive.

If the ego can hold its own in the face of the unconscious, then it goes deep. If it cannot, then it is like a leaf being blown by the winds of the unconscious forces. The ideal is like a tree. The trunk remains in this world, solid and real. The roots can reach down into the depths, gaining nourishment from the unconscious world, allowing that true centrality is in the Self. Yet the trunk must never be undermined if the tree is to survive. The branches reach up to the heavens.

I often wonder when the within becomes the without. The roots of the tree reach forever downwards and the branches forever upwards. Both are connecting with the same realities, one in the inner world, the other in the outer world. The roots connect with the unconscious world within the psyche, the branches connect with the outer-world reality, which includes the material world. But in true Irish fashion I sense that behind or within this material world are fairies and angels and spirits. The outer world reality echoes the unconscious world and is, in turn, magical.

The trunk is the part that holds it all together. Without a solid trunk the tree is lost, it will not survive. Yet, continuing with the imagery of the tree, it is best if the ego is like the tree that can bend in the wind. If the archetypal energies rip through the ego, a too-rigid ego will break with the strain. This is the paradox; the ego must be strong yet yielding. It must be sure of itself and yet humble in the face of the unknown.

A new paradigm can be – that the ego can stay conscious and still encounter the energies in the unconscious. Jung called this the transcendent function.[40] One does not let go of the ego-consciousness and then dive into the unconscious energies to emerge again into consciousness with a jewel from the unconscious. Rather, the ego holds its conscious position and at the same time allows the unconscious material to enter consciousness even though it may be at complete odds with what the conscious position is. In holding these two contrary energies together in consciousness, the battle with the beast of Otherness goes on in daylight. What happens is transformative and wonderful. A symbol appears from the unconscious depths which somehow broadens and transforms the conscious attitude so that these contrary forces are not contrary any more. They become something else entirely. This transcendent function I will speak of later. What I want to emphasise here is the vital role of the ego in this process and how important it is that the ego be well tuned and healthy. It must do the work of walking around the complexes that will influence it. It must know that it can withstand the energies of the archetypes that

---

40 Jung defines the transcendent function in *C.W.* Vol. 6, par 828. He also speaks of it, among many other places, in *C.W.* Vol. 7, par 184-186.

can flood it. It is the instrument of human salvation if it can keep its balance, if it can be poised, agile and lithe, between the worlds.

Collective Complexes in the Outer World

Complexes that exist in the unconscious play a very active role in the outer world collectively, not just in our personal lives. If a complex is held collectively it can gather tremendous power. A person has a complex in their unconscious psyche around their family. But their family is a collective entity in the material world and each member of the family has a complex around the idea of family. Thus, a collective energy is constellated. A complex is established from the core idea of being a family and each emotionally charged experience of that family feeds into this complex. The members of the family are influenced by this collective entity of family, which over the years has gathered quite an amount of energy.

We have all experienced the power that this collective family complex exerts on us within a family. It is at its most obvious when a person goes against its energy. I attended a wedding recently where only one member of the groom's immediate family was present. He had seven other siblings. They stayed away because he had made a career choice that his mother seriously objected to. Only one sibling was free enough of the family complex (and mother complex thrown in) to support her 'errant' brother. Not surprising was the fact that she was the one member of the family who lived in another country.

If we remain unconscious of the forces that influence our lives we are being driven by those forces. It is often a crisis that is our wake-up call. Members of a family can carry on, oblivious to the collective influence of the family complex that is guiding their lives, until they, or someone else within the family, step out of line. The comfort zone has been transgressed and a lot of energy is usually exerted to attempt to reestablish it. Failing that, the family can shift position and integrate this new development or it can cut off the 'errant' member. Unfortunately for many, the latter is often the path chosen.

In the story of Abraham in the Bible, it is significant that Abraham was told to leave everything, his family and home country, in order to follow the will of his god.[41] Similarly, Jesus speaks of not coming to bring peace but rather strife, to put son against father and daughter against mother.[42] The family complex, like all other complexes, needs to be 'walked around' if one is to find one's own true path. If we continue to live blindly within the family complex, we may be numbing ourselves to calls from our deeper soul. We may be. It is not necessarily so. It is possible that a family complex can support one's own true path. However, one is more in control if one becomes conscious of it, knowing what forces influence one's perception and decisions.

The Roman Catholic Church as a Complex
In Ireland up until recently, discovering and announcing that one is homosexual was one tried and tested way to shake the family complex. Another was leaving the Roman Catholic priesthood. There were many more. The latter one, leaving the Roman Catholic priesthood leads us to another major collective complex in Ireland, although not exclusively in this country. This is the complex of the Roman Catholic Church. Because of Ireland's unique history, Roman Catholicism is a very powerful complex in this country. This is rapidly becoming less so as more and more people are detaching themselves from it. Until recently the majority of Irish people were Roman Catholic and were living within a bubble that they were not altogether aware of. That bubble was the Catholic complex.[43] As with any other complexes the

41 *The Jerusalem* Bible (1968) Eyre and Spottis Woode Ltd., London. Genesis 12: 1-4.
42 Ibid., Luke 12: 51-54
43 For an insightful exploration of the time when Ireland had a unique Christian

overwhelming experience was that there was no reality outside the bubble. It was the entire world. This allows for doctrines like "outside the Church there is no salvation"[44] to be considered acceptable.

The existence of the Roman Catholic Church is not the issue here, nor the fact that people were and still are members of it. The phenomenon I am pointing out is that, because of the collective participation in the Catholic Church over the centuries in Ireland, an enormous complex has been at play. This complex has held tremendous energy. It has exerted its power and influence over each person's psyche, unconsciously. For example, often people who left the Church themselves because they could not accept its teachings, had their children baptised and receive First Communion and so forth in that same Church. Some were caught in the complex that says there is no spiritual life outside of this so, even if they do not agree with it, there is nothing else for their children. It is only fair to say that others were caught by the fact that until relatively recently in Ireland most of the schools were run by the Catholic Church. Religious instruction was automatic and was exclusively Catholic. Even if a person stepped out of the Church complex its influence in the culture was everywhere.

Within the Church complex are many archetypes (which implies that there are associated complexes clustered together to form a major one). The Father archetype is the key one. This leads to patriarchy. The Mother archetype is in there, albeit diluted down and under cover. She is seen in Mother Church, and in Mother Mary. The Family archetype

spirituality, one that had been grafted onto the earlier pagan faith and of how the Roman Church established itself in its stead see: *The Globalisation of God, Celtic Christianity's Nemesis* by Dara Molloy. Published by Aisling Publications. 2009.

44The Latin phrase *Extra Ecclesiam nulla salus est* meaning: 'Outside the Church there is no salvation', is a dogma of the Roman Catholic Church, defined in the form, "it is absolutely necessary for the salvation of every human creature to be subject to the Roman Pontiff", in Pope Boniface VIII's 1302 bull *Unam Sanctam*. It also appears in the profession of faith of the Fourth Lateran Council, "One, moreover, is the universal church of the faithful, outside of which no one at all is saved".

is present - in Father, Son and Holy Spirit and also in Jesus, Mary and Joseph. The Shaman archetype is there in the role of the priest who is the only one, chosen and consecrated, who can administer the sacraments. The priest's role also has a touch of the Saviour complex in it. Little wonder some families were devastated when their sons decided to leave the priesthood and thereby shed the projections of the collective. When all of these archetypes, and there are perhaps more, are taken into account it is also little wonder that the Church has had such an influence on people's thinking and behaviour.

Stepping out of a major collective complex like this leaves a person in a new landscape psychologically. The entire balance in the psyche shifts. In this different place, new realisations can click into place and new possibilities appear. Old doctrines like 'original sin', which inspire no trust in life or in human goodness, can look strangely suspicious. The notion that the Divine is solely male can appear unlikely. Patriarchal, institutional constructs whose sole purpose are most probably to have been to keep power within the institution can be seen for what they are.

As the years have passed, in Ireland, it has become obvious that more and more people are stepping out of the Catholic Church complex. People are beginning to mark threshold moments in a their own lives and in the lives of their children. They are beginning to independently create rituals with their families and friends and in their immediate communities. This behaviour is bound to catapult people, who are deeply immersed in this complex, out of their comfort zones. To those within the complex these actions are utterly unacceptable. Jesus had the same problem. His thinking was so far outside the Judaic complex of the time that they crucified him.

This is not to say that a person can be a Catholic without being unconsciously caught in a collective Catholic complex. What is clear is that until Ireland can separate out, as it is slowly doing, state from religion and religion from schools many who are Catholic will be Catholic not by conscious choice and thought-out consideration but because it is all about them, in the air, as it were and they cannot see beyond it. The influx of other cultures with other religions into Ireland is helping in this differentiation.

It takes a long time to 'walk around the walls' of such a major collective complex – to track the various influences and thinking that comes from being within the complex. It is especially difficult when practically the entire country has been within the same complex, as is the case in Ireland. Some remarkable people in the past have done it. James Joyce and Noel Brown come to mind. There are many others, voices in the wilderness exposing the collective belief-system. Some Irish people, James Joyce and Samuel Beckett for example, had to leave in order to be free of the collective complexes of the country.

When one has 'walked around the walls' of the Church complex, the world widens out. Not only is there salvation, and plenty of it, outside the Church, but there is also a rich diversity of thinking, all of which is reasonable and acceptable. Once outside a complex, the world becomes enlarged and perspective becomes multi-dimensional.

We are experiencing a huge shift in Western society where institutions that have held undisputable power for centuries are beginning to show serious cracks. It is not only the churches. During the years from 2000 to today people in Ireland have experienced crisis after crisis in many of our major institutions. For the Church, child abuse scandals, political scandals and the banking scandal and economic collapse are the major ones. It is hard to know what is ahead of us in collective terms but the old is passing away.

To understand our behaviour it is essential to understand the workings of complexes. We all have complexes. They are the basic working mechanisms of the psyche. They are the engines of the psyche. Without them we would not function. However certain complexes can become over-active and can begin to dominate in our psyches. Until we can get a clear sense of what our complexes are and how they work we are at the mercy of them. For better or for worse, our reactions to situations and the choices we make are defined by these complexes. At the heart of each complex there is an archetype. It is the archetypes that are the driving forces behind our behaviour and our choices. Yet we are not necessarily victim to these forces. We can choose our relationship to them. However, to do so, we must work on becoming conscious of why we do what we do.

Having looked at complexes, archetypes, the personal conscious and the personal and collective unconscious, the next major concept to explore is psychic energy. Without psychic energy everything would come to a halt in the psyche. While complexes are the engines of the psyche, psychic energy is the fuel that moves between one to the other to keep the whole psyche alive and operating.

CHAPTER TWO

Psychic Energy

The Fuel of the Psyche

Soul Peace

I know a woman
who has chosen
to surround herself with beauty
so that her soul
can find peace in the world.

I am surrounded by
tight spaces and clutter
and beautiful children
who create an endless chaos

and my soul's peace
is wrought,
as a diamond is,
from enduring extreme
pressure.

I want to look at psychic energy. What is it? Where does it come from? Where does it go when we feel completely exhausted, not from physical exertion but from psychological pressures? How can some people have such seemingly bottomless fonts of energy and others struggle along with tiredness dragging at their heels the whole time? I do not say I can answer all these questions but they are the ones that urge me to look at psychic energy and what has been said about it.

Energy in two different people can run in very different ways. Two people studying for an exam: One for the first week gears herself up and gives it her all. At the weekend she hits a major slump and is fit for nothing. Yet by the time of the next exam she is geared up again. This is her personality and her pattern. The other sets a dogged and steady pace for herself throughout her study time and when the exam time comes she continues at that consistent pace until the end. Both of these two women experience the tide of psychic energy differently. One experiences sporadic, intense spurts of energy and then a dramatic withdrawal of it. The other's experience is less extreme and easier on her system.

There is a story in Clarissa Pinkola Estés' book *Women Who Run With the Wolves*.[1] The story is called 'The Three Gold Hairs'. It tells of an old man who is struggling through a forest at the dead of night. He is ancient and exhausted and yet battles his way through the branches and undergrowth. He is in pain. Perhaps he will not make it. In the distance he sees a flickering light from the window of a small wooden cabin. He heads towards it battling his tiredness. As he reaches the door he falls down. An old woman opens the door, takes him in her arms and carries him to a wonderful warm fire. She holds him closely on her knee, sitting in her rocking chair, rocking back and forth whispering

---

1   *Women Who Run With The Wolves*, Clarissa Pinkola Estés. Rider An imprint of Random House Group Ltd. 1993.

to him - "There, there," she whispers, "there, there." She rocks him all through the night and in this time of rocking he has become younger, his limbs stronger. Just before dawn she looks down upon him and he is not an old man anymore, he is young and beautiful. And as dawn approaches he grows even younger. He is now a beautiful child with golden hair. Exactly at the moment of dawn the old woman plucks three hairs from the child's head and throws them on the ground. The little child climbs from her lap and runs to the door. He smiles at her and leaps into the sky to become the glorious morning sun.

This beautiful story has echoes of the Myth of the Sun where the hero climbs the golden chariot and travels the sky by day. At night he is devoured by the Great Mother and there he battles the beast to arise victorious at dawn. In the story of The Three Gold Hairs the old man represents the ability to focus. In Jungian terms the ability to focus is masculine energy. It is to be found in both women and men. When found in a woman, Jung calls it the animus. The man in the story represents the animus energy of the woman. In analysing this story Clarissa Pinkola Estés points out that when we lose focus we lose energy. When we lose energy, the last thing that we need to do is to gallop around chasing our tail in order to get our energy back again. This is exactly what one tends to do. Today we have become so out of touch with the natural cycles, that we do not trust that things will come around again, that the tide will come back in. Estés claims that "the assumption of eternal strength in the masculine is an error. It is a cultural introject that must be routed from the psyche".[2]

In the West we are raised in a society that, at best, ignores the natural world; at worst, it sets out to destroy it. Our perception of performance and energy are based on models that are mechanical. From the time we are four or five, and are in schools, we are sitting at desks, directed

---

2   ibid. page 331.

in our learning, and expected to perform at a pace and standard that has nothing to do with our bodies, our personal interests, or our individual rhythms. Little wonder then as adults that we are out of touch with the natural tides of our energy. We have, from day one, been trained away from them. Everything is forced to an outside beat – and so people burn out, both men and women.

The story gives an understanding of how psychic energy works. Estés writes, "Wild Woman *expects* that the animus will wear out on a regular basis".[3] This is not the mechanistic view of the world or the body, which says that one should be able to go on forever. After exertion and focus there is a natural need for sitting in the arms of the Great Mother and simply rocking, all night long. There cannot be constant daylight without dreadful results. Think of the appalling life of battery hens where there is constant light and the demand for constant production. Perhaps we could have photographs of these poor birds hanging on our walls. Deprived of night and rest they are killed off after one or two years of laying. The photographs can be a reminder of the cost of such a mechanistic projection onto the natural world. There is no tide to come back in for these birds. They are squeezed dry and then they are put on the waste heap. It is ironic that we are doing the exact same to ourselves and to our children. By ignoring the natural cycles we are putting an unholy expectation on our minds and bodies.

'Wild Woman', according to Estés, is the place of a deep nature that is conscious. She is the natural wisdom that is in our bodies and in the earth. If we look at natural cycles, sun rising and setting, moon waxing and waning, the tide coming in and going out, we see that there must be this balance.

Psychic energy for Jung flows between two opposing poles. The greater

---

3   ibid.

the tension between the opposites, the greater the energy. Without any opposition, there is no energy. Examples of these opposites are: conscious and unconscious, introvert and extravert, thinking and feeling, sensation and intuition. The natural movement of psychic energy is like the tides, forwards and backwards. The forwards movement Jung called progression. Progression satisfies the demands of the conscious and involves psychological adaptation in daily life to one's environment. The backwards movement of psychic energy he called regression and this satisfies the needs of the unconscious or the inner world. We need both the progression and regression of energy in order to be healthy.

The law of enantiodromia says that everything eventually runs into its opposite.[4] Thus if psychic energy is working in an unhindered manner, progression will naturally lead to regression. After a period of intense mental activity a person may sink into a dreamy unfocused state. The psyche demands a period of restoration. Just as the old man in the story becomes young again when he is rocked by the old woman all night, so too the psyche's tide will come in again when it is allowed to go out naturally. Once the demands of the outer world are fulfilled, it is time for a person to satisfy the needs of the inner world. If people can do this they will be in harmony themselves.

If for some reason progression becomes impossible, and one cannot adapt to the demands of life, then psychic energy becomes blocked. The energy that should be going outwards into adapting gets dammed up. The pair of opposites that worked in a co-ordinated manner come to a halt, since they now both have equal value - the scales are at a standstill. There is no movement back and forward. The longer this

---

4 In *C.W.* Vol. 7, par 111, Jung writes: "Old Heraclitus, who was indeed a very great sage, discovered the most marvellous of all psychological laws: the regulative function of opposites. He called it enantiodromia, a running contrariwise, by which he meant that sooner or later everything runs into its opposite".

stoppage lasts, the more conflict is created, since both opposing forces are receiving more value as opposed to one or the other receiving more value at any given time. Where once the opposing force worked as an equilibrating force, now it is obstructing further progress. To attempt to relieve the conflict, one of the opposing forces will be repressed. However, in repressing this opposing force a splitting off of the personality happens. According to Jung a neurosis is now very likely to happen.[5]

The stale-mate between the opposites would continue indefinitely if the process of regression, the backwards movement of the psychic energy, did not come into play. In the process of regression, psychic energy flows into the unconscious and value is given to things that have nothing to do with outward adaptation. These things are seldom, if ever, employed consciously. As the value of these unconscious elements increases, they will eventually gain influence over the conscious mind. Any number of things can happen as a result of this, depending on the contents of the unconscious that will invade the conscious mind. A person can become neurotic, can return to an infantile state of mind, or can play out primitive or even animal behaviour. Sometimes they can become suddenly violent or even psychotic. The material they are now accessing, or rather the material that is now accessing them, is unconscious and unfamiliar.

Where Jung differed from other psychologists of his time was that he saw these unconscious elements as holding the 'germs of new life and vital possibilities for the future'.[6] For him the work at hand was to track these fantasies and unconscious images in order to bring up into consciousness the psychic energy that was attached to them. Once this energy was retrieved from the unconscious, it could be applied to the

---

5 Jung deals with the movement of libido, its progression and regression in *C.W.* Vol. 8, par 60ff.
6 *C.W.* Vol. 8, par 63.

tasks of adaptation. If this energy is not used for action in the present, that is in the tasks of adaptation, it will sink back into the unconscious for want of employment.

Jung uses the example of a mountain climber as an illustration of failure to adapt.[7] The climber begins to climb a mountain and finds that a certain section of it is so difficult to cross that he cannot go on. He goes back, having admitted that he cannot succeed in this task and he uses his energy to climb an easier mountain. This is the normal utilisation of psychic energy. However, if we imagine that the difficult section of rock is, in fact, within his capabilities, and that he is simply a coward, then two things are possible. He can acknowledge his own cowardice and use his psychic energy for the useful purpose of self-criticism and self-reflection. Or he can deny the fact of his cowardice and deceive himself, allowing himself to believe that the situation is too difficult. If he chooses the latter, he falls into contradiction with himself. He knows the truth of the situation yet he refuses to acknowledge it openly. His psychic energy is split in two halves, one against the other. He regresses to an infantile mentality where he wants to stomp his foot and make people believe that he could never have climbed that mountain. The psychic energy that was progressing in his attempt to climb the mountain, has regressed into the unconscious and activated a childish, unconscious and un-adapted complex – an infantile complex. This has the man behave in a neurotic fashion. "In the later course of a neurosis, accidental events and regression, together form a vicious circle: retreat from life leads to regression, and regression heightens resistance to life."[8]

Jung uses the following image to describe the regression of energy:

---

7 *C.W.* Vol. 4, par 378 - 383
8 ibid., par 403

The libido can be compared with a river which, when it meets with an obstruction, gets dammed up and causes an inundation. If this river has previously, in its upper reaches, dug out other channels, these channels will be filled up again by reason of the damming below. They appear to be real riverbeds, filled with water as before, but at the same time they have only a provisional existence. The river has not permanently flowed back into the old channels, but only for as long as the obstruction lasts in the main stream. The subsidiary streams carry the water from the beginning, but because they were once stages or stations in the development of the main river-bed, passing possibilities, traces of which still exist and can therefore be used again in times of flood.[9]

When psychic energy is naturally flowing outwards and is being used for the purpose of adapting to life's demands then there is no question of it flowing inwards and reawakening inappropriate complexes. However, this is exactly what happens, if for some reason psychic energy is prevented from going outwards. The energy has to go somewhere. The natural rhythm of the energy going outwards and then coming inwards has been disrupted. There is a blockage and the energy goes to places deep in the unconscious.

Canalisation of Psychic Energy and the Formation of Symbols

"Will" can be thought of as disposable energy. Like consciousness, its evolution is a more recent phenomenon in the story of the human psyche. Psychic energy, or libido, is natural energy and it serves the purposes of life. When nature is left to itself, it produces natural phenomena but this production does not come under the category of "work". Energy flows instinctively along the lines of its natural gradient.

---

9 *C.W.* Vol. 4, par. 367.

Through the use of the will, human culture exploits the natural gradient. The direction of energy towards something other than instinct is called the canalisation of energy. "… A transfer of psychic intensities or values from one content to another…"[10] It happens by transferring energy to something similar in nature to the object of instinctive interest, by its "canalisation into an *analogue of the object of instinct*".[11]

An example of this is the spring ceremony of the Wachandi, of Australia.[12] These people dig a hole in the ground. They surround it with bushes, which makes it look like female genitals. The men dance around this hole, holding their spears out in front of them, simulating an erect penis. When they dance around, they thrust their spears into the hole shouting: "Pulli nira, pulli nira, wataka!" which means "not a pit, not a pit, but a -----!" No man who takes part in this ceremony is allowed to look at a woman. The hole in the ground is an analogue of the female genitals, which is the object of natural instinct. By creating this analogue, the instinctual sexual energy can be diverted toward the land. The minds of the participants are primed for the work that needs to take place for the cultivation of the land in the spring season. The instinctual energy becomes closely associated with the land and work in the land acquires the same value as a sexual act. This association secures the interest of the person working the land.

The association of sexual acts with the land and its fertility is also found in early Irish or Celtic Mythology. On May Eve, during the summer festival, Bealtaine, couples copulated in the fields. This ensured the fertility of the land. In a similar vein, the land was considered to be the body of the goddess, The Great Mother. The King had to lie with

---

10 *C.W.* Vol. 8, par 79
11 ibid., par 83.
12 ibid., par 83.

the goddess each year so that the land would produce food.[13] Jung comments that "The enormous complexity of such ceremonies shows how much is needed to divert the libido from its natural river-bed of everyday habit into some unaccustomed activity".[14]

The symbol is the psychological mechanism that transforms energy. "In abstract form, symbols are religious ideas; in the form of action, they are rites or ceremonies. They are the manifestations of excess libido".[15] A symbol cannot be produced consciously or by an effort of will. It always comes from the unconscious by way of dream, revelation or intuition. Jung points out that, for many centuries, the general tendency has been to suppress individual symbol-formation. The creation of an official state religion, and the growth of Christianity, all aided this trend. Yet he predicted an increase in individual symbol-formation as Christianity began to lose its hold. Now, well over forty years on from the time Jung wrote this, we are further along this road. The institutional churches continue to lose ground and what remains for people is exactly that individual symbol-formation that Jung speaks of. This is what can reconnect us to our souls and to the deeper layers of meaning in our lives. The collective symbols are fading in significance and the personal, individual, ones will be the ones to take us home to ourselves.

A distinction has to be made between two types of individual symbol formation. In the first type, the psychic energy is led towards something greater, towards effective work and adaptation in the world. In the second type, the psychic energy is led along old channels, activating infantile urges and archaic sexual fantasies. Symbols of the latter kind

---

13 Daithi O hOgain refers to this in his piece on Daghda in his book, *Myth, Legend and Romance, an Encyclopedia of the Irish Folk Tradition.* Prentice Hall Press, New York 1991. Page145.
14 *C.W.* Vol. 8, par 87.
15 ibid., par 91.

have to be broken down, and reduced to their natural elements, until such time as a person can live a normal life. The measure is always this – one's ability to adapt to the demands of daily life. Symbol making must promote this. If it does not, the symbols must be dismantled and the energy released from them. Once a person can live a normal life, then the inclination towards symbol making of the psyche can be seen to take the psychic energy in a positive, life-enhancing direction.

If we were to reduce symbols to their natural elements *ad nauseum* we would theoretically become like primitive peoples in a natural state. Although such a natural state may seem ideal to many, we need to acknowledge that these people were hounded by superstitions and fears. According to Jung: "Mankind was freed from these fears by a continual process of symbol formation that leads to culture".[16] So, on the one hand, we have instinct and a primitive mentality, on the other we have the regulating principle of individuation, which creates symbols. Some have named these two opposites, nature and spirit. This integrative unity, this facility to create symbols, is as real and as powerful a force as our instincts. It can, perhaps, be seen most clearly in the child. In the child there is an animal-like nature, an 'in-bodiness' that is beautiful to watch. This is a physical grace and perfect posture that is typical of most children. There is also a highly differentiated inheritance, the startling wisdom of the child's spontaneous utterances, the complexity of their dreams and the astuteness of their observations. Here we have the primitive nature and also the highly differentiated inheritance – the two opposites, which form the basis of the tension that we call psychic energy.

Jung observes that the first part of a person's life is appropriately dominated by the instincts and the satisfaction of them. Recognising sexuality and other basic healthy instincts leads a person into life

---

16 ibid., par 95.

and into the dance that is each person's particular destiny. There is a transition to be made when one gets older. It is a transition from the biological to the cultural sphere. The shift from action to meaning. Many people experience a crisis around the time of this transition. It is a transition that happens at mid-life. For many, there is little or no collective support and acknowledgement of how tricky it can be. Our Western culture has made a cult out of the satisfaction of the instincts. It has, however, failed to explore the realm of symbol and of meaning. When people reach mid-life, they are abandoned by the collective culture and must find their own lonely way.[17]

The Infantile Mentality

Jung says of the infantile mentality, "It is characteristic of children and of naive minds generally, not to find the mistake in themselves but in things outside them, and forcibly to impose on things their own subjective judgement".[18] He speaks of a young woman who suffered from acute hysteria after she received a sudden fright.[19] The story is worth retelling here because in it we can see how the psychic energy can get blocked and, in becoming dammed up, can activate an infantile mentality. The woman was coming home from a party at midnight with some friends. A cab pulled by horses came up behind them at full speed. Her friends managed to get out of the way. The woman, however, filled with terror, stayed in the middle of the road and ran ahead of the horses. The driver shouted but she kept running in his path. They were heading over a bridge and the woman was getting tired. In order not to get trampled, she was about to hurl herself over the bridge and into the water, but a passerby prevented her.

This same woman had had a worse experience years earlier when a street, where she was walking, had been cleared by shots from soldiers.

---

17 ibid., par 107-113.
18 ibid., par 382.
19 *C.W.* Vol. 7, par 8-15.

In that particular instance, she had been surrounded by people falling wounded or dead but she remained calm, found a door leading off the street and escaped from harm. Furthermore, this dreadful experience did not affect her in the future.

The question must be asked – why the lesser incident caused such a dramatic response when the much more serious incident left her unmoved? Upon further investigation, Jung discovered that it was the sound of the trotting horses that triggered the dramatic response. When questioned, the woman told of an incident where, at the age of seven, she had been with a coachman on a drive, when the horses took fright and the coachman and the young girl had to jump off before the horses and the carriage crashed down a river-gorge. Neither she nor the driver were harmed, but the horses and carriage were lost.

It seems reasonable that this childhood experience should predispose the woman to a dramatic response on hearing the sound of horses. Yet the question remains – why react dramatically to this relatively harmless event and not the other, where apparently there were horses also? Here the point of failing to adapt to the daily demands of life, and hence the blocking of psychic energy, comes into play. The woman had just become engaged to a young man, whom she loved and hoped to live happily with. On the particular night of the incident with the horses, she had been at a farewell party for her best friend. The friend, although happily married, with a husband and child, nonetheless suffered from nerves and was going off to a resort on account of this.

When Jung questioned the woman, he learned that, after the traumatic incident with the horses, she was brought back to the house where the party had been held. She was welcomed and cared for there. However, at this point in talking with Jung, the woman stopped speaking, became flustered and attempted to change the subject.

Jung discovered, after much resistance from the woman, that another strange incident had happened that night. The host, who was married to her best friend, had made a fiery declaration of love to the woman. It took Jung several weeks to piece together what exactly was going on and to discover the full story. This is what he learned.

The woman had been a tomboy while growing up and at the time of puberty she withdrew into herself and shunned all society and company. She lived in a world of fantasy and make-believe. At the age of twenty-four, two men broke through her self-imposed isolation. The first, Mr. A was the husband of her best friend. The second, Mr. B, was his single friend. The woman liked them both very much. A close relationship grew between herself and Mr. B and there was talk of an engagement.

She often came into contact with Mr. A because of her friendship with his wife and her engagement with Mr. B. She felt uncomfortable in his company, and uneasy. At the time of her engagement, she was at another party where the two men were present and a strange incident occurred. She was staring into space and playing with her engagement ring, turning it around on her finger when it fell off and rolled under the table. Mr. B found it and said laughingly, "You know what that means!" The woman was suddenly overcome by a strange emotion. She took the ring and flung it out the window in a rage. She later made up with Mr. B and things were back on track for their engagement.

Shortly after this, she was, by 'coincidence', on holidays at the same resort as her best friend and husband. It was on this holiday that Mrs. A, the woman's best friend, began to become visibly nervous and had to stay indoors because she felt poorly. The woman therefore had lots of opportunities to go walking with Mr. A. They were out boating one day when the woman became so excited and boisterous that she fell out of the boat. Mr. A saved her. It was then that he first kissed her. The woman responded by throwing herself even more wholeheartedly into her engagement with Mr. B. Mrs. A, however, guessed their secret and her nerves got worse. Hence her trip to the health resort and the farewell party, with what followed.

The unconscious attraction to Mr. A was behind the reaction to the horses and the need to return to Mr. A's house where, indeed, a further declaration of love took place. More accurately, the woman, by not consciously acknowledging her true feelings for Mr. A, was putting herself in self-opposition. She had consciously chosen Mr. B as her romantic partner and had pushed her erotic feelings for Mr. A into her unconscious. Her psychic energy, which ideally could have been used creatively to deal with her feelings for Mr. A (i.e. a healthy adaptation to a life situation), became blocked. She consciously states that her love is for Mr. B, but unconsciously she is passionate for Mr. A. The sorry reality is that a strong energy, even when it is kept unconscious, will still unconsciously drive us. This is the case with the woman. Her behaviour is driven by her unconscious desires. Her unconscious passion orchestrated the incident, which led for her to be brought back to Mr. A's house. It also orchestrated her taking the holiday in the same resort as Mr. and Mrs. A. If she were to be confronted with this, she would cry innocent. And she is innocent – as far as consciousness goes. She remains in the dark about her unconscious desires.

It is little wonder that early cultures spoke of evil spirits inhabiting people and making them behave in certain ways. The infantile mentality is similar, if not the same, as what Jung called the primitive mentality. The woman felt driven by powers outside of herself. The primitive mind also feels driven or assaulted by powers outside of itself.

It is also worth noticing that, when the woman sets herself against herself, that is, when she consciously chooses Mr. B and refuses to acknowledge or take responsibility for her feelings for Mr. A, her psychic energy becomes blocked. In not being able to flow outwards into life, it begins to flow inwards into the unconscious. This is what caused the woman's response to the sound of the horses to be so dramatic. The backward-flowing psychic energy reactivated the childhood memory of the accident with the horses and the carriage at the age of seven. Because the blockage was so intense, the energy flowing back to this memory was equally intense and thus it created the incident with the horses and the bridge.

When the energy flows backward like this the woman is in her unconscious. She is experiencing an infantile-like mentality – unconscious and driven. It is primitive and infantile in that she feels that these things are happening to her, that she is powerless. One might suspect that she knows what she is doing and she is simply being manipulative. Yet Jung comments, "If we remember that there are many people who understand nothing at all about themselves, we shall be less surprised at the realisation that there are also people who are utterly unaware of their actual conflicts."[20]

It can be seen that this woman had a tendency towards denial or fantasy. Jung had learned that, from puberty to the age of twenty-four, she had lived in a make-believe fantasy world. She had not adapted to the changes in her body and emotions. With psychic energy, as with physical energy, it must go somewhere, so if it disappears, one must ask where it will reemerge. If a young woman is lethargic and dreamy, her psychic energy is not going outward. It is activating the inner world of fantasy. Likewise, if someone has 'a bee in their bonnet' or some rabid conviction or extreme attitude, it is clear that there is

---

20 ibid., par 425.

too much psychic energy. The excess must have been taken from somewhere. The balance needs to be restored.

We can see, from the case of the woman and the horses, that the traumatic experience, although it seems to be important in tracking the cause of her neurosis or acute hysteria after her sudden fright, is in fact not the issue here. Jung makes the point that incidents like these, "merely *seem* to be important because they provide occasion for the manifestation of a condition that has long been abnormal."[21] Jung continues, "The abnormal condition ... consists in the anachronistic persistence of an infantile stage of libido development. The patients continue to hang on to forms of libido activity which they should have abandoned long ago ... The commonest (form) which is scarcely ever absent, is an excessive fantasy activity characterised by a thoughtless overvaluation of subjective wishes".[22] We came across this overvaluation of subjective wishes in the case of the woman sharing a flat with her friends in chapter one. She too was trapped in an infantile attitude and driven by the unconscious.

In a healthy version of things, if a person is blocked by an obstacle in his or her life, the psychic energy introverts and causes a state of reflection. This reflection will then help the person overcome or deal healthily with the obstacle. In the unhealthy version, the psychic energy still goes inward but the person gets stuck in the introverted attitude because he or she prefers the infantile mode of adaptation as being the easier one. The introverted world of fantasy, which in the first case is a source of inspiration and repose, in the second case becomes an escape route and hide-out.

---

21 *C.W.* Vol. 4, par 303.
22 ibid.

If a person tried always to adapt himself fully to the conditions of life, his libido would always be employed correctly and adequately. When that does not happen, it gets blocked and produces regressive symptoms. … The neurotic's bondage to fantasies (illusions, prejudices etc.) develops gradually, as a habit, out of innumerable regressions from obstacles since earliest childhood … and this bondage to fantasy makes reality seem less real to the neurotic, less valuable and less interesting, than it does to the normal person.[23]

The Parental Complex

Jung says that a regular concomitant to the infantile mentality is the parental complex.[24] When the psychic energy introverts and remains introverted, it invests large areas of memory. These memories then acquire a vitality, which they would not otherwise have, since they are past and done. The person, in whom this has happened, lives in the world of the past. They perceive the present world through the lens of these activated memories. The most influential aspect of our very early past tends to be the personalities of our parents. We have all experienced the mother or father in our head — the voice of the parent constantly rattling away in our minds, be it positive or negative. This is most clearly seen when the parent is long dead and a person is still behaving as if that parent was a major part of his or her life. The parent in our head often bears little resemblance to how that parent now would be, if he or she were still alive. It was because of this discrepancy that Jung referred to the "imago" of the mother or father rather than "mother" or "father". "…These fantasies are not concerned any more with the real father and mother but with subjective and often very much distorted images of them which lead a

---

23 *C.W.* Vol. 4, par 410.
24 ibid., par 304.

shadowy but nonetheless potent existence in the mind of the patient".[25]

For a person to develop and adapt, they must move beyond the world of just mother and father. The narrow restriction of a life to mother and father is played out in the myth of Oedipus. In this myth, Oedipus marries his mother and slays his father. The infantile conflict is magnified to adult proportions. The child's world is limited to its parents, but the world of the adult is not. At a certain point in a person's development, detachment from the parents is required for growth. This is the time of puberty when sexuality drives the person away from family and pushes him or her towards independence. It is often only with the greatest difficulty that a person can separate from the family. However difficult this may be physically, it is much more difficult psychologically. Psychologically it involves freeing oneself from the infantile milieu.

The symbolic idea of sacrifice helps with this separation. It is no accident that the idea of sacrifice is at the centre of many religions, including the Christian religion. The symbolic idea of sacrifice, in this case, involves the surrendering of infantile wishes. Religion provides the symbol, which then becomes the bridge for the psychic energy to cross. The child moves away from the parents and the infantile world and towards the adult world. "(Religion) leads his libido away from the infantile objects (parents) towards the symbolic representatives of the past, i.e., the gods, thus facilitating the transition from the infantile world to the adult world. In this way the libido is set free for social purposes".[26]

Religion however is merely a stepping stone on the journey to growth. For the power that the parents had over the person gets transferred,

---

25 ibid., par 305.
26 ibid., par 350.

in the transition to adulthood, onto the–institutions which promote the collective symbols. The path of individuation, if persisted with, leads a person to a place of independence where one relies on the power within oneself for authority over one's life. This goes beyond the Father and Mother of the collective symbols to a place of the Self. I will deal with this in more detail later.[27]

Transference

One could rightly ask what is the way out of the infantile mentality and the parental complex. To varying degrees we all suffer from it. It is not only people with neurosis who put the blame outside of themselves and force their own subjective view onto reality. What separates most people from being seriously neurotic is the ability to respond to the demands of life. The ability to function in the world. This is the ability to use psychic energy to connect with the world and with other people and to forge a place for themselves in the world. How 'real-ly' each person relates to the world varies enormously. Many relate to the world through webs of their own projections and transferences and fail to see "reality" separate from their own inner history. In fairness, we can only know our own unconscious psyche by projecting it out onto the world. The work then begins of claiming it back again and separating it out from what is in fact 'otherness'.

According to Jung there is a biological demand in the task of adaptation and that demand is to connect to people outside of our family.[28] It is not necessarily a sexual relationship that is demanded but rather that meaningful connections are made outside the bonds of family. This is both a physical and a psychological demand. Many of us manage physically but are slower to separate from the infantile

---

27 Chapter Six of this work looks at the process of psychic growth and the path of individuation. In this process, as one individuates the various archetypes, one progresses towards a relationship with the Self, the regulating principle of the entire psyche, the centre of the psyche, of both consciousness and the unconscious.

28 *C.W.* Vol. 4, par 439.

mentality psychologically. It is in looking at extreme cases that we can see the situation more clearly.

A neurotic person lives in a world of fantasy where their introverted psychic energy has activated their unconscious complexes. Everything is viewed through the lens of these fantasies, which consist of early memories of their mother and father (or mother and father figures). The task of adaptation requires them to relate beyond the limits of these fantasies. It would have them relate to the real world, with real people and respond to real situations. When a neurotic person goes into analysis, the first task of the analysis is for the analyst to listen to the client in order to discover the complexes at play in the person's neurosis.

During this stage of analysis transference is likely to occur. This is where the libido that was locked into the fantasies of mother and father gets transferred onto the analyst. On the one hand, this can be a positive thing because the transference to the analyst can act as a bridge upon which the person can get away from their family and into reality. It can also be a negative thing, in that the analyst merely becomes established in the client's psyche as another god among the family gods. That is, he or she merely becomes assimilated into the client's infantile milieu. What makes the difference between it being a good or a bad thing is the skill with which the analyst can encourage the person to recognise the transference and to break it. Here too there is danger, for the energy attached to the transference, once snapped, can slip back to the unconscious bondage of the parental/infantile complex. What the analyst tries to encourage is that that energy, once freed from the transference to the analyst, will be used to live life in reality. This means that it will be used to establish real relationships to people in the world and to connect to the world in real situations. The energy must be used for action or else it will slip back into the unconscious and the client's state will not have shifted.

Once transference is established it is extremely difficult to disentangle it and set the psychic energy on its right path. What can happen for the analyst is that a counter-transference takes place. This means that something in the psyche of the analyst has a corresponding hook for the transference that the analyst is not aware of. When this happens the analyst becomes the 'blind' leading the 'blind'. Jung, along with Freud, was adamant that if a person was to practice psychotherapy, that person must undergo analysis himself or herself. Only then can an analyst remain even remotely objective and clear of the psychic material that a client is putting on him or her.

For people to break such a transference they must, as Jung says, conquer themselves completely. People in the infantile mentality feel that, in the name of love, they can make demands. Jung says that they behave no differently to 'normal' people, except that, in the case of 'normal' people their capacity to fulfil their duties to life, which in turn satisfies their psychic energy, prevents the tendency of their energy to reach too high a pitch. The neurotic person does not exercise psychic energy in adapting to life. This requires self-discipline. Rather he or she makes infantile demands and begins to bargain. From the bargaining perspective, there is nothing in the infantile mentality that will benefit from breaking the transference. Thus the person must act from outside the infantile mentality while still being at the mercy of it. This is what 'conquering oneself completely' means. When a person is caught in a complex the same thing is required. The person must walk around the walls of it and act from outside of it, even when one is within it.[29]

---

29 Jung discusses transference at length in *C.W.* Vol. 4, *Analysis of the Transference*, par 436 - 451.

We have been looking at transference that is created through the analytical situation. These transferences also happen outside of analysis. Transference is used by all of us to shift the psychic energy away from the family and parents and outwards onto the world. We are all familiar with the experience of meeting someone and something coming alive inside of us… a teacher in school, a lecturer in college, a boss at work whom we admire and look up to. The experience is a feeling that we are living more fully in the presence of this person. The experience can be a very powerful one and can help greatly in our development if we are wise to what is going on. If we are not, it can oftentimes turn nasty.

What is happening in these instances is that the other person has become a hook for our inner material and we transfer or project onto them what truly belongs to ourselves. If it is parental material then the person becomes a carrier for our parental images. The classic example of this is the case of the young woman transferring her image of Father onto the wise professor as is the case of the young man transferring his image of Mother onto his female partner.

Two things can be happening here. Firstly, the personal experience of mother and father can be transferred onto another. It is a common situation for a person to realise that one has partnered up with someone who is very like one's parent. A person, who has grown up with a violent parent, often attracts a violent partner. Whatever you put out onto another person, that person must have a hook for it. If you have had an experience of a very loving father, you could very well attract a man who is also very loving. It works both ways. A person who is likely to be emotionally absent in a relationship will probably end up with someone who was accustomed to living with an emotionally absent parent during childhood. The list of possibilities is as numerous as there are people in the world.

The second thing that can happen is that one can experience an archetypal parental energy in someone else. This goes beyond one's personal historical experience. It is an experience that comes as a result of being a member of the human family. Experiencing this kind of transference can be very powerful and numinous. There are sometimes blessed pockets of experience where you feel so loved by another that it is as if an almighty goddess has taken you to her abundant breast and has held you close. Or, when you receive a look from another and you feel that a god has entered your soul and has accepted you to the core. The same principles apply to these experiences as to a personal transference. If you can recognise it for what it is, you can claim it for your own; if not, you are then vulnerable to the person you have transferred it onto and that person is vulnerable to you.

When a transference is not recognised, love can turn to poison. Often charismatic people can be like magnets for other people's transferences. Charismatic people can be put on pedestals and can be looked to for guidance. It is difficult for these people to live up to the expectations put upon them. They are individual people living their lives, yet because of the transferences put on them, they are often called upon to support others more than is humanly possible. To those who transfer onto them, these people can become the worst in the world having started off as the best in the world.

A man, whom we will call Mr X, was very idealistic, but struggled with alcoholism. Mr X met, and began to work with, a charismatic leader type whom we will call Mr A. Mr X transferred onto Mr. A, his own 'good father'. He felt good in Mr. A's presence. He felt he could do things right. This relationship lasted a few years, and during this time Mr X was able to keep his alcoholism under control. But Mr. A did not come up to scratch in the long run. He was not Mr. X's 'good father' and he could never, even if he had wanted to, fill that gap for Mr. X.

When the disillusionment set in, all Mr. X's good feelings towards Mr. A turned negative. The transference was unconscious in the first place and the swing into the negative was equally unconscious. The god had become the devil. Perhaps something in Mr. X's unconscious was trying to protect him by swinging into the negative and thereby cutting off the transference. This could have been good for both of them. To have persisted in the transference would have left Mr. X bound to Mr. A. Also Mr. A himself was stumbling under the weight of such an uncontained transference.

In the long run, Mr. A was hurt by the poisonous material that began to surface in the relationship. Although he had a hook for Mr. X's unconscious material, he had done nothing to deserve either the transference or the poison. Also, the energy that was made accessible to Mr. X, through the transference onto Mr. A, sank again into the unconscious and was lost to him once the transference was cut. He reverted to alcoholism.

A woman moved house very soon after her mother died. Her new neighbour was an older man with whom she became friendly. The man became her counsellor and confidante. He helped her through that very difficult time. She transferred her image of "Mother" onto this man. She became dependent on him. Although he was unavailable to her as a partner she went to him at every turn to fix things and to advise her. He continued to act as her counsellor. Eventually the transference got too much for the man. He felt smothered by her continuous presence in his house and in his life. She seemed to extract energy from him simply by being in the same room. Eventually the man felt that this woman had a huge suction pipe and whenever she was with him she would attach the suction pipe to him and drain all his energy. This is an appropriate image for what happens when anyone transfers onto another. Because of the transference, unconsciously the woman felt that the man was her Great Mother. Therefore, unconsciously, she felt justified sucking all his energy from him. The sorry fact was that he was not her Great Mother but a mere mortal and he felt sorely the loss of his own vital psychic energy.

In this particular instance, the man decided that he had to end the relationship. He asked the woman not to come and see him again. The woman reacted very badly and for a while she was suicidal. However, over time she recovered her balance in life.

In the first instance a man transfers Father material onto another man. In the second instance a woman transfers Mother material onto a man. In both instances, the break-up of the transference caused a lot of pain, hurt and angst. It is possible, however, to become aware of transferences and to deal consciously and less destructively with those that occur outside of the analytical situations. This is why a working knowledge of the dynamics of our psychic energy is extremely useful.

Transference on to Institutions
Jung points out that a church and its priests also fulfil the role as surrogate parental figures for people. The priest and the institution replace the parents. To this extent, "they free the person from the bonds of the family".[30] However, because a church does not often encourage personal psychological development or independent intellectual pursuits it only fulfils this role for those who would surrender their psychological and intellectual independence. Jung comments: "The more highly developed men of our time do not want to be guided by creed or a dogma".[31] For those who would be so guided, the transference onto a church works. Their psychic energy moves away from family and parents and onto the church. Their psychic scope is broadened. However, in the case of analysis, the transference will

---

30 *C.W.* Vol. 4, par 434.
31 ibid.

be analysed and the person will be challenged to break it, therefore leading the psychic energy to be reintegrated and reclaimed back into the person's own psyche. In the church and priest situation, the aim is to maintain the transference. While the transference remains on the church, the person will remain captive, albeit on a higher and healthier level of development.

It could be argued that advanced psychic development, or individuation, is only for a few and that most people need some religious container wherein they can be guided. However, church institutions, in general, are losing their hold over people. Something is happening collectively to many religious institutions. The time of them carrying peoples' psychic energy is drawing to a close. Perhaps we are experiencing a crucial moment on the psychic evolutionary path of humanity where we are being pushed towards individual psychic maturity and responsibility.

It is not only the churches or analysts that receive transferences from people. Other institutions also have transferences put on them: a work place, a government, a medical institution or an educational establishment. People can also transfer onto the many individuals who are within these institutions.

One very poignant example of a woman's transference of her father onto an institution is to be found in the story of Judy Garland. This story shows very clearly how we can become trapped by a Father transference and how we can suffer from the lack of a positive Mother image. In Judy Garland's story, as told by her daughter, Judy did not have a strong positive connection with her mother. From the very start, her mother connected with her as a child star, not as a daughter. She was not a mother-loved child.

Judy Garland adored her father. When he died, she was thirteen years old and already working for Metro-Goldwyn-Mayer Studios. The executives of the studio became her parental figures. She overworked to please. She took pills in order to be able to overwork to please. Judy Garland had a brilliant voice, but her appearance was not considered 'right'. Much work had to be done to make her 'presentable', according to those who were controlling the situation. Nothing in that industry affirmed Judy Garland as a person, as someone valuable in herself. She was an object. She became an obsessed woman who longed to be loved and minded. Five husbands could not give her what she wanted. She died from accidental drug overdose. Judy Garland transferred her positive father and negative mother onto the film industry and it became the 'god' and the 'bad witch' that drove her.

Judy Garland was a remarkable woman, despite it all. Time and time again she lifted her career out of oblivion. Time and time again she rose from the ashes of her own destruction and she sang again. Most moving about the story is how her third husband truly loved her and how her three children truly loved her. She was the living testament to Maya Angelou's's poem "And still I Rise".[32] She was spirited to the end.

Judy Garland had lived with a gaping wound within her. She suffered from a lack of true mother love. No amount of loving by human beings could fill the gap. Only the healing of that wound could have changed her life. She transferred that parental situation onto the world and wanted outside things and other people to make her happy. It did not work. Her life was tragic. Yet it was filled with the nobleness of her spirit and the indestructibility of her soul, which came through again and again in her singing. She is a living testament to how a damaged

---

32 Maya Angelou's poem *And Still I Rise* is published in the book of the same title. Virago Press Ltd. London.1986. *Me and My Shadows: A Family Memoir* was written by Lorna Luft, Garland's daughter. 1998 Simon & Schuster.

life can be controlled by that damage. She is also a living testament to how the beauty of a human soul can shine through all the damage.

It is only today that the psychological skills and tools are available to ordinary men and women to do the work of owning the scale of damage and wealth of beauty that is in each one of us. Psychic energy is within each one of us. How we use it is ultimately our responsibility. More is known now of the inner world of the psyche, and how it interacts with the outer world, than ever before. We have, as human beings, the resources now to become great, to be responsible, to step out of the infantile mentality and to be in the world as true adults. One of the most enduring resources we have is our dreams. These are the messengers of the unconscious. They connect us to the collective unconscious and they show us how things are in our personal unconscious. The trick is to know what they mean and this is no easy task.

CHAPTER THREE

Dreams

The Messengers of the Unconscious

How Much Tenderness Can You Bear?

i

How much tenderness can you bear
after the desolation
of no one being there to catch you
in the free fall into life?
No one to instinctively put their finger
on the one small hole in the dam of your soul.

To touch your heart
and whisper tenderly –
"It's alright, you are mine".

ii

I dream of a huge green luminous snake
that is coming towards me
and I wake screaming.

Jung at Heart

When an inner situation is not made conscious,
it happens outside, as Fate.

Jung, Aion *C.W.* 9 II

The unconscious by definition is unknown. So, how can we know it? Dreams are the songs of the unconscious. Like most music they are of benefit to us even if we do not truly appreciate them. The more we appreciate them the greater their healing and transforming powers. Working on our dreams is like learning a new language. The more we practice it the more the meaning reveals itself to us. Working on dreams is not an easy thing. The images used often seem mundane or irrelevant. Sometimes dreams seem to be merely repeating our daytime lives with nothing new to offer. Often the action or scene within a dream can completely change, giving the dream a surreal feeling. Dreams can appear disjointed and nonsensical. Yet the thing to realise is that everything in a dream is there for a reason. Even the tiniest element has a meaning. Nothing is there by accident. The unconscious is a wonderful orchestrator of images and symbols, often with a tremendous sense of humour.

A student who was writing his thesis for the Jungian Institute found that he could not proceed with the work. He dreamed that he was being pursued. Marie-Louise von Franz was working with the student on his dreams. She interpreted the dream to be about the man's creativity. He, however, felt it was about his sexuality. Von Franz defended her interpretation by pointing to the fact that the man had a woman friend and that all his sexual needs were being fulfilled. The man, however, remained unconvinced.

The student later dreamed that a bull was chasing him. In the dream he ran away from the bull and jumped a fence. The bull stopped and went onto its hind legs. The writer saw the erect penis of the bull and it was a ballpoint pen! After the dream he finally admitted that his dreams were about his creativity and he finished his thesis for the Institute.[1]

No one can tell you what your dream is about. One can only suggest. The real answer has to click with you, the dreamer. However, you can resist or reject an interpretation because you do not like what it is telling you. Dreams show you your back. They tell you what you are blind to and what you are, perhaps, resisting.

The Compensatory Function of Dreams

Dreams are about energy – they tell us where energy is and where energy wants to go. They are compensatory to the conscious attitude of the dreamer at the time of the dream. If the dreamer's conscious attitude has become rigid or unhealthy, the dream will compensate by creating the other side of the story in dream image. This compensatory function is extremely important and is totally unique to each individual. It is impossible to interpret this compensatory function in any general way, for the interpretation relies on the temperament of the dreamer. What a particular object means to one person may mean something else entirely to another. The compensatory function does two things. It keeps a balance in the person's psyche. It also attempts to stimulate the dreamer into action to adjust the conscious attitude. The intensity of the compensation and the images used depends on the degree of unhealthiness or rigidity in the conscious attitude.

Therefore, in analysing a dream of another person, a thorough knowledge of the person's conscious attitude is necessary. Compensatory dreams happen when the conscious attitude of the dreamer is more or less adequate. They attempt to adjust or fine-tune the perspective. Jung himself was working with a client, a woman,

1   Marie-Louise von Franz in conversation with Fraser Boa. (1988) *The Way of the Dream*. Windrose films Ltd., Toronto, Canada. Page 128.

and the analysis was going nowhere. He dreamed that he was at the bottom of a long stairway and had to crane his neck in order to see the woman, his client, at the top of the stairs. He interpreted the dream to mean that he had been looking down on the woman, unknown to himself. When he adjusted this attitude the analysis began to get somewhere.[2]

Few dreams are that delightfully simple. However, someone who has split off their sexuality may dream of a prostitute and sleazy bars. Someone who keeps himself or herself tightly controlled may have dreams where there is chaos everywhere. If a person's conscious attitude is too rigid then energy becomes blocked in the unconscious. The dream points to this energy and indicates where it needs to be released.

It is important to understand how dreams and the unconscious work in relation to consciousness. Jung warns against over-rating the unconscious. The two are intimately connected and respond to each other as sensitively as two people dancing a minuet. If we are inclined to believe that the unconscious always knows best, then we would have to rely on dreams to make decisions for us in our lives. Jung points out that we will be disappointed. The corresponding response of the unconscious is likely to be that the dreams will become more and more meaningless and trivial. It is the conscious mind that is and must be in the driving seat of the psyche. "The unconscious functions satisfactorily only when the conscious mind fulfils its tasks to the very limit".[3] A dream will help round off and fill out our conscious attitude. It will show us our blind spots. But, were the unconscious to be considered superior to the conscious attitude, we must ask what would be the advantage of consciousness at all. The two are in

---

2   C.G. Jung, *Memories, Dreams, Reflections* (1983 by Fontana Paperbacks) page 155.

3   *C.W.* Vol. 8, par 568.

relationship. Consciousness is what we know and what we must trust to lead us. The unconscious provides the balancing mechanism when our conscious attitude needs it.

The unconscious is not superior to the conscious mind, but neither is it a monster. It is not a dark space with lurking shadows and pits full of misery. Here again it is important to see how the relationship between the two works. The unconscious only becomes dangerous when our conscious attitude to it is wrong. "To the degree that we repress it, its danger increases".⁴ By assimilating the contents of the unconscious into consciousness, the danger diminishes. Unfortunately, the attitude that sees the unconscious as a monster, and therefore avoids it and represses it, creates that very reality. When the unconscious can be embraced it ceases to be threatening. "The unconscious is not a demoniacal monster, but a natural entity which, as far as moral sense, aesthetic taste, and intellectual judgement go, is completely neutral."⁵

Many of us have had the experience of that which we most fear becoming that which actually happens. People who have mental illness in their family and are in horror of becoming ill themselves, get depressed and are soon in a terrible and familiar place despite their resistances. A similar dynamic can be seen in dealing with young children. Often parents will say to a child climbing on a wall – "don't fall" and the child falls. It would be better to embrace the danger positively and make a positive statement: "Be careful, it is very high up there". The child's attention is drawn to being careful as opposed to trying not to fall. With the unconscious, if we can direct our attention towards what it might be saying, rather than expending energy on trying to avoid it, ignore it, or repress it, we are less likely to trip.
A woman dreamed she was being gang raped by a group of men. She

---

4   *C.W.* Vol. 16, par 329.
5   ibid.

awoke in a sweat, terrified. The shock of the dream startled her into seeking advice about the dream. It emerged that she had a large amount of creative energy that she was not accessing. When she began to take up her talent, the male figures in her dreams became more benevolent and helpful. The unconscious is morally neutral and obviously has no problem shocking us into growth. The more violent or dramatic the images the more urgent the need to respond accordingly. Shocking and disturbing dreams can visit our night time sleeping – brother and sister can be inappropriately sexually intimate; you can discover that the toilet upon which you are defecating suddenly has no walls around it and you are in a public place; a stranger is fondling a young child; a bishop is torturing a victim who is tied down, by slitting him from anus to below the neck; your partner is in bed with another woman, or man.

The unconscious has no conscience and often has the strangest sense of humour. We often awaken from these dreams feeling sick to the stomach, frightened, and uneasy. It is perfectly natural to want to forget them. Strangely though, the only way we can shake off the unease is to tell someone the dream. By telling someone else our dream, we somehow put it outside of ourselves, we remove it or distance it from ourselves. This is the wise thing to do. By distancing ourselves from the dream we can begin to try and fathom what the message might be.

Another woman dreamed that her youngest son of two years was run over three times by a huge articulated truck. In the dream her other three children and she herself watched on, horrified. When someone asked her in the dream why she had not saved the boy from harm, she responded that in order to save her other three children she had to let it happen. Upon waking reflection the woman commented that this particular child who had been run over was very tuned into her, almost intuitively so. She also acknowledged that her own intuition, which was very strong, had been completely put aside so that she could get by in life. The dream was a wake-up call to her that she needed to rescue her mangled intuition and adjust her conscious attitude to life.

All the shocking dream images cited above appeared because some attitude in consciousness was not right. By not right I mean that it was damaging the overall psychic health. When we want to look at a dream we must ask, *"What conscious attitude does it compensate for?"* The woman who repressed her creative energies dreamed she was being gang-raped. Too little masculine focused energy on the conscious side led to too much aggressive masculine energy on the unconscious front. The woman who lived with no intuition in her conscious life had her attention violently drawn to intuition in her dream.

And so too with the more shocking examples; the dream of the bishop torturing his victim was dreamed by a young woman who had a conscious attitude that was much too aligned with her father and with masculine intellectual values, to the detriment of more base chakra energies (the cutting from the anus). The theory of compensation is the basic law of psychic behaviour. Too much on one side means too little on the other.

Before any dream interpretation can be attempted a detailed knowledge of the situation of the dreamer needs to be known. A young man brought Jung the following dream: *My father is driving away from the house in his new car. He drives very clumsily, and I get very annoyed over his apparent stupidity. He goes this way and that, forwards and backwards, and manoeuvres the car into a dangerous position. Finally he runs into a wall and damages the car badly. I shout at him in a perfect fury that he ought to behave himself. My father only laughs, and then I see that he is dead drunk.* [6]

---

6   *C.W.* Vol. 16, par 335. The original text is in italics.

In analysing the dream Jung points out that the dream has no foundation in fact. The young man holds his father in high regard and the father would not behave in this manner even if he were drunk. The relationship with the father is a very good one. Perhaps the young man secretly despises his father and cannot acknowledge this fact. But nowhere in Jung's interviewing of the man can any evidence of this be found.

Jung then asked, not *why* the young man had the dream but rather, *what was the purpose of the dream?* Why discredit the father? What point was the unconscious trying to make? If the young man's relationship with the father was good, why try to take the father down a peg or two? With regards to compensation, Jung realised that the young man's relationship with the father was not only good, but that it was too good! Because it was too good, it was damaging the young man's perception of himself. He could not separate himself out from the father. The light emanating from the father, in the young man's psyche, was blinding him to his own separate reality. The unconscious decided to snuff out the light by discrediting the father so that the young man could get a sense of himself. In the dream he was shouting at his father. He was furious. He was separate and distinct. He needed to establish this separateness from his father for the sake of his psychic health.

When Jung suggested this interpretation to the young man, it immediately clicked with him.[7] Without a knowledge of the conscious situation between the son and his father, the real meaning of the dream would not have been discovered. A dream, free-floating as such, without the knowledge of the dreamer's life situation, cannot be interpreted with any accuracy.

---

7   ibid., par 337.

Interpreting Dreams – Establishing the Context of the Dream

To interpret a dream one must establish the context of the dream very carefully.[8] A dream does not pop up out of nowhere. It is remarkably well crafted. The unconscious chooses images or situations with which one has associations and it allows these images to convey a message. Yet it is not a facade. If the image were a facade for the message, it would need to be stripped away before the message becomes clear. The dream is what it needs to be in the moment it is dreamed. It is important to remember this when one is in the throes of frustration wondering what a particular dream could possibly mean. The relationship between consciousness and the unconscious must be remembered. The two are intimately tuned to each other. The unconscious must use the images it does in order that the conscious mind can begin to grapple with its message. It cannot be explicit. If it could be, the conscious mind would know it already and it would not need to make the point at all. Another way to put this is to speak in terms of language. If the unconscious spoke the same language as the conscious mind, then it would be the conscious mind. It would not be a compensatory, balancing entity. The language the unconscious speaks is the language of symbol and image. This then needs translation for the conscious mind. The unconscious is not presenting a facade, which we must then get behind, it uses a language which we must learn.

To establish the context of a dream, we must look at the associations that the dreamer has with the images used in the dream. Jung cautions that one must not look at free associations,[9] for these will only show up a person's complexes, in general.[10] They will not tell you the specific meaning of the dream. You must stay as close as possible to the actual dream images. For example, I was looking at someone's dream, where

---

8 ibid., par 320.
9 Free associations are the ideas or thoughts a person has connected to particular words or objects.
10 *C.W.* Vol. 16, par 335.

he dreamed of a certain house he visited as a child. When I asked for associations, he said: "place of freedom, we had good fun playing there, it was like a soul home for me." If I had left it at that, we would have missed something important. I asked him if the house or the area in the dream was the same as it is now, or if the image gave any indication of time. He remembered that in the dream another house, which had been built later, was missing. In the dream, he had parked his car on the site of the house that was missing! So, his unconscious was drawing attention to the fact that the neighbouring house was missing and that this meant something. I asked when that second house had been built. It was built when he was ten years old. The dream was dealing with something before he was ten years of age. It was a crucial insight in the interpretation of the dream.

Jung emphasises this point. If, he says, someone dreams of a wooden deal table it is not enough for the person to associate it with her writing desk, which does not happen to be a deal table. It may happen that the person can become blocked when attempting to say specifically what she associates with a deal table. This must be seen as suspicious. Ordinarily a person might have many associations with a deal table. To have none means that you have run into a resistance and this indicates a complex. Jung keeps on returning to the specific image. "I usually say to my patient, "Suppose I had no idea what the words 'deal table' mean. Describe this object and give me its history in such a way that I cannot fail to understand what sort of a thing it is".[11]

A temptation when working with someone on their dreams is to presume that your associations with objects are the same as the dreamers. There is a very strong tendency to do this. It is only when you see, over and over again, examples of how other people have entirely different associations with familiar objects that you begin to realise

---

11 ibid.

what a mistake it is. At a dream workshop once, when working with a woman who offered her dream for interpretation, we were looking at the symbol of a chalice. I was mulling over my associations with chalice. These were: sacred offering, holy. I was surprised to hear that the woman's association with the chalice was of men and patriarchy and overbearing and boring services in church. Needless to say, my associations, unchecked, would have taken the interpretation in a totally wrong and pointless direction. Another example was a person who dreamed of a political figure going into an underground shelter that is surrounded by soldiers. My immediate association on hearing the image was of the film, 'Independence Day', when the president was led underground to a secret laboratory which had information about aliens. The dreamer's association with the political figure was of someone running for cover when something disastrous happens. Again, my interpretation, if allowed to dominate, would have led the dream interpretation in an irrelevant direction, of no use whatsoever to the dreamer.

This point cannot be emphasised enough. One must not usurp the dreamer's associations with one's own. If one does, it makes a nonsense of the interpretation. Neither can one stray from the dreamer's actual associations. Jung also points out that a single dream, taken alone, is very difficult to interpret with any certainty. It is much better to have a series of dreams. In the series, the theme becomes clearer, important images are repeated and misinterpretations are corrected by the following dreams.

Marie-Louise von Franz suggests that, if you are interpreting your own dream, you write the dream on one side of the page and, on the other, you write all your associations with the dream images. Then you can see if any connection between the dream and the associations strikes you.[12] One should also see if the dream connects to anything that happened the day before. Sometimes things happened the previous day that stirred emotions, which went unnoticed because of distractions at the time. If we can remember these things, they will help us with interpreting the dream.

There is no doubt that talking to someone about a dream can help us get a little distance from the dream. It is said that Jung once complained that he had no Jung to speak with about his dreams! So, he would tell his dreams to the gardener. The gardener would say what he thought about the dreams and Jung would think "No, that is not it, but this is what it is!" It was only in speaking about the dream and hearing someone else's wrong ideas that he could get to his own right ones.[13] We have all probably had that experience. Someone, on hearing our dream, says that it means something. While the interpretation is not correct, it triggers our own insights.

It can also be helpful to hear what images can mean for others. There must be a warning here against the many books that outline dream images and what they mean for everyone. These are anathema to proper dream analysis. They give a static interpretation. Yet it can be helpful to hear Marie-Louise von Franz say, "Burglars very often represent something breaking into one's conscious system".[14] Or that if one is urinating in a dream, it can be to do with one's authentic self. If one has to pee one has to pee, there is no holding on to it.

Often dream images can seem banal. Shoes in a dream might appear banal, yet shoes, especially for a woman, can be about what persona one wishes to present to the world. Whose shoes do you wish to wear or are you wearing? A woman dreamed she was helping out in a shoe

---

12 Marie-Louise von Franz in conversation with Fraser Boa, (1988) *The Way of the Dream*. Windrose films Ltd., Toronto, Canada. Page 46.

13 Ibid., Page 14 also mentioned on page 51.

14 ibid., page 45.

shop and the till was clogged with receipts and needed to be cleaned out. This woman was a writer and was trying to make her way in the world as a writer. The dream was telling her that before she could get all these shoes (stories/personas) to walk, she had to unclog her attitudes around money and receiving money.

Making associations and tracking links in dream interpretation can be exciting and even wonderful. When a significant insight is attained one can have a 'Eureka' experience which releases a surge of energy. A man dreamed of driving a very fast car along a road. The road was thankfully free of traffic. There were metal signs across the road but they did not hit the car. The feeling of the dream was of being overwhelmed by the speed of the car. The man identified the feeling with feeling overwhelmed with the amount of things to be done that 'came at him' every day. On discovering the message of the dream, he resolved to take time out twice a day to meditate, so that he could counteract the feeling inside of himself of being 'driven too fast'. The following day he felt elated. A large amount of energy had been released through his insight and his decision.

Jung claims that dreams in themselves are naturally clear. We can have the experience of looking back over them after a long period of time and wondering how we could have been so blind not to have seen their meaning before.[15] However, I have copybooks full of dreams which are as obscure to me now as they were when I dreamed them! I have no doubt that, like any language, practice of it is what gives one fluency in it. The more I work with dreams, on a regular basis, the more I can understand how they work.

A woman once told me of how she had broken up with her partner because he was cheating on her with another woman. Ten years later

---

15 *C.W.* Vol. 16, par 313.

she was looking through her dream journals dating from before the time of the break-up. She noticed two dreams in particular. The first one she had dreamed when her partner was away on a business trip with the woman that he was to leave her for. The dreamer did not suspect the relationship between the two. She dreamed that she was in her bedroom with her partner. When she and her partner went to lie on the bed they realised that this woman was in the bed! In the second dream, a month later, still before the dreamer knew of the affair, she dreamed that she was looking for her partner. He was with this woman and he was kissing her on the lips. He was looking past the woman and was watching the dreamer. The dreamer walked away very angry. She met up with her partner again in the dream and he had his arm around her. However, in the next piece of the dream she was in a room with a corpse and her partner was in the room also, sitting beside her. On rereading the dreams the woman was amazed that she did not interpret them to mean that her partner was cheating. When the truth finally came out she had been stunned. Yet her dreams were telling her the situation long before the time of the breakup.

Subjective or Objective Interpretation?

In part, this demonstrates the problem in dream interpretation that we must constantly grapple with. Is a dream about our outer, objective life or is it about our subjective inner experience? If I dream about a person I know, is the dream saying something about that person and his or her life or is it simply using that person, and my associations with that person, to represent some aspect of my own psyche. So, for example, a woman Jung worked with dreamed that her mother hanged herself. Should this be seen as a warning to watch out for the mother, that she is unstable and may commit suicide? The following dream clears this up and again shows how a series of dreams is much more helpful to work with than a single dream. In the follow-up dream a horse jumped out of the fourth story window. It is a similar act of suicide yet it is not the mother this time, rather it is a horse. This led Jung to conclude that the mother and the horse represent some aspect of the woman that is destroying itself. The woman, in fact, was discovered to have a terminal physical illness.[16]

There is a general rule, which is merely a rule of thumb, regarding this. If the person you dream of is someone whom you have not met for many years, then it is likely that that person represents some aspect of your own psyche. If you dream of someone with whom you have daily contact then there is a chance that the dream will have some bearing on that person and will be telling you something about that person and your relationship with him or her. However, these things are not clear-cut. The people that we work with, or live closely with, are the very ones who carry the projections of our inner psyche material. Therefore, the chances are that the dream is about both things; it is telling us about the person, commenting on our relationship with that person and it is also using that person to tell us something about ourselves, for the person has a hook for the inner content that we put onto him or her. This gives rise to the very tricky question – where does the inner leave off and the outer begin?

It is wise, when looking at a dream, to look at it every-which-way and to watch for what finally clicks. Jung tells the story of a colleague of his, an older man, who would tease Jung about his dream analysis and interpretations. "Well, I met him one day in the street and he called out to me, "How are things going? Still interpreting dreams? By the way, I've had another idiotic dream. Does that mean something too? This is what he had dreamed: *I am climbing a high mountain, over steep snow-covered slopes. I climb higher and higher, and it is marvelous weather. The higher I climb the better I feel. I think, 'If only I could go on climbing like this forever!' When I reach the summit my happiness and elation are so*

---

16 ibid., par 343.

great that I feel I could mount right up into space. And I discover that I can actually do so: I mount upwards on empty air, and awake in sheer ecstasy. [17]

Upon hearing the dream Jung implored the man not to go mountain climbing again without taking guides and being very cautious. The man dismissed his advice and Jung never saw him again. Two months later the man was out climbing alone and was buried by an avalanche. He was dug out just in time by a military patrol that happened to be passing. Three months after that he went out again, this time with a younger friend. They took no guides. A guide who was standing below them saw the older man literally step out into the air while descending the rock. He fell on top of his younger friend and the two fell to their deaths.

The man's unconscious was crying out a warning to take more care while rock climbing. It may also have been showing him that he was looking to rock-climbing to achieve some spiritual experience and that if he pursued his passion of rock-climbing without becoming aware of what drove him to do it, he was in mortal danger. This we will never know for certain. What is certain is that the dream was a literal warning to the man to be more careful when mountain climbing. If the man had not had such a resistance to dreams and their meanings, he might have taken heed.

Jung gives another example, this time of a man suffering from the symptoms of mountain sickness. The interpretation Jung gives is symbolic and not literal. Jung was approached by this man who was very successful in the world. He was suffering from anxiety, dizziness sometimes causing nausea, heaviness in the head, constriction of breath. The man had come from very humble origins as the son of a poor peasant. He had reached a certain level in his profession and

---

17 ibid., par 323. The original text is in italics.

was at a point where he could climb even higher had his neurosis not afflicted him. He had two dreams, which he brought with him to the first session. The first was where he was once again in the village in which he was born. He passes some men that he had gone to school with. They are peasants. The man passes them by and ignores them. He overhears them saying that he does not come back to the village often. In the second dream he is in a great hurry to go on a journey. He is rushing to pack things but cannot find them. Time is running out. He finally arrives at the train station yet the train has left. He watches it go. It is a strange S shape and the man knows that if the driver does not watch out then the train will be thrown off the rails. This happens and the man wakes up in terror.

Jung interprets that the man has exhausted his strength in achieving what he has in his career and suggests that he should rest content with what he has gained. However, the man's ambition is driving him on. He is too high and in an atmosphere where the air will not sustain him – therefore he experiences feelings of mountain sickness and a neurosis. The man refused to listen to the analysis and did push on in his career. The outcome was disastrous.[18]

The first dream of the man revisiting the village where he was born and ignoring the men he went to school with was showing the man that something in his conscious attitude was ignoring the reality of where he had come from. It was a simple, earthy, peasant place that he had come from. He was ignoring and neglecting this aspect of himself. The dream of the train crash was a symbolic image for the actual crash in his own life if he were not to heed the warning that he was over-stretching his energy. The man's symptoms of mountain sickness were an attempt by the unconscious to urge him not to climb any higher in his business.

---

18 ibid., par 297ff.

It is often the case that dreaming of death is of no great matter. When actual death is indicated by the unconscious the language is symbolic. So, for example, I dreamed numerous times of my father dying long before he actually died. The dreams were indicating a shift I was making away from the patriarchal intellectual mentality. The passing on of the old mindset. Whereas the young woman who came to Jung with the dream of her mother committing suicide and of the horse jumping out the window was actually diagnosed with having a fatal physical illness and she subsequently died. The dream images of her dying were symbolic.[19]

In analysing this last dream, Jung could only know if his interpretation was correct, that the woman's instinctive, physical body was destroying itself, by the confirmation of a medical examination. Likewise, with the dream where the ambitious man overreached himself and destroyed his career. When Jung presented this interpretation to the man, having heard his associations, the man reacted strongly saying it was not the case. Jung's interpretation was borne out in time when the man's career went off the rails. Until that actually happened, Jung could not have known for certain that his interpretation was correct.

No matter how clever you may think your interpretation of another person's dream is, if it does not click with the other person, preferably releasing some energy for them, or stirring some emotion, it cannot be known to be correct. Failing the positive response of the dreamer, the interpretation can only be proven in time, in reality. It is the same with an intuition. You can only know an intuition to be correct when it is played out in time, in reality. Such is the nature of these things.

---

19 ibid., par 343 - 348.

Assimilating the Dream Contents

The dream contents must be consciously assimilated if the person is to benefit fully from it. Dreams do benefit a person, even if they are not understood, because dreaming is a natural occurrence and has a value by its very happening. The value of a dream to a person can, however, be enhanced hugely by understanding the dream and assimilating the contents. This does not work if the dream is approached from an exclusively rational perspective. A person may hear an interpretation of their dream that "makes sense" at a rational level but if it does no more than that the interpretation has not really "hit home" and nothing in their psyche has changed. Something has to shift in the dreamer's understanding. " 'Assimilation' in this sense means mutual penetration of conscious and unconscious, and not – as is commonly thought and practiced – a one-sided evaluation, interpretation, and deformation of unconscious contents by the conscious mind".[20]

The unconscious contents must not be manipulated in order for to arrive at an interpretation. Nor can an interpretation be forced upon the conscious mind. The conscious mind must not be damaged or, worse still, destroyed by an interpretation. If this were to happen then there is no one left to do the assimilating. For example, if we consider the young man mentioned earlier who dreamed that his father was recklessly driving his car and was drunk. If Jung had forced the suggestion on the young man that he secretly hated his father, the young man would have been seriously disturbed by the suggestion. His ego awareness of himself could have been undermined by such a suggestion and the analysis would have gone badly off track. The integrity of the conscious mind must remain and the contents of the unconscious, via the dream interpretation, must become assimilated When this happens everything shifts, incorporating the new contents. Again, the intimate connection and interplay between the conscious

---

20 ibid., par 327.

and the unconscious is clear. It is not a matter of 'either/or' but of 'both/and'.

The Prospective Function of a Dream

Jung considered that the unconscious psyche is creative and compensatory to the conscious mind. Every neurosis[21] has an aim and that aim is to compensate for a one-sided attitude to life. It is a voice drawing attention to a side of the personality that has been neglected or repressed. He reasoned that dreams have the same function. The source of a neurosis is a failure to adapt to the demands of life, therefore the energy gets blocked and builds up in the unconscious This blocked energy activates unconscious complexes. Restlessness is the first sign of neurosis. It means that the energies in the dream-world, the unconscious, are bottled up. Energy is not integrated and the person can experience irritability, meaninglessness, aggressiveness. The dreams will indicate what complexes are being activated and will also point to what area in day to day living that needs to be addressed.

If we are living against our instincts, or our true self, the dream-world has no choice but to appear in the negative. Thus, we have dreams of being pursued, of being attacked. These simply mean that something in the unconscious desperately wants to be recognised. The unconscious is telling us that we are in psychological danger and the degree of danger will correspond to the awfulness in the dream content and the feeling-tone of the dream. Jung says of the compensatory function:

> ... the unconscious, considered as relative to consciousness, adds to the conscious situation all those elements from the previous day which remained subliminal because of repression or because they were simply too feeble to reach consciousness. This

21 Neurosis: disorder of nervous system producing depression or irrational behaviour. *Oxford English Dictionary*

compensation, in the sense of being a self-regulation of the psychic organism, must be called purposive.[22]

He goes on to speak about the prospective function of a dream. This is "...an anticipation in the unconscious of future conscious achievements, something like a preliminary exercise or sketch, or a plan roughed out in advance. Its symbolic content sometimes outlines the solution of a conflict."[23] This does not mean that these dreams are prophetic. Merely they present probabilities. In speaking of prospective dreams, Jung is at pains to say that even though it is tempting to allow the unconscious greater value than consciousness, and therefore to put great weight on these dreams, it is wrong to do so. The importance of the unconscious is equal to that of the consciousness but not greater. Therefore, in general where the conscious attitude of the dreamer is seen to be adequate, this means that the dreamer is well adapted to the demands of life, then the meaning of the dream can be confined to the compensatory function. If the conscious attitude of the dreamer is obviously defective, the dream can be seen to be "...a guiding, prospective function capable of leading the conscious attitude in a quite different direction which is much better than the previous one. ... It is obvious that dreams of this sort are found chiefly in people who are not living on their true level".[24] Jung does however admit that such incidents of defective conscious attitudes are very frequent and that this prospective function in dreams comes into play a lot. How many of us are actually living on our true level?

It has often been said by both Jung and Marion Woodman, a Jungian analyst working in Canada, that just before analysis a client can have a major dream that can outline the issue and the probable solution. This would be a prospective dream. It does not indicate that analysis

22 *C.W.* Vol. 16, par 492.
23 *C.W.* Vol. 8, par 493.
24 bid., par 495.

will be easy. Rather it seems to be a gift, a graced touchstone to keep coming back to during analysis. A young man in his twenties came to Jung to work on his homosexuality. He was intelligent and had a strong sense of aestheticism. He was girlish and immature for his age. Jung described him as a clear case of retarded development. Thus, he was not adapting well to the demands of life. The night before he came to Jung, he had this dream: *I am in a lofty cathedral filled with mysterious twilight. They tell me that it is the cathedral at Lourdes. In the centre there is a deep dark well, into which I have to descend.*[25]

This dream has a strong feeling-content. It feels numinous to the dreamer. It is, in fact, a dream about initiation. Remember that the dreamer had this dream the night before he began analysis with Jung. The analysis was to become his initiation into manhood. Something that had not until then happened. Jung analysed the dream as follows, working on the young man's associations. Lourdes represented healing. The cathedral, which reminded him of Cologne Cathedral, which his mother had spoken to him about as a child, represented the mother archetype. The young man had a very close bond with his mother. Not a conscious one, but an unconscious one. This unconscious tie expressed itself consciously in his behaviour, his retarded development of character.

According to Jung, the developing personality strives towards consciousness. An infantile unconscious bond, such as this, obstructs this development. *Therefore, instinct will replace the object of the infantile bond, in this case the mother, with another object.* This is an important process to understand. Something in the human psyche, the striving towards development of personality, towards consciousness, pushes us beyond unconscious infantile bonds. The mechanism it uses is *transference* or *projection*, replacing the mother or father with another object or person outside of ourselves. In the dreamer's case, in this

---

25 *C.W.* Vol. 7, par 167. The original text is in italics.

dream, the mother, and the infantile bond with her, was replaced by the church – Mother Church. "The Church represents a higher spiritual substitute for the purely natural, or 'carnal', tie to the parents".[26] Often the Church will become the replacement object for the infantile bond, yet this is not unique to the Church. Earlier societies have had complex initiation ceremonies for their young people, the purpose of which, psychologically, is to enable them to move into another stage of development. The tribe or community in these cases replace the infantile bond and the young person is freed to move on psychologically.

In the case of the dreamer, although as a child he had heard of Cologne Cathedral and since then the image had stirred in him as a replacement for the mother bond, he had no priestly teacher to enable him to develop it further. He therefore remained locked psychologically with his mother. The longing for a male teacher, or guide, is expressed eventually in his homosexual leanings. The analysis represented the deeper meaning in his homosexuality, his entry into manhood. Jung's analysis was confirmed by a second dream where, again in a cathedral, a priest stands at the altar and a baptism ceremony is about to begin for the dreamer.

This dream cannot be taken as a comment about homosexuality *per se*. It simply outlines the area of psychological development that this particular young man was grappling with. The dream might suggest that from then on, having had the dream, the analysis went smoothly and the young man had made progress in a short space of time. In fact, this was not so. The young man was antagonistic and full of resistance. This shows how the dream compensates for the conscious attitude, rather like the two sides of a scale. The unconscious drive towards development, as shown in the dream, is in direct relation to

26 ibid., par 172.

the conscious attitude of infantilism, which the dreamer displayed in analysis. This dream has a prospective function in that it proposes where the dreamer might go, psychologically speaking.

Negative Compensatory Dreams

There are dreams that are negative compensatory dreams. These are dreams that appear in the person who has a conscious attitude that exceeds their actual capacity. The problem for them is not their adaptation to the environment but rather that they appear to be better than they actually are. To ask how this could be so is a fair question. The answer is that these people feed off collective suggestion. A familiar example is the clergy. The collective projection of holiness, wisdom, moral purity is projected onto men who are priests. It is all the stronger if celibacy is part of the priesthood. Priests can succumb to the lure of this collective energy and live out of it rather than living within the limits of their own personalities. If they appear to be larger than life, holier than thou, untouchable saints, it is very likely that their inside reality does not match their outward eminence. In cases like this, dreams play a negatively compensatory function. This can happen not only to priests but also to anyone who is in a position to access collective esteem. Doctors, surgeons, politicians, bankers also tend to be the targets of collective projection in our very patriarchal society.[27]

The negatively compensatory dream does not simply present the opposite picture to the conscious attitude. This would certainly make the point but it may not bring down the inflated attitude of the dreamer. The negatively compensatory dream constellates repressed infantile-sexual wishes and infantile claims to power, which are retrospective and deeply personal to the dreamer. They are retrospective as opposed to prospective and can be traced back to the past, which the

---

27 The collective esteem given to such people is now on the wane, as a result of public revelations of child abuse by clergy, bishops covering up, banks being exposed for corruption and tribunals exposing the wrongdoings of politicians. I believe this augurs well for a new level of collective maturity.

dreamer thought was buried. These dreams are in such contrast to the dreamer's conscious attitude, and to how she or he is perceived in society, that the dreamer is likely to awake in the morning feeling deeply disturbed!

Negative compensatory dreams or reductive dreams have a tendency to tear down, to devalue, or to destroy. What they are attempting to undermine is not the entire personality of the person but the attitude of consciousness that the person has. They are trying to bring the dreamer back home to himself or herself away from a collective inflation.

Reaction Dreams

For the sake of completion, it is necessary to mention another possibility in dream interpretation. This is the *reaction-dream*. After the various wars in the world, it was discovered that men had dreams that re-enacted the traumatic scenes of war faithfully each night. No amount of interpretation at a deeper level had any impact on these dreams. They repeated themselves until they wore themselves out, or until the traumatic stimulus exhausted itself. It seems that these dreams were the result of a traumatic incident that was not just psychic but that caused a physical lesion of the nervous system. It is difficult to know whether a dream is recreating a traumatic event symbolically, so that the dreamer can change something in his or her conscious attitude, or whether it is, in fact, a reaction dream. What actually decides it is that, if it is the former, then correct interpretation of the dream will stop the dream reoccurring. If the latter, then no amount of interpretation will affect it until it has run its course.

The Structure of Dreams

According to Jung, complexes are the authors of dreams. The dream can tell you what complexes are activated in your conscious day.

As was said earlier, dreams are about energy, where it is and where it needs to go. Complexes are the engines of the psyche. They can generate energy, drain energy away or block energy. Dreams are a valuable way into discovering what our complexes are and, therefore, where our energy may be blocked or sluggish. This is why it is of great value to look at the structure of a dream and to begin to gain access to the insights they offer us. Dreams are often overwhelming with their abundant images and bizarre events. It is, therefore, helpful to note that there is a definite structure that can be perceived.

Jung names four phases in a dream:
1. The introduction or exposition. This involves a statement of place and protagonist, the naming of the problem. 2. The development of the plot. 3. The culmination. Something decisive happens or something changes completely. 4. The result, solution or *lysis*.[28]

A woman has the following dream: I am eating dinner with my husband. A young woman, whom I do not now recognize, is also with us. We are sitting at a round table. I know this woman is in love with a friend of mine, an older man. He has been in America and is presently on a flight back home. He should be arriving at the airport any moment. I decide that I will ring him on his mobile phone on behalf of the woman. I leave the table between dinner and desert and go to a bedroom, which was my bedroom when I was attending college. In the dream, the room now belongs to my brother. I attempt to phone my older friend but I cannot. I phone a woman friend and ask her to try, while I stay on the line to her. She asks for the number. I cannot find it in my address book.

I am then walking with this woman friend through trees and green grassy gardens and fields. She is finding a path back to her own home.

---

28 *C.W.* Vol. 8, par 561 - 564. (*Lysis* - from Latin, from Greek *lusis* 'loosening', from *luein* 'loosen', Oxford Dictionary).

We pass by my home (where I actually live with my husband). I ask her to look at it for she has not seen it since I had changed it. She is delighted by it. I say I want to extend it but that I need more land. She points out that there is plenty of land! I realise that she is right and I wonder why I did not notice it before!

If we look at this dream, with the dramatic structure outlined above in mind, we are firstly looking for the place, protagonist and the problem. The place of the dream is not clear except that it is at a round table. This suggests that the round table and the meal are the significant points and that the dream refers to the present state of the dreamer. The dreamer associated a round table with King Arthur and the Round Table. A place of wisdom and decision and a place to go forth to action. They are eating a meal. Dinner. It is an important meal, the main meal of the day. When there is eating in a dream it can often point to the digesting or breaking down of a complex. It can refer to the fact that a dreamer is working on a complex, cooking up a complex, at the time of the dream. Because the meal is dinner, we can assume that the complex is a major one in the woman's psyche. The round table seems to suggest that the dreamer is on the right track in working on this complex (a place of wisdom).

We discover what the complex is and the problem that is set up in the dream by looking to the young woman who is sharing the meal. She is in love with an older man. The dreamer associates this older man with a positive father figure. He is unavailable for any intimate relationship.

The dreamer had, in reality, worked with a father complex for quite some time at the time of the dream. The dream is stating that there is an aspect of her psyche that is still caught up in it (in love with it). The dream acknowledges the fact that the dreamer is currently working well on this – hence the meal (digesting the complex) and the round table (place of wisdom from which to go forth and act). But it also presents a problem — this aspect of the dreamer's psyche that is still in love with the father figure. (Note that the dreamer did not recognise the young woman on waking i.e. she was not aware of her in her psyche).

The development of the plot, the second phase of the dream, reinforces this problem, for it is the dreamer herself who interrupts the meal to go to phone the older man on behalf of the young woman. She goes to a bedroom, which she used when in college. The dreamer associates this time with when she was immersed in academic pursuit. It was at this time that she met and developed a friendship with this older man, her academic lecturer. The room, in the dream, now belonged to her brother. She associated him with being bound up unconsciously with their mother. It is from this room that she attempts to make the phone-call. There is a hint here as to where in the dreamer's psyche she is still ready to entertain and encourage her negative father complex. It has to do with the part of her psyche that, like her brother, is still bound up unconsciously with the mother. The dreamer's mother, in reality, would not let the brother leave home. She also encouraged her children to adore the father. A negative father complex does not necessarily mean that her relationship with the father was negative. It refers to the fact that the complex has a negative effect on her as a person.

When the dreamer was asked if the interpretation, so far, triggered any memory of events during the day before the dream, she related the following experience. "I had done something that I was quite proud of. Rather than leaving it at that, I said to my husband something like 'who is a clever girl to do that'." I realised, once I had said it, that I was looking for approval from my husband, approval that I had longed for from my father. I could have kicked myself. I thought that that was something like my mother would have said."

It is important to note that the older man (father figure) is on a plane, returning from America. Exhausting though it may be to sift through every part of the dream, each piece is there for a reason. Each part is an important piece of the jigsaw, not to be dismissed or overlooked. The dreamer associated trips to America as transformative. Her previous trips to America changed either her or her circumstances significantly. This seems to imply that the aspect of her psyche that is the father figure is in transition (on a flight) and is about to be changed significantly.

Next, in the dream, comes the culmination, or the place where something changes. In the case of this dream, the change takes place when the dreamer cannot phone the older man. She phones a woman friend. Then comes what Marie-Louise von Franz calls a dream absurdity. The dreamer asks her older woman friend to call the older man while leaving the line open to her. This is not possible in the real world (at least it was not at the time that the dream had been dreamt) but is an example of how the dream world differs from reality. The dreamer, however, cannot find the number in her address book. This is the change in the dream. The dreamer is being blocked and in comes a new figure. The older woman. Then the scene changes completely to where the dreamer is walking with the older woman in a country-like place.

The dreamer has dual associations with the older woman. She recognises that she has some kind of negative mother projection onto the older woman that has made her uncomfortable with her in the past. She also associates this woman with the fact that this older woman had freed herself from a partnership with a man much older than herself.

The dream presents this older woman as someone to whom the dreamer has turned for help in continuing to encourage the connection between the younger woman and the older man (i.e. the father complex). The older woman agrees to help. It is not here that the attempt is foiled. Rather the dreamer cannot find the number in her address book. This seems to imply that it is simply not appropriate, objectively speaking, to continue the relationship with the father figure. Hence the number is not there. However, the older woman is not the one to challenge the dreamer not to connect with the father figure. So, what does she represent?

The setting lends some clues. It is the countryside, green fields with trees. The dreamer associates this with nature. Her experience of nature has provided her with a positive mother/feminine/nurturing experience. The older woman is trying to find a pathway to her own home. She too, the dream implies, is trying to find the right path. The two women, the dreamer and the older woman, are contained/situated in a nurturing and beautiful place. This seems to imply that the dreamer is being supported by an archetypal feminine presence in her psyche. Nature representing the archetypal feminine. The older woman represents that aspect of the dreamer's psyche that is recovering from a mother complex, who has separated from the father figure herself and is attempting to find her path home.

The lysis or solution or conclusion to the dream comes next. The two women pass by the home of the dreamer. She wants to show it to the older woman since she has changed it. The older woman is impressed. This again seems to point to what the dreamer has achieved already in her work with this father complex. Her home represents herself, where she is at. She has already made changes. However, she explains to the older woman that she wants to extend some more but needs more land. The older woman points out that there is already plenty of land there in order to extend the house. The dreamer wonders how she did not see this before.

This is the solution, or resolution to the dream. The dreamer thinks that she needs to get more land. This leaves her powerless, vulnerable to the owner of the land who, in reality, has already said that he would not sell. So, the dreamer is stuck. She cannot extend her house because she cannot get the land. In the dreamer's psyche there is still a dependency on the masculine/father figure. The older woman points out that she already has plenty of land. The dream is saying that the dreamer has, within herself, an older woman who is, as yet, imperfect but is 'searching for the path'. This older woman may still be negatively connected to her mother complex but she can help the dreamer to see that she can use what she has got inside to make the personal extensions/growth leaps that she feels she needs to. Basically, the dreamer's own imperfect feminine aspect is what enables her to see how she can grow/extend beyond the limits of what remains of her father complex.

The dream seems to imply that this imperfect feminine aspect (the older woman) is contained by the feminine archetype (the walk in the countryside) and is in a state of transformation (trying to find her path home). The dream already implied that the father aspect is also undergoing transformation (by the flight from America). There is a clear indication in the dream that the mother and father complexes are shifting and changing and transforming. The challenge for the dreamer is to continue this by believing or seeing that there is the necessary space/land within herself to grow psychologically (expand her home space).

Often, with dream interpretation, because dreams are so complex, it is difficult to see where the dream may be compensatory to the conscious attitude of the dreamer, as Jung claims. Marie-Louise Von Franz says that a dream "corrects one's attitude".[29] In the dream and interpretation above, the compensatory function can be seen in the way that it corrects the dreamer's attitude the previous day. She admitted to feeling despair when she found herself looking for her husband's approval. She felt that with all the work she had done, she had not, after all, come very far. The dream shows just how far she has come and it does more than that. It shows the other energies that are being transformed in her psyche that she was not aware of. It encourages her to keep on track and to believe in those aspects of herself that she most doubts (the older woman whom she initially associates with her negative mother complex).

It seems to me easier to think of dreams as showing the whole picture rather than limiting oneself to discovering, in black and white terms, what they compensate for. As a line in a song by The Waterboys says – "I see the crescent, but you see the whole of the moon"[30] – the unconscious uses dreams to give us the larger picture. Our conscious attitude can, because of its very nature, give us only a section. We must function in the world. We cannot embrace everything and still function. And so our dreams give us glimpses of the full picture. It shifts the camera lens from the narrow focus to the wider angle.

Dreams also give us information on how our psyche and our attitudes are shifting. A man dreamed that he sent his three spinster aunts west in a car and told them that he could still be contacted until they got as far as Athlone, a town in the Irish midlands. He then found himself in a hotel with a beautiful young woman sitting with her head in his lap. They were having a deep and sincere conversation. He associated

---

29 Marie-Louise von Franz in conversation with Fraser Boa, (1988). *The Way of the Dream*. Windrose films Ltd., Toronto, Canada. Page 47.
30 The Waterboy's song *'The Whole of the Moon'* is on the CD entitled: *The Whole of the Moon: The Best of Mike Scott and the Waterboys*. (1998) Ensign Records Ltd, London.

his maiden aunts with dried up femininity. He associated the West of Ireland with new life and with the golden road of the setting sun, which leads to the Otherworld. Athlone and the River Shannon marks the border to the west. The dream was indicating that the man had reached a new relationship with the feminine. He had mindfully sent off the old dried feminine to be renewed in the magical west and he now was in a new place (hotel - neutral venue) with a young feminine energy to which he was relating deeply. The man in reality was making progress in his relating to his feminine side. The dream shows this. He has further to go. This is implied through the hotel venue. It is not a private home space, rather it is a non-committal type space. On tracking further dreams, this push to take his feminine into private space, and his resistance to do so, is played out.

Dreams expose the larger reality. They tell you the situation as it is. If in your conscious attitude you have striven to respond to unconscious aspects of your psyche, your dreams will tell you this. If you still have further to go, they will tell you this also.

One of my most treasured dreams came after a series of dreams where I was in my mother's house, or parked outside it, or trying to get out of it. These dreams indicated a struggle with the mother complex. In this particular dream, I woke up in my own bed in my own home. I went outside and saw a beautiful new dawn! I interpreted the dream as saying that I had finally stepped outside of the mother complex and psychologically I had caught up with my physical whereabouts.

Another delightful dream is related in *The Way of the Dream* by Fraser Boa. It goes:

> A six-year-old girl dreamed she was with her grandmother. In the dream she said, "Grandma, I

can make myself disappear!" "Nonsense, child!" the grandmother replied. "Nobody can do that". At that point the child woke up, sat up in bed, looked around her darkened bedroom, then lay down and went back to sleep. As sometimes happens, she re-entered the same dream, whereupon her dream grand-mother looked at the girl and said, "Lord, child, how did you do that?[31]

What a lovely image for how the unconscious realm and the conscious realm interplay with each other.

Little Dreams and Big Dreams

Jung makes this distinction between little dreams and big dreams: "Looked at more closely, 'little' dreams are the nightly fragments of fantasy coming from the subjective and personal sphere, and their meaning is limited to the affairs of everyday. That is why such dreams are easily forgotten, just because their validity is restricted to the day-to-day fluctuations of the psychic balance."[32] Big dreams on the other hand come from the collective unconscious and are not easily forgotten. Rather they are often remembered for a lifetime with the same strong affect as on the night that they were dreamed. "The dream uses collective figures because it has to express an eternal human problem that repeats itself endlessly, and not just a disturbance of personal balance".[33]

Jung points out that little dreams deal with the day-to-day imbalances in our psyche while the big dreams tend to occur in people during critical phases of their life, in early youth, puberty, middle age and before death. Little dreams pertain to the personal life and unconscious

---

31 Marie-Louise von Franz in conversation with Fraser Boa, (1988). *The Way of the Dream*. Windrose films Ltd., Toronto, Canada. Page 39.
32 *C.W.* Vol. 8, par 554.
33 ibid., par 556.

of the person while the big dreams have relevance and meaning for all of humankind. The material in the little dreams is purely personal. The associations in these dreams are from the personal realm. The material of the big dreams, however, comes from a much wider field. This field is mythological and can be seen to be repeated throughout the history of humankind. Motifs within these big dreams are archetypal and often the associations of the dreamer alone cannot unlock the meaning of the dream for us. We must look to mythology. "A young man dreamed of *a great snake that guarded a golden bowl in an underground vault.*"[34] The young man did see a huge snake in the zoo but that was the limit of his associations. This association and the lack of any other did not add up to explain the degree of emotionality that accompanied the dream. When we look to mythology we see there the snake or dragon, and the cave, as part of the hero's ordeal or journey. He has to slay the dragon. It is a story that has relevance to all humanity, not just this dreamer. Perhaps the dreamer has this image coming to him in his dreams because he is about to face an ordeal such as this, or he is refusing to face such an ordeal.

In indigenous tribes the shaman or the king often dreamed for the whole tribe. There is a report about the Polar Eskimos, where one of the tribe had a dream which instructed him to lead the tribe to another place that was many days journey over the ice. He did so, but some of the people lost faith and turned back. Food and shelter were found in the new site, while those who turned back perished from starvation.[35] The way society is structured in the West, it is hard to see how an individual could dream for the collective. Archetypal dreams are more likely to come to us during times of transition in our personal lives. They have meaning for us as individuals. They can, however, have significance for the rest of society. Even if we have lost the avenues for

34 ibid., par 555.
35 Knud Rasmussen, (March 1999). *Across Artic America, Narrative of the Fifth Thule Expedition* . University of Alaska Press.

communicating them to the rest of society they can still be important for that society.

There are worlds within worlds. We have our personal lives which is one world. Then we have our personal dreams, which show us the fuller picture. These dreams attempt to help us to integrate the 'more' of the personal unconscious into our conscious attitude, which by very definition must be one-dimensional. And then there is the even bigger world in which our personal unconscious resides, the collective unconscious. The dreams that come from the collective unconscious show us an even bigger picture of balance, integration and assimilation. These dreams set us in the context of the repeating story of all of humanity and of psychic meaning and growth.

When we work on our dreams, we learn how our complexes work and we bring some of them into better balance. When complexes are out of balance they are using up too much psychic energy. They are therefore draining our life force and they need to be looked at and adapted. Our dreams help us to do this. They tell us what the complex is and what can be done about it. They are the basic nuts and bolts of how to achieve balance in one's life. When attention is paid to these dreams we gain more respect for the symbols and the language that they use. It is hard to judge where the little dreams end and the big ones begin for even in the little dreams we have visitations from snakes and dragons, wise old women and semi-divine children. Granted, we rarely have dreams that pertain to the whole of society but we do have dreams which echo the great struggles and stories of humankind. For these are also our struggles.

Jung divided life into stages. The early stages of a person's life were concerned with action and with establishing oneself in the world. In the middle of one's life meaning becomes an issue. Striking archetypal images are more likely to appear in our dreams during this time in our lives. Jung discovered a common pattern in dreams after he had analysed many thousands of them. Often the people he worked with were in their middle years. The pattern presented itself in the type of archetypes that people dreamed of and in the order of their appearing. Initially the shadow archetype appears. The shadow is that which we are unaware of. It consists of the parts of our psyche that we do not perceive or will not perceive. It appears in dreams as the same gender as the dreamer. When this archetype has been grappled with by the dreamer the animus and anima archetypes appear (anima for a man and animus for a woman). The animus and anima are the counter-sexual aspect of a person's psyche. It is when these archetypes have been experienced and somehow assimilated that the archetype of the Self, the inner organising principle of the entire psyche visits a dreamer. Some of these archetypes will be looked at more closely in the latter part of this work. What is relevant here is that there is a pattern. Jung called this pattern the Individuation Process.

The process of individuation does not begin in middle age or with the onset of some dreadful crisis. It is there from the beginning. There is a grand pattern being woven by our experiences. How we deal with our life experiences dictates how we progress on our journey through life, both the outer journey and the inner journey. Perhaps it is in middle age or with some crisis that the process becomes accelerated significantly. However, we can accelerate the process consciously by looking at our dreams and by becoming aware of our complexes. It is our inner world that directs and orchestrates our outer life. Our life is like a spiral. Keeping a journal of dreams can seem overwhelming, for there will be hundreds of dreams within a few years. Yet I am sure that when I am an old woman, I will look back over the big pile of journals and begin to recognise the motifs. I will see the times when I was dealing with shadow, or when I was learning to relate positively to animus energy, or when I began to get a sense of the wise old woman, or the nurturing earth. Nor do I think it impossible that I might find all of this in one year's journal, as well as seeing it stretch over an entire lifetime. For this is how the unconscious works. Time is a conscious construct. In the unconscious, everything is happening at once. There are concurrent realities. This is reflected in our dreams.

Active Imagination – A Tool to Explore Dreams.
Active imagination is a very effective tool that allows us to explore the images that have emerged from the unconscious. It is an invaluable way to actively explore what a dream might mean or where the energy in the dream can go. It is simple and easy and extremely useful. Jung developed the idea of active imagination over time. He refers to it in Vol 8, 166-175 though he does not use the term. Here he recommends its use as a way of accessing psychic energy that is 'in the wrong place' and suggests that it is possible to track the misplaced energy through a 'mood' or 'emotional state'. The first time he uses the term, active imagination is at The Tavistock Lectures where he describes a young artist whom he was treating who was having great difficulty in understanding what Jung meant by active imagination.[36]

With active imagination Jung distinguishes between daydreaming, which is a conscious activity and dreaming at night, which is an unconscious activity and proposes a combination of the two as a way of getting both the unconscious content and the conscious ability to focus, to interplay in such a way as to gain further insight into the unconscious. In *C.W.* Vol 9, par 319 he provides this account of active imagination:

> … a method (devised by myself) of introspection
> for observing the stream of interior images. One

---

36 *C.W.* Vol 18, par 392

concentrates one's attention on some impressive but unintelligible dream-image, or on a spontaneous visual impression and observes the changes taking place in it. Meanwhile, of course, all criticism must be suspended and the happenings, observed and noted with absolute objectivity. Obviously, too, the objection that the whole thing is "arbitrary" or "thought up" must be set aside, since it springs from the anxiety of an ego-consciousness which brooks no master besides itself in its own house.

We have all experienced a daydream that, without our being aware of it, seems to take off on its own. In this experience we have ceased directing the daydream and it develops a life of its own ending up in a place that sometimes surprises us. Active imagination is a tool that harnesses this natural tendency. Firstly, we begin with a dream or dream image that we would like to learn more from that has a strong emotional content or interest for us. We re-enter the dream and step back, that is, we relax our conscious mind and allow the images to develop, to act, to come alive. In order for this to happen: "Critical attention must be eliminated".[37] The role of the conscious mind is openness and observation. The material takes on a life of its own and the conscious mind goes with it. In active imagination the conscious and the unconscious are not antagonistic, they are not set against each other but rather a synthesis occurs because of the cooperative attitude of the conscious mind.

For Jung the unconscious was creative and in active imagination we have a tool whereby we can access and cooperate with that creativity. The archetypes are the orchestrators of the dream world and we can experience what Jung refers to as a "kind of spontaneous amplification

---

37 *C.W.* Vol 8, par 170

of the archetypes".[38]

A woman dreamed that her kitchen was filled with people whom she did not invite. The room was crowded. There were people over at the kettle and she wanted to make a cup of coffee and was angry and frustrated that the people were there because she could not get near the kettle to make the coffee. In the dream she asked one of the people why they were there and he told her that her husband had said they could all stay. The woman felt furious and powerless. She thought in the dream that she would have to talk to her husband and suffer the presence of the people until she did. When she awoke from the dream the woman felt disturbed. She could not understand why in the dream she did not just tell everyone to leave. She could not understand why she hesitated. The woman decided to do active imagination on the dream. She intended to re-enter the dream with guns blazing and tell everyone to leave and give her husband a piece of her mind to boot. However, before reentering the dream she realised that she could go into the dream like this, angry and assertive or she could go back approaching the matter differently. She could consciously step back and observe a little more, perhaps relate to the people a little more. She decided to be less defensive and reactionary and to be more open. She did this. Upon re-entering the dream she saw that the people at the kettle were making coffee and they offered her a cup! It was really good coffee. When she sat at the table to drink it she noticed a young man opposite her and when she spoke with him he offered to help with some tricky renovation that she had been planning. Then the people all simply disappeared and the kitchen was filled with light that shot up into the sky. The woman described it as a cathedral of light and her entire body felt shot through with this light.

The new insight that the experience of active imagination gave the

---

38 *C.W.* Vol 8 par 403

woman was that her old conscious attitude of feeling victim to and inwardly but silently resisting her inner masculine's (husband's) openness to the world had become a sticking point for her psychic freedom and growth. While the logical response was to get all those people out of her kitchen, to make an assertive stand, the active imagination was showing her that if she could let go of the defensive, assertive stance and relax into what was happening everything could shift, transform and move on. She could be shot through with light.

Jung sums up what happens in active imagination by saying "a product is created which is influenced by both conscious and unconscious, embodying the striving of the unconscious for the light and the striving of the conscious for substance".[39] There are other ways to make the dream images substantial: you can draw them, paint them, sculpt them. One of Marion Woodman's's amazing contributions to Jungian psychology was to dance them and to use awareness of the body and where sensations appeared in the body to explore dream images.

I urge people to record their dreams. But not only this. If you have an interest in your personal growth then you will benefit greatly if you look at dreams and begin to learn the language. It was only after recording hundreds of my own dreams that I eventually began to work hard at interpreting them. In doing this, I discovered a new respect and awe for the cleverness and integrity of the images and the messages within the dreams. I felt myself move more swiftly through issues with the help of the dream images. I got into the practice of writing the dream and then working on the associations I had with each part of the dream. I would track the form of the dream; the introduction, development, culmination and result. I would try to locate the complex or issue that the dream was dealing with. It was

---

39 *C.W.* Vol 8, par 168

always interesting to see if it was triggered by anything that happened in the previous day. Some dreams called for all of this work and still I would be left wondering what they were really about. I would, sometimes, tell the dream to someone who could listen generously to it. It might take days before I would realise what a dream was about. Some dreams had enough energy or carried enough emotion to stay with me for days. They would nag at me repeatedly. Other dreams I would simply write down and not bother much further with.

Dream interpretation is a strange task. Some dreams take a lot of effort and there may be little noticeable result. Other dreams just click. It is like breaking up slabs of limestone, which I have had to do to level a foundation for building. You can hit away for a long time, swinging with a very heavy crowbar and finally only break off a small piece. Or you can sometimes get a lucky strike and an entire slab falls away. The dreams that simply click are the lucky strike ones. More often than not we need to keep chipping away at them hoping they will reveal their message. The dreams that need to be worked on are the ones that call to us. They are the ones that we remember, the ones that nag at us, disturb us and excite us. They are loaded with emotion. They are the ones to try to crack.

It is extremely difficult to analyse one's own dreams. Our dreams show us our backs. They show us what we do not know, or do not want to know, about ourselves. Yet many of us do not have the benefit of an analyst. Like Jung himself, we must rely on ourselves and the 'gardener' in our lives, the person, or people who have the patience to listen with generosity, so that our backs might be revealed to us. These are the people who can give us an opinion no matter how off the wall it might be, so that we can say, no that is not it, but this is it! A friend once, on parting, said to me – "Look after your dreams". It strikes me as the best advice he could have given me.

CHAPTER FOUR

A Psychology of Types

Befriending the Other

The Dinner Party

Gobsmacked
by the mime act
of pleasantries at the party –
the Asperger-y voice
in my head
said
(loudly) –
'BORED,
I WANT TO GO HOME
NOW'
And I think
'Holy Cow,
how come nobody
heard that?'

Carl Jung drew up a psychology of types.[1] Even though the terms he used are now in our common use of language, their meaning is not always understood. First, there are the attitude types. These consist of introvert and extravert. Then there are the function types. These are thinking, feeling, intuition and sensation. How an introverted person experiences the world is very different to how an extraverted person experiences it. The same is true for people of different function types. A person who is a thinker will value very different aspects of life than a feeling type. In this chapter I will explore the attitude types of introvert and extravert. I will also look at the structure of the function types. Each person has a dominant function, auxiliary functions and an inferior function. The former lies in the conscious psyche, the latter in the unconscious, the auxiliaries lie somewhere in between. It is important to discover what our relationship is with each of our functions and to observe how they play out in our lives. It is also valuable to begin to recognise that other people who work from different attitude types and different function types to ourselves, experience the world very differently than we do.

The Attitude Types: Introvert and Extravert

"The one achieves its ends by a multiplicity of relationships,
the other by monopoly".[2]

To understand these terms, one must distinguish between subject and object. The subject is the person and that person's inner world. The object is the outer world. Jung talks of a person's relationship to the object and asks the question: does that person have a positive relationship to the object or a negative one? The answer indicates

---

1 Volume 6 of the *COLLECTED WORKS*, Psychological Types. (1971) Princeton University Press, N.J., U.S.A.
2 *C.W.* Vol. 6, par 559. Italics mine.

whether one is an extravert or an introvert. The extravert has a positive relationship with the object. The introvert has a negative relationship with it.

If something is suggested to the extravert, a project, a plan, even a suggestion that they go out somewhere, the extravert's initial response will be "yes, let's do it". Only after that response will other considerations come into play and be considered. For the extravert, the outer world carries all the weight of importance. The inner world is to varying degrees ignored. In an extreme extraverted attitude, the subject himself or herself will receive no consideration whatsoever. The person is so identified with the object that he or she will not even be aware that a subjective dimension needs to be considered. This is in very extreme cases. For the extravert, the libido, or psychic energy, constantly and habitually flows towards the object. Just how identified one becomes with the object, to the detriment of one's subjective self, defines how healthy, or unhealthy, one is as an extravert.

On the other hand, when something is suggested to the introvert, the immediate response is "no". Only after consideration will the suggestion be processed and perhaps deemed acceptable. The introvert experiences the world as something to protect oneself from. If an introvert is healthy, that person will be able to consider the outer world, the object, in the scheme of things and act accordingly. The introvert has a rich inner life and a keen sense of themselves in the world. In an unhealthy state, the introvert constructs such defenses as to withdraw entirely from the outer world.

Being introverted or extraverted is basically a mode of adaptation to one's experience of life. Jung claims that these psychological modes of adaptation are founded in the two fundamentally different physical modes of adaptation found in all living organisms. In nature, some species survive by propagating profusely and have a very low defense system. Fleas, rabbits and lice are in this category. These are the extraverts! They cope with reality by pouring themselves into it, conquering it and overcoming it. The other type of species has few offspring and has a powerful defense system. Hedgehogs and elephants are examples of this type of species. These are the introverts! They protect themselves from the world while getting on with their lives.

These are the two different ways in which species cope with reality in order to survive in the world. Marie-Louise von Franz gives examples in nature of how the introvert and extravert attitudes work. In her excellent work *Lectures on Jung's Typology*, which she presented as a series of lectures in 1961, she refers to a study done by a professor of Zoology.[3] This professor stated that "the higher anthropoid apes are incapable of performing the sexual act, unless they have observed another ape and learned that way, whereas with many other animals it is quite the opposite: without ever having seen animals of their species mating, the urge from within is sufficient".[4] She goes on to give another example of how animal behaviour consists of both inborn disposition and external stimuli:

> Experiments have been made by incubating stork's eggs and keeping them from contact with the social group. When birds produced from such eggs are released, those bred of eggs whose group fly over Yugoslavia to Africa will fly over that country, and those produced from the eggs of birds, which fly over Spain, will fly over Spain to Africa. This proves that they rely completely on an inborn disposition, which tells them how to reach Africa.

---

3   Marie-Louise von Franz and James Hillman. (1986) *Lectures on Jung's Typology.* Spring Publications, Putnam, C.T. U.S.A. Page 8 ff.
4   Ibid, page 8

> But if a stork bred from the Yugoslav group is put with the birds, which fly over Spain, the bird will fly with them and not follow his inborn disposition. This shows the two possibilities very clearly – being influenced by outer factors and social pressure, or simply following the inborn disposition.[5]

Everyone has both the introvert and extravert attitude. When one or the other is predominant, and is the habitual response, then it becomes a type. Because it is possible to see in very small children a particular type, it cannot be the struggle for existence that determines a particular attitude. Therefore, it must be the individual disposition of the child that determines it. One seems to be born with these attitudes, the same way as one is born with a certain colour hair or eyes. Jung speaks of abnormal cases where the mother's own attitude is extreme, and is forced on the child, thereby distorting the child's own natural orientation. Such cases invariably lead to a neurosis in later life, which can only be cured by re-establishing the person's original attitude. This shows how essential it is to stay true to one's own attitude, for to do otherwise is detrimental. "I do not think it improbable, in view of one's experience, that a reversal of type often proves exceedingly harmful to the physiological well-being of the organism, usually causing acute exhaustion".[6]

In describing the two attitude types, it is important to cover both the attitude of consciousness and also the compensatory attitude of the unconscious. To look at one without the other would be too simplistic and would be to draw a one-dimensional picture with no depth. The consciousness is counterbalanced always by the unconscious. When consciousness becomes too extreme, the unconscious will come into

---

5   ibid, page 9
6   *C.W.* Vol. 6, par 560.

play in order to balance things out again. As indicated earlier, the term used is enantiodromia [7]. This is a term first used by Heraclitus. It means that everything in time swings towards its opposite. Jung describes it as "the emergence of the unconscious opposite in the course of time. This characteristic phenomenon practically always occurs when an extreme, one-sided tendency dominates conscious life; in time an equally powerful counter-position is built up, which first inhibits the conscious performance and subsequently breaks through the conscious control".[8] Thus, when the conscious attitude becomes too extreme the unconscious counter-position begins to interfere with the conscious attitude. It calls attention to the imbalance. If, however, this warning is not heeded and the conscious attitude is not brought into some kind of balance, the unconscious contents will erupt into the conscious attitude and will cause havoc. Basically, they will take over.

A good example of this was in a Western film I watched. The teetotaling, non-smoking, law-upholding governor of a men's prison hunts down the heartless bank-robber, who has escaped to find the stolen money he has hidden and who plans to run for Mexico. The governor finds the bank-robber who is dead from a snake bite. The bank robber's dead body covers the stolen money. The governor brings the body back to the prison, but at the gates turns around and heads for Mexico himself with the money! He turns his back on his life as a governor, smoking and drinking all the way!

Extraverted Type – The Conscious Attitude
Both the extravert and the introvert, in their conscious attitudes, orientate themselves according to the outer world. However, the difference is that the extravert takes the given facts in themselves and responds to them. The object receives the weight of value. The

7   See Chapter 2 of this work, footnote 4.
8   *C.W.* Vol. 6, par 709.

introvert, on the other hand, "holds in reserve a view which interposes itself between him and the objective data".[9] The value is placed on the person in relation to the given data, not on the data itself.

In every situation there is subject and object. For the extravert, the determining value lies in the objective conditions, for the introvert it lies in the subjective conditions. For the extravert, the essence of reality is found in the outside world, he or she will therefore not look for this essence within. This value placed on the outer world allows the extravert an awareness in relation to the outer world. The extravert will tend to know what the proper behaviour is in various situations. Take, for example, at a funeral. The extravert will usually know what is expected of him or her. The introvert, on the other hand, will have to watch carefully what other people are doing in order to get their lead. Being an extravert has to do with awareness and information. The extravert, because of the value he or she places on the outer world, receives more information in relation to the outer world.

The extravert's actions are "recognisably related to external conditions"[10] in terms of actions, interests and moral standpoint: "Objective happenings have an almost inexhaustible fascination for him, so that ordinarily he never looks for anything else".[11] And "The moral laws governing his actions coincide with the demands of society, that is, with the prevailing moral standpoint".[12] Extraverts often want the radio on as a background stimulus. They need outside input. An extravert can have the interest to watch the news every day and to tune into regular current affairs programmes while an introvert may rest content to listen to a random catch-up news report and/or a weekly newspaper perusal.

---

9   ibid., par 563.
10   ibid.
11   ibid.
12   *C.W.* Vol. 6, par 564.

Ironically, the body is not objective enough for the extravert's attention. The extravert can become absorbed by objective demands and ignore the most basic needs of the body, not to mention those of the psyche. When this happens, the body kicks back with physical and/or nervous disorders attempting to draw attention to the subject. Jung gives a dramatic example of this: "... a man about to marry a woman of doubtful character whom he adores and vastly overestimates is seized with a nervous spasm of the esophagus and has to restrict himself to two cups of milk a day, each of which takes him three hours to consume. All visits to the adored are effectively stopped, and he has no choice but to devote himself to the nourishment of his body."[13]

Unconscious Attitude of the Extravert

The attitude of the unconscious in the extravert is a compensatory one and it is therefore egocentric, placing all emphasis on the subjective. This is the underside of the extravert's character. If the extravert is to be healthy he or she needs to allow for this underside and incorporate it into one's life in a healthy and conscious fashion. If one cannot or does not do this, if the conscious attitude becomes too extreme, then this underside will make itself felt. Marie-Louise von Franz points out that: "In the extravert the conscious libido habitually flows towards the object, but there is an unconscious secret counter-action back towards the subject."[14] When this secret self is given some room in the person's life, it will provide a fresh flow of libido into the person's psyche. If, however, it is ignored or repressed severely, then it takes on a regressive character. The less acknowledged it is, the more infantile it becomes.

If an extravert thinker makes time in his life, for example, to follow an inclination to look at classical art, by going to galleries and browsing

---

13 ibid., par 565.
14 Marie-Louise von Franz and James Hillman. (1986) *Lectures on Jung's Typology*, Spring Publications, Putnam, C.T., U.S.A. Page 3.

through art books, he is making room in his life for introversion and for the subjective feeling that is experienced through art. If the same extravert ignores these inner urges, he can become driven by an obnoxious and deluded inner demon that urges him to give up his real work in the world to become an art critic! Jung cited a similar example of a business man, a printer, who, rather than using art as a way of exploring his own inner world, incorporated his artwork into his business products and very swiftly went bankrupt.[15]

There is a process of disintegration that takes place in extreme forms of extraversion. The unconscious loses its compensatory character and appears in open opposition to the conscious attitude. Once the unconscious is in open opposition, the conscious attitude responds by becoming even more extreme, attempting to repress the unconscious contents even more. The conscious attitude can then begin to disintegrate. This can happen in the world, objectively, as in the example of the businessman above, where the unconscious contents flowed over into the real world with disastrous results. Or it can happen subjectively in the form of a breakdown. The unconscious paralyses all conscious action. The person either does not know what he or she wants and nothing interests them, or the person wants what is impossible.

Introverted Type - The Conscious Attitude
In western culture the extravert attitude is the one that is most accepted and understood. In schools, the extravert feeling children are often the most popular. This carries on into adult life. Who fails to be impressed by people who can be sincerely charming socially? Even when we come to look at each of the functions we will find that the extraverts are the ones who are most easy to describe. Their frame of reference, that is, the outer world, is more obvious.

---

15 *C.W.* Vol. 6, par 572.

Just as there is a bias in our culture towards extraversion, so too is there a bias towards objectivity. However, perception and cognition are not purely objective. The subjective plays a huge part in all experience. Jung said: "The world exists not merely in itself, but also as it appears to me".[16] Therefore, the subjective factor influences how we see things. For the introverted type, that subjective factor, as opposed to the objective data, receives most of the value. The subjective factor is what the introvert orientates himself or herself by. The extravert will respond to what comes to him or her from the object; the introvert will rely on what is constellated in himself or herself by the object. Something is, of course, constellated in the extravert by the object but he or she puts little value on it. For the introvert it is all-important.

This subjective factor needs to be looked at. It is not synonymous with the ego, for the ego is but a small part of the subjective factor. Basically, when Jung speaks of the subjective factor he is speaking of the collective unconscious as well as the personal consciousness and the personal unconscious. Therefore, for the introvert the frame of reference is not merely personal, rather it is a whole world within. Jung had to argue very hard in his day that this world actually existed. Jung said of the subjective factor: "It is another universal law, and whoever bases himself on it has a foundation as secure, as permanent, and as valid as the man who relies on the object".[17] The subjective factor is the world of the collective unconscious/personal unconscious and personal consciousness. The ego is included in this. It is like the piece of the iceberg that is above water and is conscious. Under water there exists energies and archetypes and complexes. It is from this world that the introvert gains energy, meaning, and definition. But not exclusively so. Introverts have an unconscious connection to the objective world and although they withdraw their energy from

16 ibid., par 620.
17 ibid., par 622.

the objective world, unconsciously they direct their libido towards it. Marie-Louise von Franz writes: "In the case of the introvert … he feels as if an overwhelming object wants constantly to affect him, from which he has continually to retire; but he is unaware that he is secretly borrowing energy from and lending it to the object through his unconscious extraversion".[18]

Jung is at pains to point out that the value of both, the subjective factor and the objective data, is relative and therefore *in extremis,* neither are ideal. A balance is needed to achieve something close to an 'accurate' experience of the world.[19]

Two factors reveal to us what type a person is: whether a person puts more value on the inner or the outer world, and where a person gets his or her energy. Extraverts get their energy from the outer world. Introverts get their energy from within. Introverts need to make time in their lives to be alone, for the sake of their psychological health. Every introvert knows the feeling of being dry, of having no psychic energy left to go on. Every introvert also knows the feeling of being refueled after having had time alone. It is like drinking clear water from a well after being in the desert for too long. The introvert connects with his or her energy supply by being alone. It is only by experiencing solitude that introverts can process their subjective experience of the world.

Because introverts put more value on the inner world they will look to themselves when something has bothered them, before they will look at the outer event or person. Two women were talking and one said something that seriously disturbed the other. The disturbed woman was an introvert and carried on as if nothing had happened. She went away from the meeting with strong feelings of dislike for the other

---

18 Marie-Louise von Franz and James Hillman. (1986) *Lectures on Jung's Typology,* Spring Publications, Putnam, C.T. U.S.A. Page 3.
19 *C.W.* Vol. 6, 556ff.

woman. If the disturbed woman had been extravert, it is unlikely (but not impossible, depending on function) that she would have said nothing. The disturbed woman knew that she had to do something with her negative feelings towards her friend. She decided to track the negative feelings and in doing so she discovered that she had not wanted to meet the friend at all, initially. She had a busy life, was feeling drained and what she needed in order to renew herself was to be alone. She had acted against this deep need when she had agreed to meet the person. Once she realised this, her negativity towards the person lifted! She never had to address the issue overtly with the other woman. She dealt with it entirely on the inner plain. This is typical of how introverts deal with situations. They will deal with them inwardly firstly, and then they will only address them in the outer world if they absolutely have to.

Extraverts will, most likely, do the opposite. They will, whether there and then, or later, address the person who disturbed them and only then, if absolutely necessary, will they look within to what was actually disturbed in themselves. For the extravert, the disturbance exists in the outer world and they will either address it there or ignore it there and live with it. It rarely occurs to them to look within and try to change things from that perspective. The opposite is the case for the introvert. The outer world merely triggers the disturbance, which exists in the inner world, and that is where it must be dealt with. In fact, both perspectives are true. In an ideal situation, both realms need to be addressed when a disturbance takes place.

Unconscious Attitude of the Introvert
The health of the introvert depends on being able to make the distinction between the ego and the Self. The ego is the organising principle of the conscious psyche and is in the personal conscious of an individual. The Self, however, is the organising principle of

the entire psyche, both conscious and unconscious. It resides in the unconscious. If the introvert is not identified with the ego, and has a sense of the greater unconscious and the Self therein, then this subjective factor, that is, the subject, is equal to the outer world, to the object. If, however, the introvert becomes identified with the ego, and excessive importance is attached to the ego, then the ego is not an equal match with the object. "Self and world are commensurable factors: hence a normal introverted attitude is as justifiable and valid as a normal extraverted attitude. But if the ego has usurped the claims of the subject, this naturally produces, by way of compensation, an unconscious reinforcement of the influence of the object."[20] This is played out, in reality, by the person desperately trying to remain separate from the object, yet finding themselves bound to it. It is felt as "an absolute and irrepressible tie to the object."[21] Jung gives some examples: "The individual's freedom of mind is fettered by the ignominy of his financial dependence, his freedom of action trembles in the face of public opinion, his moral superiority collapses in a morass of inferior relationships, and his desire to dominate ends in a pitiful craving to be loved".[22]

The process of this disintegration is worth looking at. The ego has taken over the subject's claims. It is not a match for the object. It degrades the object and there is an extreme compensatory response on behalf of the object. The unconscious now is in charge of the relation to the object. The object assumes terrifying power despite the attempt of the ego to degrade it. The ego, therefore, becomes even more aggressive in an attempt to assert itself and degrade the object. It surrounds itself with various systems of defense to preserve some illusion of dominance. This results in obsessional behaviour – an attempt to order the world to make it less frightening. This attempt to order the world is found also

---

20 ibid., par 626.
21 ibid.
22 ibid.

in normal introvert behaviour. Marie-Louise von Franz writes: "Jung once told of the case of a child who would not enter a room before it had been told the names of the pieces of furniture in the room – table, chair, etc. That is typical of a definitely introverted attitude, where the object is terrifying and has to be banished or put in its place by a word, a propitiating gesture by which the object is made known and cannot misbehave".[23] In the case of the adult who is struggling to degrade the object's power over the ego, this behaviour becomes truly extreme. The person becomes completely alienated from the object, while being totally dominated by the object. The neurosis that results from this is called psychasthenia and it consists of chronic fatigue and extreme sensitivity. The object holds frightening power, almost magical power, because it is contaminated by the unconscious contents.

We need to consider a person's habitual behaviour when considering introvert and extravert types. It can be the case that an extravert type will claim that they are introvert. A woman was quite noticeably an extravert in her habitual behaviour, yet she was adamant that she was an introvert. Her reason for this was that, when she does behave in an introverted manner, she feels most real to herself. She feels that she is in touch with her deeper self. This may be true. However, the fact remains that for the hour or two that she is introverting in a week, there remains the other one hundred and sixty-six hours she is extraverting! Therefore she is much more likely to be an extraverted type.

One must ask: where does one habitually place value? On the inner world or on the outer? On the subject, oneself, or on the object, the world? Where does one get one's meaning and definition? From what does one get replenished, from where does one get one's energy; the inner or the outer world? Understanding whether one is an introvert

---

23 Marie-Louise von Franz and James Hillman. (1986) *Lectures on Jung's Typology*, Spring Publications, Putnam, C.T., U.S.A. Page 5.

or an extravert helps one to understand why one behaves in certain ways, why one experiences the world as one does. It also empowers one to be conscious of how one lives, challenging one to allow for time apart if one is introvert in a culture that does not readily accept introversion, or understanding why, as an extravert, one may feel uncomfortable on one's own.

The Structure of the Functions: Dominant Function and Auxiliaries

In his observation of the human psyche Jung initially outlined two functions: sensation and intuition. He later added two more: thinking and feeling. When you combine these functions with the introvert and extravert attitudes you have eight functions: extravert thinking, introvert thinking, extravert feeling, introvert feeling, extravert sensation, introvert sensation, extravert intuition, introvert intuition. Before going into a detailed description of each of the eight functions in Chapter 5, I want to look at the way in which Jung suggested that the functions appear in the psyche.

Thinking and feeling are opposites. One cannot think and feel at the same time. A man with a dominant thinking function was at a meeting. A person at the meeting attacked the enterprise that the man was responsible for. The man defended his enterprise with clear information and facts. It was much later, when the meeting was over, that he began to process what he felt about the experience. He could not have done both at the meeting. At any given moment, one is either thinking or feeling, but not both. Similarly, sensation and intuition are opposites. They cannot be used at the same time. Sensation, as understood in this typology refers to the ability to relate to the sensate world through the senses. When a person is concentrated, at a given moment, upon making a wooden table, that person cannot, at that moment, be sensitive to unseen possibilities around him or her. Similarly, when in the grip of intuition, a person is often oblivious to the sensate reality around them.

Thinking and feeling are both rational functions. This means that in order to think and feel one needs to go through a rational process. Feeling, in the context of this typology, must not be confused with emotion. Emotion occurs when a complex is stirred in the psyche. Feeling is a rational process. Even when we separate out feeling from emotion we see that Jung's use of feeling involves a much narrower definition than in ordinary usage. In the English language the word 'feeling' is used in many different ways. According to the *Oxford English Dictionary*[24] it means: "capacity to feel; sense of touch; emotion; emotional susceptibilities; opinion or notion; sympathy with others…" The closest meaning for our purposes here is 'opinion or notion'. The same dictionary says of 'reason' that it is an "intellectual faculty by which conclusions are drawn from premises". People who are feeling types know what they like and what they do not like, they have a keen sense of what is right and what is wrong. It is a high thinking person who will tend to confuse feeling with emotion. This is because feeling, for them, is their inferior function, deep in the unconscious and therefore closest to the complexes of the unconscious. It is, perhaps, easier to understand how thinking and feeling are rational functions when we consider how sensation and intuition are not. The latter are irrational functions. This means that one simply has a sensation or an intuition. It comes to us raw from the world. We do not need to put it through any rational process to experience it.

A person develops one of the four functions early in life and uses it as a way of experiencing the world. It becomes a tool, a *modus operandi*. A person will become proficient with this function as with any well-practiced skill. It will reflect the person's conscious personality. When

---

24 *The Pocket Oxford English Dictionary.* (1969, 1978, 1984) Published by Oxford University Press, New York.

a function is used habitually, it is a dominant function. This means that the least used and least conscious function will be the one on the opposite end of the pole to the dominant one. If a person has developed thinking as their dominant function, feeling will be their least conscious, least dominant function, that is, their inferior function. Often it is easier to discover a person's inferior function, since this is sometimes more obvious. One can then infer the dominant function when one knows the inferior one.

The other two functions act as auxiliaries. If one thinks of the points of a compass, one cannot go north and south at the same time, but one can go north-east, or north-west, south-east or south-west. This is how the auxiliaries work. They back up the dominant function. They are next in line in terms of how conscious they are. In the first half of a lifetime, a person will develop a dominant function. Many, but not all, will have the back up of a reasonably developed and differentiated auxiliary function. Some will even have dabbled in their second auxiliary function. To differentiate a function means to work from that function and in so doing this draws it up from the unconscious into consciousness. This is not as easy as it sounds, for in order to put energy into a less dominant function one must take energy from the most dominant one. This can be disorientating and can leave one feeling unsure in the world. Also, the more a function is in the unconscious, the more the unconscious contents attach themselves to it. Therefore, one can find oneself in complex after complex, when one tries to use the less differentiated functions.

Jung writes: "The superior function is always an expression of the conscious personality, of its aims, will and general performance, whereas the less differentiated functions fall into the category of things that simply 'happen to one'."[25] This echoes what Jung said

---

25 *C.W.* Vol. 6, par 574.

about the things that we refuse to face, which then meet us as our fate. That which we do not see, that which is in the unconscious, whether we simply cannot see it, or will not see it, has the potential to become the very thing that effects our lives the most. When it is said that our thoughts create our reality, it is important to note that it is more often our unconscious thoughts than our conscious thoughts that create our reality. This is how energy works in the world. Many of us believe that, if a negative thought crops up in our conscious mind, and if we pay heed to it and give it attention, then this very thing will happen. So, we try not to think negative thoughts. We put them away. Ironically, this very act of putting them away gives them even more power. By ignoring them we make them more powerful.

When we have negative thoughts, it is good to look them in the eye and track them to their source. If we look hard enough, they will lead us to the complex which generated them. We can then deal with the complex and de-power it. This means re-establishing it as a normal complex rather than one that has too much energy, with no conscious means of expression. Discernment is called for, however, when working on recurring negative thoughts for sometimes to focus upon them too much can trap us in the very complex that we are trying to address.

It is the work of the first part of one's life to establish a dominant function. It is often possible to observe what the dominant function is in a person early on in childhood. We have all seen in small children how one child will be socially interactive with other children (high feeling), another child will push past other children and go straight for the toys (high sensate), another will sit in the corner and draw pictures of angels or monsters (high intuition), another will do jig-saws (high thinking). If their specific type of behaviour is repeated over and over, we see a dominant function beginning to be established. A friend recently told me of her niece who was seven years old. The child was clearly intuitive and spoke of ghosts and visions as naturally as of her breakfast and toys.

Jung said that one's introvert or extravert attitude was innate and that one seems to be born with it. "Since the facts show that the attitude-type is a general phenomenon, having an apparently random distribution, it cannot be a matter of conscious judgment or conscious intention, but must be due to some unconscious, instinctive cause. As a general psychological phenomenon, therefore, the type antithesis must have some kind of biological foundation."[26] It is possible to notice in very young children their orientation towards the world, whether it is introvert or extravert. With the functions, however, what makes a child develop one over another? It seems, in watching young children, that each child has his or her specific strengths and weaknesses. Children will naturally work on their strengths and veer away from their weaknesses. This is the beginning of the development of a dominant function. What a child's strengths and weaknesses are seem also to be innate as opposed to being dependent upon environment and circumstances. Twin girls reared in the same home, who experience the same environmental conditions, by the age of two clearly demonstrate that one is an introvert and the other an extravert. By the age of three it is evident that the introvert child is a feeler and the extravert one a thinker. It does not appear that each began as an empty slate. It is much easier to believe that each had within them latent strengths that then developed in a certain way.

It sometimes happens that a person would have naturally developed as one type, but circumstances, or the surrounding atmosphere, forced that person to develop another function instead. This person becomes a distorted type and will have trouble later on, trying to establish his or

26 ibid., par 559.

her true type.[27] For example, a girl is naturally a feeling type, yet she is born, as an only child, into a family where the father is a high thinker, academically successful and ambitious for his child. The mother is a dominant sensate type with a thinking auxiliary function. She too is intellectually ambitious for her daughter. The child's surroundings will put enormous pressure on the child to become an intellectual. The feeling function, which would have been her dominant function, will be pushed aside as inferior. It would be too much of a jump for the girl to develop her thinking function in place of her feeling function. They are polar opposites. She can, however, develop one of the auxiliary functions, for example sensation, so that she can blend in somewhat with the expectations put upon her. For this child, her main function, feeling, was not acceptable in her home, so she developed an auxiliary function instead in order to be acceptable.

A person who is a distorted type will spend the first part of his or her life feeling that he or she can never truly excel at anything. This is because the person is using an auxiliary function in the dominant place, and the dominant function has been shoved back to second or often third place. The joy of living from one's dominant function is that one develops in a one-sided and exclusive way and one feels the benefit of that. Without that, one tends to be able to work on various fronts, but not in an outstanding way. When a distorted type, like this girl, discovers her true dominant function she feels as if the scales have fallen from her eyes. She suddenly understands why she felt so held back in her life and she can now relish the experience of running with her dominant function and excelling in it. Also, there is a time when the distorted type will reap benefit from his or her past distortion. This is in the second part of one's life when it is time to develop the lower auxiliary function and the inferior function. By the time this happens

---

27 Marie-Louise von Franz and James Hillman. (1986) *Lectures on Jung's Typology*, Spring Publications, Putnam, C.T., U.S.A. Page 6.

the distorted type has already a much more developed auxiliary function (for the person had used it in a dominant place for years) and the likelihood is that the second auxiliary is also well developed.

The Inferior Function

It is important to understand the nature and workings of the inferior function when one looks at the structure of the functions. This allows one to perceive the personality as a totality rather than merely from the perspective of the dominant function. It also makes one see how the inferior function plays a role in our daily lives and how it comes out in our behaviour despite ourselves. We have our conscious personality, yet we also have an unconscious compensatory dimension and this dimension is also at play all the time.

The dominant functions behave in a certain way. They are conscious. With the dominant function, a person is in control and is aware of what he or she is doing at all times. The dominant function is quick to work. When people are working out of the dominant function they are able to respond well and promptly. A high feeler will know what to say in a difficult situation. A high thinker will be able to think a problem through on the spot. In relation to ascertaining whether a function is dominant or not, Jung writes: "We must observe which function is completely under conscious control, and which functions have a haphazard and spontaneous character".[28]

The inferior function, despite being haphazard and spontaneous, does have general characteristics, and can be described. It is the bridge to the unconscious. It is always directed towards the unconscious. However, this does not mean that it does not prompt us towards action in the outer world. Marie-Louise von Franz gives an example of this.[29] If an introvert thinking man says he need not phone a

28 *C.W.* Vol.6, par 576.
29 Marie-Louise von Franz and James Hillman. (1986) *Lectures on Jung's Typology,*

certain woman because she is simply an anima figure, (that is the counter-sexual feminine aspect of his psyche), for him, he will never come to grips with his inferior function. The reason this is not an appropriate response to his inferior function is this – he is dismissing the significance of the outer world and is dragging all experience into the inner world. His inferior function is extravert feeling and, as such, it is genuinely extravert. It actually wants him to begin to experience life in an extraverted manner. Therefore, for the man to come into proper relation with his extravert feeling, he must respect this need to extravert and he must ring this woman in the real world. He cannot drag the inferior extravert feeling into his dominant introvert thinking realm, for that is cheating. In order to experience the inferior he must take it on its own terms – therefore, in this case, in the actual outer world. This is what assimilating an inferior function actually means – that we live according to that function's priorities and values and integrate that experience into our lives.

Another characteristic of the inferior function is that it is slow. Compared to the dominant function, which is well adapted and well-practiced, the inferior function is frustratingly slow. It does work, and often it can perform well enough, but it will be slow and will not be able to work well under pressure. I spoke with a man, a high intuitive who, for a time, earned money working as a carpenter. I remarked on how unusual this was since sensation was his inferior function. He replied that he felt extremely limited in carpentry, that he could only do the job if someone instructed him on exactly what had to be done, showed him how to do it, and left him to do it in his own time. Under pressure, the job was a nightmare. Likewise, I watched a high feeler describe a well thought out ceremony for her son's christening. When, however, she was asked about incorporating a new piece that would change the order of the ceremony, she fumbled a reply. She was not

Spring Publications, Putnam, C.T., U.S.A. Page 11.

being asked to consider how she felt about it, whether she liked it or not, rather she was being asked about the structure of the ceremony and whether it would work logically or not. She was caught off guard and she realised that she did not know what she thought of the new idea. Later, in her own time, she was well able to incorporate the new idea, but at the time her inferior function was simply not up to scratch. It could not work fast enough nor could it function under pressure. Similarly, a high thinker may take days before he realises that he did not like doing what he had been asked to do. Having done it, mildly enough at the time, he may end up being furious that he was even asked. Too late! This is what is so disheartening about working with the inferior function. On the spot, there is simply not enough time for it. Unfortunately, day-to-day living is very much on the spot.

The inferior function is very touchy and tyrannical. With a practiced eye, you can usually spot when a person's inferior function has been activated. The person begins to behave in a childish manner. This is because the person has been hit on a sore spot. A high intuitive man organising a meeting may get very irritable when he is asked about the details of the meeting. He may begin to feel attacked and will come out with an attack of his own. This kind of behaviour is typical of the inferior function dynamics and it takes the person being attacked totally by surprise.

It pays to be aware of these things because if one realises that the person is in inferior function mode, one will not bother to argue, for it will only go from bad to worse. The best thing is to back off as gracefully as possible and to wait for the person to come back to himself or herself. To argue with a person possessed by his or her inferior function is like arguing with an hysterical child. It is unwise to take to heart what has been said by someone when the inferior function is at play. It is to deny the person the rest of his or her personality. Certainly, there is a seed of truth in what is said in the heat of emotion that accompanies the inferior function but it must be considered within the wider context of the person's personality, i.e. their dominant function and their more conscious auxiliary functions.

Unfortunately, some people, when in crisis or under great stress, can get locked into their inferior function. This is very difficult, for you are not dealing with a conscious person who has had a brief lapse into the unconscious. Rather you are dealing with someone who is staying fully in the unconscious and is more than likely of the opinion that he or she is quite conscious!

There is a great deal of sensitivity around the inferior function. Sensitivity and tyranny are connected. Marie-Louise von Franz claims that sensitivity or touchiness is a secret form of tyranny. "Sensitive people are just tyrannical people – everybody else has to adapt to them instead of them trying to adapt to others".[30] If one has worked on a project with the inferior function one has worked with a function that one is unsure of. One is bound to be highly sensitive to criticism or any comment in relation to the work. If one is not conscious of the limitation of the inferior function, and therefore has not given it the necessary handling, one can get possessed by the inferior function, or more accurately, by the complexes that are lurking around with the inferior function. These complexes can be negative or positive. What is definite about them is that they are unconscious.

A woman was at a meeting in an organisation. The woman was a high thinker. She was always in her head spinning up ideas. At the meeting, however, she strayed into inferior feeling and made some critical comments, which surprised people. After the meeting, one

---

30 Marie-Louise von Franz and James Hillman. (1986) *Lectures on Jung's Typology*, Spring Publications, Putnam, C.T., U.S.A. Page 13.

man privately confronted the woman about her comments. Much to his amazement she completely exploded. She attacked him and gave him a list of all his faults over all the years that she had known him, even telling him what other people thought were his faults too! The woman obviously had strayed into inferior function territory during the meeting and rather than becoming conscious of this and backing down, she merely went deeper in, becoming possessed by it and by the various complexes that were close to the inferior function.

This demonstrates another characteristic of the inferior function. The amount of emotion that is connected with it. Emotion is connected with complexes and complexes are connected with the inferior function. So, it follows that emotion comes with the inferior function. What surprises people is just how much emotion can come up through it. People can literally be explosive, or at least feel explosive.

I have said that it is often easier to discover one's inferior function than it is to discover one's dominant one. This is so because the dominant function can become weary and can wear thin and the person will not be quick to claim it as a dominant function. The dominant function is identified by discovering where value is placed. However, a distinction has to be made. It may be that what you feel you value right now, and what you have been valuing throughout your life as a consistent pattern, are not the same. A woman may feel that she values people, and right and wrong and so forth, which would make her a high feeler. However, when one looks back over the pattern of her life, it is clear that most of her energy has gone into projects and ideas. This would make her a high thinker. It is also clear from the various relationship casualties in her life that feeling was her inferior function. The discovery of the inferior function confirms the naming of the dominant function.

The inferior function can be found by asking the question – what has hurt you most over your life? What function has caused you most suffering? This is sure to be your inferior function. A related question is – how have you most hurt other people in your life? Jung said that evil can creep in through the inferior function. It is the blind spot. It is the place where you are most unsure, most unconscious, most dangerous and most creative. Most 'eureka' moments come through the unconscious inferior function.

Many people may not be able to distinguish between a dominant and an auxiliary function. A woman thinks of herself as both intuitive and feeler. Yet which is dominant? If she asks the question what has hurt her most – sensation or thinking, she can find which is her dominant function. Let us say that her sensation is poor. She has a bad sense of direction. It is something about which her family and friends laugh and joke with her. However, this has never hurt her, or caused her to get upset. She laughs at it herself. On the other hand, her thinking, which has also been poor, has caused her to make decisions which have led to real hardship in her life, real suffering. Her thinking then, rather than her sensate abilities, has hurt her the most. Her thinking function is therefore her inferior function. This means that feeling and not intuition is her dominant function. Intuition is her auxiliary.

There is extreme subtlety involved in this typology. Discernment of one's type can be complicated. A woman who initially thought of herself as a high intuitive with a feeling auxiliary discovered that she was off track when she considered what had most distressed her in her life. During her childhood it had been necessary for her to develop intuition in the place of what turned out to be her more naturally dominant function, thinking. What led her to consider feeling as her auxiliary function was that she experienced the world with a lot of emotion. She was, however, confusing emotion with feeling. It is significant to note that high feeling types do not experience the world with an excess of emotion. That is more likely to be the high thinkers. This is because their feeling is in the unconscious and very close to the complexes therein. Therefore, it can get contaminated with the emotion of them more easily. Once the woman separated emotion from feeling she saw that her feeling was not highly developed. Quite the contrary. By considering what had caused her most pain in her life she was able to conclude that it was feeling and not sensation (which would be the opposite inferior function to a dominant intuition), that was her inferior function.

This woman had, in fact, been involved in many sensate projects. Considering as she did that sensation was her inferior function she took much care with it. She knew it was not a strength and she developed it slowly. It was only when she had the following dream that she realised that sensation was not the lowest function at all, rather it was an auxiliary function.

She dreamed that an aunt who had shared a house with another aunt's family bought her own house and was radiant and happy. The woman interpreted this to be addressing the sensation function, which she had molly-coddled and treated as an inferior function for so long. The dream was announcing that its day had come. It was now independent and did not need to be treated with such care! As we will see elsewhere, this cannot happen with an inferior function. The inferior function will always remain in the unconscious. It will always need to be treated with care. It cannot come into consciousness like the other three can. One can never get control of it as with the other conscious functions. It is the doorway to the unconscious and therefore must always be in the unconscious. The work that the woman had done with sensation was work with a second auxiliary. It could therefore come more fully into consciousness. However, the work of coming to terms with the inferior function of feeling was a whole other kettle of fish.

When one does not take on the challenge of coming to terms with the inferior function one finds oneself covering up for it. Life is ruthless with inferiority of any kind and that is why most people will try to avoid this side of themselves for as long as possible. People 'cover up'. High feeling types, when pressed to think, will borrow from the collective thinking. They will churn out commonplace opinions or they will dogmatically argue a point that they have picked up from somewhere else and have learned by heart. To dive for their own thoughts would take too long. Thinkers also will form the habit of learning off conventional expressions of feeling. Marie-Louise von Franz, a thinker, admits to having a form letter of condolence in which she has put all the nice phrases that she has heard over the years. She claims that if she were to have to write a letter on the spot, it would take three days. She writes: "One must not be deceived by these adaptive reactions, if one is to connect with another person. You can always observe these 'covering up' reactions by the fact that they are impersonal and banal and very collective. They have no convincing personal quality about them".[31]

The response of the dominant function, when it is confronted with the inferior function's reaction to a situation, is to try to control it. The dominant function will try to bring the inferior function over to its side. Not to do this is to risk losing control, which is paramount for the dominant function. And, in fairness, to lose control to the inferior function is not a pretty sight!

A high extravert thinking man gets a dream message that there is a fire in the attic of a building of one of the businesses that he is responsible

---

31 ibid., page 17.

for and there is no fire escape. As opposed to interpreting the dream in any way personal to himself (which is what his inferior introvert feeling function would call for) he interprets that he must, in fact, put a fire escape in the attic of the building. This practical interpretation is of course valid, however, it may not be all that the dream is trying to convey. Another interpretation is worth considering along the lines of what such a fire in the attic, the topmost part of the house (thinking) might mean for the man's psyche.

There is a fine line to be walked with the inferior function. I would not recommend that the dominant function simply hand over to it. As has been said earlier, it can lead to touchy, emotional and volatile behaviour. The dominant function can learn ways to relate healthily to the inferior function and this is to be recommended. Firstly, it is best to learn what it is. Then one can learn to recognise when it interferes with one's living. One can work with it in active imagination[32] and ask it what it needs and how one can incorporate these needs into one's life. Then one can respond by doing these things. Because the inferior function cannot function well on the spot, it is best to have a sense of play with it. It is important to be willing to waste time with it. In a way, one can imagine it to be like a difficult child. One can humour it and play with it and draw it out, without letting it get into any kind of tantrum, without letting it take over. It is important to be firm with the inferior function. It will try to bring you over to its side. In doing so, it will destroy what you have done so far in your life with your dominant function. The life you have created with your dominant function is not satisfactory to the inferior function, for the inferior function was, most likely, not included in the making of it. So, to let the inferior function get free reign is to threaten to lose what you have already achieved.

---

32 For description of *Active Imagination* go to the end of Chapter 3 of this work.

A woman, an introvert thinker, began to dialogue with her inferior function shadow character. The shadow is that part of a person that the person is unaware of consciously. It resides in the unconscious and appears in dreams as the same gender as the dreamer. This woman's shadow character was extravert feeling. She announced that she hated the woman's husband and she wanted the woman to leave him and her life with him and do something else entirely! The woman was very shocked but she remained firm. She sympathised with her shadow having to live in such an unsatisfactory situation, but she stated that she herself loved her husband very much, she had no intention of leaving him and she said that the shadow would have to work within those confines. She asked her shadow what, within those confines, she could do for her. Her shadow backed down and said she wanted the woman to paint, and to create some time and actual physical space for painting. The woman did this. But she still had to watch for spontaneous eruptions from her inferior feeling in unguarded moments. She had to constantly go back to her shadow in dialogue, keeping her in line and trying to negotiate in order to give her some expression and satisfaction. If she had not done this, her shadow could easily have disrupted the woman's life and relationship with her husband. It takes great strength of ego consciousness to be able to contain such an articulate representative of the inferior function. However, at the heart of the shadow's discontent was that she wanted the woman to have a life separate from her husband. In this, the inferior function had a point. The woman did need to develop a life for herself separate from her husband. The shadow held the pearls that come from the unconscious. How to get those pearls, without destroying what you already have, is the difficult thing.

When the dominant function is under severe stress, or when it has burnt out, or worn out, it is all the more difficult to contain the inferior function, and dialogue with it. In these instances, the unconscious inferior function will rise up and falsify the dominant function. When this happens life can no longer flow. The inferior function is primitive and tends towards the negative. When it invades the dominant function, it gives it an "un-adapted, neurotic twist".[33] So we have thinkers who cannot think any more. Even worse, they come out with an inferior feeling which is full of superstition. We have feelers who cannot discern feeling value any more, and who fill the gap with bad thinking, and so forth. These people are in a psychological limbo. Their dominant function has collapsed and there is nothing to fill the gap. They have not yet reached a new level.

Assimilating the Inferior Function and The Middle Realm

A person in early childhood will begin to develop a dominant function. Over time he or she will develop an auxiliary function, which will back up the dominant one. If the person is well differentiated, he or she will include a second auxiliary and develop that too. Assimilate is a better word for it. "To assimilate a function means to live with that one function in the foreground. ... Assimilation means that the whole adaptation of conscious life for a while lies on that one function".[34] For the years that I was building a stone house with my friends, I, who has thinking as a dominant function, was assimilating an auxiliary sensation function. I was eating and drinking and sleeping the sensation of building. I experienced dreams during this time where I would wake myself up moving around the room lifting pillows to 'build' in my sleep!

Moving to another function, in order to assimilate it, is rarely, if ever, an abstract decision. Two things tend to happen at the same time. The dominant function wears down and degenerates and the ego simultaneously becomes bored with it. In the development

---

33 Marie-Louise von Franz and James Hillman. (1986) *Lectures on Jung's Typology*, Spring Publications, Putnam, C.T., U.S.A. Page 20.
34 Ibid., page 73.

of personality, one cannot jump from the dominant function to the inferior one. The leap is too great. One needs to go through the auxiliaries. These give depth and perspective to the personality, which tends to be dictated to by the dominant function. Each of the functions exist in the unconscious and one draws them up one by one. However, when one comes to the inferior function one finds that one cannot draw it up. The more one tries, the more one gets pulled down into the unconscious. So, what do you do? If you cut off the inferior function again, it simply means that you regress. If you ignore it, it can pull you down into the unconscious. What option is left?

If you imagine that consciousness is like a room and it has four doors that lead out into the unconscious. Each door represents a function. The dominant function in time can become a lockable door. That is, we can control it. We can control what comes in through it. Each of the auxiliaries, as they become conscious and developed, also become lockable doors. The inferior function is the fourth door. It is unlockable. It is through this door that the unexpected comes in. To attempt to bring up this inferior function to consciousness, is to attempt to bring up the entire unconscious into consciousness. It is impossible. The inferior function is the bridge to the unconscious. If it were possible to shut it off, or close it down, conscious life would stultify and stagnate. It is worth considering this when we experience our inferior function tripping us up again and we curse it. Without it, we would die of boredom and our lives would become predictable and unbearable.

But what do we do with this fourth door? These are the options, as stated already: 1. Cut it off and regress: 2. Get pulled into it entirely and live at the animal primitive level. Marie-Louise von Franz comments that "People who have a great primitive courage for life can do this".[35] She tells the story of one of Jung's cases where a sixty-year old man

---

35 ibid., page 76.

who had a successful business and a wife and family began to get restless. He awoke one night exclaiming that he had the answer. He declared that he was a 'bum', left his wife and home, and wandered homeless, drinking himself to death! Such a drastic embracing of the inferior function is hardly to be recommended. To do this is not to assimilate the inferior function. Rather it is to become swallowed by it and to lose the upper structure of the former personality. Marie-Louise von Franz comments: "The fourth function is always life's great problem: if I don't live it, I am frustrated and half dead and everything is boring; if I live it, it is of such low level that I cannot use it, unless I have the pseudo-courage of this man. Most people do not have that courage, others would have it but they see that this is not the solution either".[36]

There is a third option. It is to take the inferior function on board, but not in the outer world where it could ruin one's life entirely. It is to take it on board in the imagination, in the realm of fantasy. It is to deal with it in the middle realm. This means painting it, dancing it, writing it, Lego building it, playing it out through music, clay building it. Whatever manner one chooses should be appropriate to the inferior function itself. "Jung found that active imagination was practically the only means for dealing with the fourth function".[37] So, for example, an intuitive type would have sensation as his inferior function. He or she may need to fix the inferior function in concrete material, in clay or stone. The thinker, with feeling as an inferior function, may dance it, or paint it with strong colours, sing it with strong feeling or play music passionately. A sensation type may create bizarre fictional stories with their inferior intuition. The high intuitive might, with inferior sensation, build small villages with clay. The person with high feeling might chose a course to study and actively

---

36 ibid., page 77.
37 ibid.

imagine their lower function as the 'professor'. Whatever one does with it, the active imagination allows one to touch it and experience it without it entering one's life in a chaotic and destructive manner.

When people get to this stage of dealing with the inferior function they must take energy from their dominant functions. So, they must drop down, as it were. However, it is not wise to drop down entirely into the inferior function. Therefore, a middle place, or middle realm, is called for. It is the only possible solution. Few people manage to do this, but when they do the results are usually remarkable. Rather than keeping one's value locked in, or identified with, a dominant function, which has the back-up of the auxiliaries, one transfers it to another place, to an inner centre, to the middle ground. When this happens, the functions become mere instruments and they cease to be something you identify with. Marie-Louise von Franz writes:

> The ego and its conscious activity are no longer identical with any of the functions. ... There is a complete standstill in a kind of inner centre, and the functions do not act automatically any more. You can bring them out at will. ... At this stage the problem of the functions is no longer relevant. The functions have become instruments of a consciousness, which is no longer rooted in them or driven by them. It has its basis of operation in another dimension, a dimension that can only be created by the world of imagination. That is why Jung calls this the transcendent function. This right kind of imagination creates the uniting symbols.[38]

When this happens, the three functions do not become four, rather, added to the four there comes a fifth, which is beyond the four but

---

38 ibid., page 78.

consists of all of them. This is what the alchemists call the philosopher's stone. This happens when a person lives from the middle realm and is not identified with any of the functions. The best description is that of the Zen master who can live fully either teaching or meditating or working with any of the functions but who remains detached from them all.

At this stage another kind of development begins. It is, however, remarkably difficult to even get to this place. Most people when they get to the problem of the fourth function will experience it as if they were getting into a bath that is too hot! They will jump out again! Then they will go on as they had been, living from the three functions, aware of the fourth like the devil in the corner. When things get too disturbed, they may jump into the bath again and get out again. Many people who undergo analysis have had this experience of jumping into the hot bath and of leaping out again. To stay in it is extremely difficult, yet to fail to do so is to prevent further growth. To continue growing at this stage requires an understanding of the process of individuation and of the problem of the fourth function in relation to this.

If this seems abstract, try imagining the thing that makes you most uncomfortable, embarrassed, afraid, or angry. Now try to imagine consciously choosing to draw that to yourself over and over again. To freely put ourselves in the most difficult, frightening, awful situations – that is what the hot bath feels like. If we invite this into our lives, albeit in the imagination, this is what it is to deal with the fourth door. It is the process of calling up the very things that we have suppressed. We have suppressed these contents so that our dominant function can work in the world as it does. We must call them up to the middle realm so that we can still function in the world with our dominant function. However, in this middle realm we can look at these contents and somehow find some creative expression for them in our conscious psyche.

Active imagination is the process whereby we look at our undeclared devils and create some relationship with them. To do so, we must give up on the idea that it is even desirable as a human to achieve moral perfection. I will look at this idea later in Chapter Seven on Shadow. Suffice it to say here that it is psychologically healthier to embrace completeness as opposed to perfection. I often wonder was Jesus grappling with the archetypal issue of creating a middle realm when he said "Seek first the Kingdom and then all things shall be given to you".[39] For this is what happens when the middle realm is established. "The centre of gravity shifts away from the ego and its functions, into an interim position, into attending to the hints of the Self".[40]

In summary, one develops a dominant function and lives from that function. Backing up this dominant function is an auxiliary function. The way the functions work is similar to a compass. Let us imagine that the dominant function is thinking and this is north. Then the polar opposite function is feeling, and this is south. One cannot go north and south at the same time. Therefore, if thinking is the dominant function, feeling is what is called the inferior function. While one cannot go north-south, one can, however, go north-west, or north-east. The auxiliaries are like east and west. They back up the dominant function.

So, a person can be a dominant thinker with a backup of intuition. The inferior function is feeling and the second auxiliary is sensation. Being one of the four function types as opposed to another causes us to experience the world very differently to our fellow humans who

---

39 The New Testament, Matthew 6:33.
40 Marie-Louise von Franz and James Hillman. *Lectures on Jung's Typology* (1986) Spring Publications, Putnam, C.T., U.S.A Page 85.

may be of another dominant type. Each type values something that the others do not. It is important to go through them one by one to get a sense of what exactly they value and in doing so to understand why people can seem so very 'other' in their experience of the world.

CHAPTER FIVE

The Function Types Described

There are Many Ways of Seeing the World

Suffer Fools Gladly

There is a danger
of sickening everyone's arse
by being repeatedly assertive.
'No'
'No thank you'
'Why do you keep asking questions?'
'Could you please stop that!'
'I feel X when you do Y because of Z'.

Yet
the alternative
seems to be
a constant sickening
of my own sweet arse
for
after years of trying,
I simply cannot
suffer fools gladly!

Description of the Functions

Having worked with the various function types for a long time I have learned to appreciate that other people, especially if they have an opposite dominant function to my own, experience the world with an entirely different value system. What they attach importance to will simply not be the same as what I consider significant. When we consider the inferior function discussed in the previous chapter, we see that people of opposite dominant functions are a little like fish are to birds. How strange would it be for a fish to be constantly out of water and flying? This might be like what a dominant thinker might experience at an unfamiliar social situation. Or how a high intuitive might react when handed a technical graphics assignment and told to draw a three dimensional train to the set measurements. When we begin to understand the various perspectives, skill sets and value systems of people with dominant functions that are different to our own we can begin to allow people to be themselves. We can begin to appreciate their otherness. This is the importance of looking at each of the functions closely.

The four functions consist of thinking and feeling, sensation and intuition. When you attach introvert and extravert to these functions, you end up with eight personality types. Four of these are rational types: extravert thinking, introvert thinking, extravert feeling, introvert feeling. Four are irrational types: extravert sensation, introvert sensation, extravert intuition, and introvert intuition. As it has been stated previously, thinking and feeling are both rational functions. They are rational "…because they are characterised by the supremacy of the reasoning and judging functions".[1] Sensation and intuition are both irrational functions. You experience sensations and intuitions without any need for a rational process. I will describe each of the functions beginning with the rational functions of thinking and feeling.

---

1 *C.W.* Vol. 6, par 601.

The Four Rational Types

These are extravert thinking, introvert thinking, extravert feeling and introvert feeling.

Extravert Thinking Type

Extravert thinkers are orientated by objective data and not by the inner world of subjective data. This means that their thinking relates to objects in the outer world. There are, in fact, two types of extravert thinkers, the practical kind and the philosophical kind. The first is much easier to recognise. The practical thinker can be seen among business people, politicians, in law firms, and among scientists and teachers. They establish order in the outer situation. They are people who get involved in projects. They are logical and rational and clear-sighted. These people look to the situation at hand and see it purely from a rational, logical perspective. Their driving energy is towards outer projects, towards doing things.

When an extravert thinker tends more towards philosophy and ideas, it is harder to recognise that she or he is an extravert. One must ask the question — does this thinker make judgements using external or internal criteria? From where are the conclusions drawn, outer or inner? If a philosopher takes his thinking from the collective tradition or intellectual atmosphere, then she or he is an extravert thinker. Introvert thinking is neither orientated by immediate experience of objects, or by traditional ideas. Rather it starts from the subject and moves towards subjective ideas or facts. Its realm is the subjective inner world and its relation to the outer world is as confirmation of ideas rather than inspiration. But more of this later when I look at the introvert thinker type. For now, looking at extravert thinkers, we see that they are inspired by the object, by the outer world. Their ideals are taken from the collective, be it the dominant collective or a minority collective. It is important to remember that each person has both extravert and introvert tendencies. What makes one an extravert or introvert type is the habitual value put on either the outer world or the inner world.

Charles Darwin is an example of an extravert thinker. His thinking was concerned with the outer world. His reflections on the outer world led to humanity understanding the nature of this world in a whole new light. This kind of thinking can be seen "… when the life of an individual is mainly governed by reflective thinking so that every important action proceeds, or is intended to proceed, from intellectually considered motives".[2]

These people see objective reality as the ruling principle, not just for themselves, but for the whole environment. They see that their ideal is the best conceivable version of objective reality and therefore believe that it must be a universally valid truth, essential for the survival or wellbeing of humanity. As teachers, they can believe that there is only one way to teach. They can be quite petty, insisting, for example, that there is only one right way to wash your teeth, or make a bed, or bake bread. This pettiness, or narrow-mindedness, can also be seen in wider contexts, such as politicians insisting that there is only one right way to run the economy. "If the formula is broad enough, this type may play a very useful role in social life as a reformer or public prosecutor or purifier of conscience, or as the propagator of important innovations".[3] John the Baptist, preaching in the desert, is an example of the purifier of conscience – someone so sure of his own vision that he gives up everything to follow it and live it out. There are two extremes with this type of person: the innovator or inspired person, convinced of his or her own truth and the dominant or self-assured person, who will force himself or herself onto others and attempt to

---

2   ibid., par 584.
3   ibid.

force others to live within a particular mold.

At a Jungian workshop I gave on the functions, there was one extravert thinker in the group, and he was a judge. His interests were photography and movies, church and community activities, and keeping up to date with politics and new scientific developments. All of these activities were an expression of his dominant function. His interests involved the outer world. Some of them involved projects (the community activities) and others were concerned with ideas (politics and new scientific developments).

The vocabulary of an extravert thinker often contains a lot of 'oughts'. When it becomes extreme, the person exhibits tyrannical behaviour. Those who live further afield may find benefit in this, but those closer to home usually do not. What works at a public level and translates as innovative, socially aware, reformer-type energy can be torturous in the home space. Someone with a keen sense of what should be done in the larger social picture can be oppressive in the home. This belief that certain things should be done and often that they should be done in one particular way can translate to more mundane things. If a person attempts to live rigidly in accordance with their ideal intellectual formulae all the time, a large amount of experience must be repressed. Life does not comply with intellectual formulae, no matter how broad. Most healthy people of this type will allow themselves exceptions, albeit disguised in a suitable, rational form, in order to be acceptable to themselves. They will therefore live out their lives incorporating energies and ideas wider than their 'notion' of the world. They will see that one must compromise in order to promote one's ideal in the long run.

If a person does not allow this safety valve in his or her life, then he or she must repress an enormous amount of material, in this case feeling, because feeling stands contrary to thinking. When this happens "... the subliminal feeling then functions in a way that is opposed to the conscious aims, even producing effects whose cause is a complete enigma to the individual".[4] There are classic examples of this: the judge found with pornographic material in his home (not the man in the workshop I mentioned above I hasten to add!) or the scientist who is so convinced that his findings are true that he lies in order to defend it. Jung comments: "Only an inferior feeling function, operating unconsciously and in secret, could seduce otherwise reputable men into such aberrations".[5]

For the extravert thinking type, the inferior function is introvert feeling. Such a person could spend his or her entire life starting new innovative projects. These projects could even be beneficial for all of humankind. But if this person was never challenged to look at the inferior function, and his or her own personal feelings, the person may never know how he or she ever felt about any of it. People like this appear to be driven. The dominant function drives them, so that they often become workaholics. Extravert thinking, as a dominant function, does not allow for one's own feeling in relation to things. Neither does it incorporate the feelings of other people. The focus is on the idea and the objective. One's health, one's feeling about things, other people's feelings, are not in the picture, until some crisis hits. When the crisis hits one is forced to look to the other side of one's psyche.

The feelings of the extravert thinker are deep in the unconscious and the person is often not aware of them. Yet they are there. They are primitive and pure. The extravert thinking type has "a kind of mystical feeling attachment for ideals and often also for people. But

---

4   *C.W.* Vol. 6, par 588.
5   ibid.

this deep, strong, warm feeling hardly ever comes out".[6] Marie-Louise von Franz speaks of a man she knew who was an extravert thinker. When he once came out with his feelings for his wife in a rare moment, Marie-Louise von Franz was truly moved. She was, however, later shocked to learn that the wife had no notion of her husband's feelings. Being forever occupied with the outer world, and with his projects, he had never told her! "She did not realise the depth of his feeling for her and that, in a deep sense, he was loyal and faithful to her; that was hidden and not expressed in his life. It remained introverted and did not move towards the object."[7]

An extravert thinker can have very strong feeling, but, because that feeling is inferior and introvert, it does not move towards the object. While it has an influence, it is not expressed. Thinking types are often seen as having no feeling or as being cold. Yet this is far from the truth. Because feeling is the inferior function, it is not adapted and it does not click in at the appropriate time. Therefore, a high thinker can weep openly when he hears a friend has died, yet at the actual funeral he will perhaps feel nothing. His feeling does not work for him at the appropriate time. This hidden introvert feeling of the extravert thinker means that the person can establish strong invisible loyalties. Extravert thinkers may not be great communicators among their friends but they will be faithful to the last.

There are two sides to having such strong unconscious feeling. Take the example of a politician. In the positive, it could translate as a deep loyalty and love for one's country. In the negative, it might allow the self-same politician to drop a bomb on another country. Unconscious feeling can be barbaric and absolute.

---

6   Marie-Louise von Franz and James Hillman. (1986) *Lectures on Jung's Typology*, Spring Publications, Putnam, C.T., U.S.A. Page 48.
7   Ibid., page 49.

The introvert feeling of the extravert thinker is deep in the unconscious and therefore very close to the complexes of that person. It is almost certain that this feeling will be contaminated by these complexes. The type most likely to confuse feeling with emotion is the dominant thinker, whether extravert or introvert. Feeling, as we will see later, has nothing directly to do with emotion. Emotion is what is experienced when a complex is triggered. Feeling is a rational function that enables a person to discern what he or she likes or dislikes, what he or she feels is right or wrong. Because, for the thinker, inferior feeling is close to the complexes, emotion contaminates that feeling. The feeling can then appear in this type to be childish and irrational. However, feeling as a dominant function is highly differentiated and sophisticated. It is not in the least childish. This is not the case with the inferior feeling of the extravert thinker. "Because of the highly impersonal character of the conscious attitude, the unconscious feelings are extremely personal and oversensitive, giving rise to secret prejudices … or a constant tendency to make negative assumptions about other people in order to invalidate their arguments in advance".[8]

When attempting to discover which is the dominant function in an individual, often the behaviour of the inferior function confuses the picture. You may have an extravert thinker who is good at his work, clear headed and effective, and who comes home to his wife and children and appears fuzzy and emotional. He, basically, switches to his inferior function at home. His wife and children probably would not recognise him at work! An extravert thinker would not be inclined towards overt shows of primitive emotion because his or her feeling is introverted and private. The person can, however, be swamped in moods, trapped in negative, inferior feeling. One could be fooled into thinking that such a type was obviously a high feeler, because of the effect that feeling has on him or her. But one could not be further from

---

8 *C.W.* Vol. 6, par 588.

the truth. It is because that feeling is inferior that it is so primitive and emotional. Ironically, when one sees a person either swamped by moods or prone to uncontrolled outbursts of emotion, one is dealing with a high thinker and not a feeler at all!

Introvert Thinking Type

When one is looking at thinking types, it is often possible to tell whether they are extravert or introvert by looking at their relationship to things in the outside world. By looking at where they place value and meaning, on the outer or the inner, one can establish whether this relationship is fundamentally positive or negative. Extravert thinkers will habitually say yes to proposals, plans and so forth in the outer world. Later they may consider things in more detail and perhaps vary their response. I know of one extravert thinker who often upset and confused people by acting in this way. When a person made a proposal to him, he always sounded very positive and enthusiastic. But later he was capable of coming back with a whole list of reasons why the project should not go ahead. Introvert thinkers are likely to do the reverse. They will say an adamant no, or will shrink away from an initial proposal but later, after some consideration, may come around and be all in favour! A person's habitual response to the outer world indicates whether that person is an extravert or an introvert.

The difference between extraverted thinking and introverted thinking is not easy to understand. The introvert thinker may look to be concerned with the object, however, on investigation, the thinking "… begins with the subject and leads back to the subject, far though it may range into the realm of actual reality".[9] For an introvert thinker, the outer facts must not be allowed to dominate. The introvert thinker will raise questions and make theories but the facts will only be used as evidence for the theory and not for their own sake. In the

---

9   ibid., par 628.

area of science, the extravert thinker will be involved in projects and experiments. The introvert thinker will grapple with the basic concepts. In physics, the extravert thinker deals with practical physics; the introvert thinker will look to theoretical concepts. And in the area of the history of art, the extravert thinker will ask when one picture was painted and how the history of the time relates to the artist; the introvert art historian will question various established opinions about art and come up with his or her own opinions.

The realm of the introvert thinker is in the logical processes of the human mind and the building up of ideas. If the introvert thinker has an interest in psychology, he or she is fascinated by ideas about the psyche and how it works. The person will look to reality to confirm and support these ideas. The introvert thinker will be less interested in clients in and for themselves but rather as material for his or her ideas. Jung says that with introvert thinking:

> It's aim is never an intellectual reconstruction of the concrete fact, but a shaping of that dark image into a luminous idea … It wants to reach reality, to see how the external fact will fit into and fill the framework of the idea, and the creative power of this thinking shows itself when it actually creates an idea which, though not inherent in the concrete fact, is yet the most suitable expression of it. Its task is completed when the idea it has fashioned seems to emerge so inevitably from the external facts that they actually prove its validity.[10]

The realm of the introvert thinker is the inner world of ideas, archetypes and primordial images.

---

10 ibid.

The introvert thinker has a negative relation to the object and this can come across as indifference. In a more extreme form it comes across as aversion. This type of person may be polite and friendly yet, if one is sensitive to such things, one might pick up a feeling that one is being kept at bay, or that one is being pacified, just in case one becomes a nuisance. However, with very close friends this reserve disappears and the person is warm and relaxed. The threat of strangeness is not there.

Introvert thinkers will shrink from nothing in order to build up their world of ideas, or system of thought. They will not worry whether it will be heretical, unpopular, subversive or even disturbing to other people. The outer world does not carry such influence for them. They are, however, riddled with anxiety when they are called to make their system of thought an objective reality. Jung says, "… that goes against the grain. And when he does put his ideas into the world, he never introduces them like a mother solicitous for her children, but simply dumps them there and gets extremely annoyed if they fail to thrive on their own account".[11]

Introvert thinkers have a horror of publicity. They will not go out of their way to gain people's appreciation of their ideas or work. They simply wish to be left alone in order to be able to continue. They also feel that the truth of their work is so self-evident that if it is not appreciated then it merely reflects the dimness of the other people. They are the type *par excellence* who do not "suffer fools gladly". "In pursuit of his ideas he is generally stubborn, headstrong, and quite unamenable to influence".[12] These kinds of thinkers, because they are so free from the outer influences, can come up with the most original work. Nietzsche is an example of one, as is Kant. However, if they

---

11 *C.W.* Vol. 6, par 634.
12 ibid.

become extreme, their work can become irrelevant because it is so unrelated to the time and to objective reality.

The inferior function of the introvert thinker is extravert feeling. Therefore the introvert thinker has the same strong, loyal and warm feeling that the extravert thinker has. This type of feeling is peculiar to dominant thinkers. It is different to the differentiated feeling of a dominant feeler. The inferior feeling of dominant thinkers is more raw and child-like. The difference between the inferior feeling of an extravert thinker and that of an introvert thinker is that the feeling of the introvert thinker flows outwards towards the object and is not private and inward like that of the extravert thinker. The inferior feeling of the introvert thinker is characterised by having:

> …very black and white judgements, either Yes or No, love or hate. His feeling can be very easily poisoned by other people and by the collective atmosphere. (It is) sticky … and has that kind faithfulness which can last endlessly … You could compare (it) to the flow of hot lava from a volcano – it only moves about five meters an hour, but it devastates everything in its way.[13]

On the positive side, as I have said above, the inferior feeling of the introvert thinker is very genuine and warm. There is no calculation in their love. This is an attractive quality as the love is primitive and intense. This can, however, be their downfall, as in the classic case of the professor, in midlife crisis, who falls completely in love with a younger woman and leaves everything to be with her.

The inferior feeling of the introvert thinker is deep in the unconscious and therefore very close to the complexes of the person. Because this

---

13 Marie-Louise von Franz and James Hillman. (1986) *Lectures on Jung's Typology*, Spring Publications, Putnam, C.T., U.S.A. Page 52.

feeling is extraverted, it is more likely to be experienced as projected out onto the world. The introvert thinker will experience this inferior feeling not so much as moods, but as extreme emotions attached to situations. If a situation triggers an introvert thinker's inferior feeling, the feeling function will work away discerning the right and wrong of the situation. However, because it is deep in the unconscious, it will be slow. It will also be bogged down by the complexes close by, which will hitch a ride and clog up it's working. Such feeling will appear in the person's mind loaded with emotion and primitive superstition. Unless the person knows what is happening and can deal with it appropriately, it will be far from helpful.

I knew of an introvert thinker whose partner was wrongly accused by an outside party. The partner responded calmly and went about proving her innocence. The introvert thinker, however, got caught in the grip of his inferior function and came up with the most primitive fears. He felt that his partner, though he knew her to be innocent, would go to prison and that they would lose their home. These fears were outrageous – what his partner had been accused of did not merit jail and there was no question of losing their home. This man was caught in a victim complex. The emotion and fears he was feeling came from the complex and had nothing, whatsoever, to do with the situation. His inferior feeling could not function in any way beneficially for him, because it was contaminated by his victim complex. He had to clear that complex before his feeling could be applied helpfully to the situation at hand. Introvert thinkers can use their feeling in the world once they clear it of the complexes and accompanying emotion. This involves a great deal of consciousness and hard work and is a very slow process.

Extravert Feeling Type

Feeling is very often confused with emotion. The two are not the same. Emotion is what is experienced when a complex is activated. Feeling is a rational function based on judgement and reason. The French people are collectively a nation with high feeling. In the French language, the word for feeling, *'sentiment'*, does not carry the interpretation of emotion but rather implies a judgement. The English language uses the word feeling for when one is emotional – someone was feeling upset, for example. Yet, the English language has no other word to convey feeling as a rational function. For example, someone can say: "I felt that it was wrong to say something about the woman's husband because she would be hurt" and this is a judgement statement as opposed to an emotional statement. Because of this lack of distinction in using the word 'feeling', high feelers are often described as emotional, gushy people. This is not the case. The more differentiated the feeling, the less likely one is to have strong emotional responses. High feelers are normally well-adjusted and reasonable people who are able to say the right thing at the right time and can make other people feel good in their presence. The feeling function allows them to ascertain what they like and what they do not like. It allows then to know if something is right or if it is wrong. It enables them to make a value judgement. High feelers can make friends easily. They are people's people.

Marie-Louise von Franz says: "The extraverted feeling type is characterised by the fact that his main adaptation is carried by an adequate evaluation of outer objects and an appropriate relation to them".[14] The extravert feeler values things in the outer world and is able to adjust to a smooth and right relationship to them. Extravert feelers are the ones who are often the favourites in the eyes of Western society. Because they are extraverts they are comfortable in the outer

---

14 ibid., page 54.

world, in social situations and with other people. They are sensitive to the social atmosphere and are aware of the current fashions. Jung claims that it is this kind of feeling that has people going to theatre or concerts and even to church. Fashions owe their existence to it, as do social, philanthropic and cultural institutions. "In these matters extraverted feeling proves itself a creative factor. Without it, a harmonious social life would be impossible".[15]

This kind of feeling is interesting in that, being extraverted, it is the object that holds most of the value, as opposed to the subject. It is not "I, the subject, feel x, y, or z because of this object" rather it is more like "the object impresses itself upon me and these are the feelings I have". The process begins with the value on the object, then to the subject and then back to the object. For an introvert feeler the process would be different. The value would begin with the subject, then on to the object and then back to the subject. This process of valuing is played out for instance in an extravert feeler's choice of partner. Conventionality will play a large part in the choice. Extravert feelers are sensitive to the collective conscious attitude around them and therefore are greatly influenced by it. Jung comments:

> ... the 'suitable' man is loved, and no one else; he is suitable not because he appeals to her hidden subjective nature – about which she usually knows nothing – but because he comes up to all reasonable expectations in the matter of age, position, income, size and respectability of his family, etc. One could easily reject such a picture as ironical or cynical, but I am fully convinced that the love feeling of this type of woman is in perfect accord with her choice. It is genuine and not just shrewd.[16]

---

15 *C.W.* Vol. 6, par 596.
16 ibid., par 597.

A woman goes to an exhibition of modern art and meets the artist. Because this woman is an extravert feeler, she speaks with high admiration of the art, how she likes it and how wonderful it is, even if, from another person's perspective, the art may be strange and obscure. This person's feeling comes from the appropriateness of liking the art in the face of the creator of the work. She is also influenced by the fact that this artist is popular and that the art is now fashionable. Such 'correct' feeling can only work if it is not interrupted or disturbed by anything else. What will disturb it is thinking. A high extravert feeler will try to keep thinking at bay.

If the extravert feeler's dominant function becomes worn down, or if the person is under stress, then that person regresses to habitual responses. When this happens, the connection between the person and the response disappears and the object gains ascendancy. The person is pulled into the object and the personal quality of the feeling disappears. There is no charm in the person's response, no warmth of feeling. It appears mechanical, cold, unfeeling and untrustworthy. One gets the impression that the person is acting. "Over extraverted feeling may satisfy aesthetic expectations but it does not speak to the heart".[17] It appeals only to the senses and/or reason. It has become sterile. In this case the subject has disappeared in the feeling of the moment and all that remains is the influence of the object. People who experience this can then enter into many different relationships which are all at odds with each other. They experience many varying feeling states, each one different to the one before. Their feeling no longer appears as a personal expression of the subject but seems more like a series of moods. These people appear unreliable and fickle and, in the worst-case scenario, hysterical.

It is only when the object gains too much value, to the detriment of

---

17 ibid., par 596

the subject, that the high extravert feeler seems hysterical and gushy. This happens when the person is under pressure, or when his or her dominant function is wearing thin. Marie-Louise von Franz gives an example of this: "I once noticed an extraverted feeling type, on a dreadful day when there was a horrible fog outside, saying mechanically: "Isn't it a wonderful day!" I thought: "Oh dear, your main function is rattling!"[18] Yet, when the extravert feeler is not worn down, you will find no better person to feel into another person's situation. They have the ability to see exactly what needs to be done and they will just go and do it.

Extravert feelers dislike thinking and especially dislike introverted thinking. They wish to avoid the deeper questions in life. Philosophical and abstract thought are anathema to them. Unfortunately, one cannot not think these things. Because we are human, these questions surface all the time. Extravert feelers, because they neglect such thinking, end up with a pile of neglected, negative, primitive thinking judgements. For such amiable types, herein lies the sting in the tail. Anyone who has been stung will know what it is like. One feels wrapped in the warm atmosphere that such a person creates when suddenly a crass and cynical comment will be made, which will hit you like a ton of bricks. Von Franz writes:

> If one analyses an extraverted feeling type and is somewhat sensitive to the atmosphere, one very often gets a bit frozen or cooled down in spite of his amiability. One can sense these negative thoughts swarming around in his head. Such thoughts hit one in a disagreeable way. One sometimes sees a cold flash in the eyes and knows that there is a very negative thought about, but the next

---

18 Marie-Louise von Franz and James Hillman (1986) *Lectures on Jung's Typology*, Spring Publications, Putnam, C.T., U.S.A. Page 55.

minute it is gone. It gives one the creeps. Such thoughts
are generally based on a very cynical outlook on life…[19]

Extravert feelers experience thoughts like birds landing on their
heads and flying off again. They feel that if they somehow catch these
thoughts, if they are negative, then the negative thoughts will, like
some kind of black magic, have power over them and will affect their
life. And so, they attempt to ignore them. Unfortunately, the reverse
is the case. It is by ignoring the negative thoughts that they give
them the power to affect their lives in unconscious and destructive
ways. The challenge to the extravert feeler is to catch the thought and
follow it through to some insight. This challenge can however seem
overwhelming.

An example of this was of a woman, an extravert feeler, who decided
that she would catch her thoughts and look at them. She found
herself thinking that if her son-in-law died then her daughter would
return home! The woman was terribly shocked at such a thought
and she refused to look at her thoughts any more. However, had she
dug deeper, she would possibly have looked at her desire to have
her daughter home and perhaps understood where that desire had
sprung from. She would then have realised that she needed to figure
out the purpose for her life, now that her daughter had left. In looking
at the meaning of her life, now that she was not actively mothering her
daughter, she would have been confronted with the deeper questions
of the meaning of life in general. To be fair to her, facing that one
thought would have led her into very deep waters, but the process
would have enriched her life hugely, and made use of her inferior
thinking function.[20]

---

19 Ibid., page 57.
20 Marie-Louise von Franz and James Hillman. (1986) Lectures on Jung's Typology,
    Spring Publications, Putnam, C.T., U.S.A. Page 56.

Often extravert feelers, rather than doing some genuine thinking of their own, will circumvent the problem by adopting some established system of thought — lock, stock and barrel. This can be seen in people who take up a religion and who will then repeat the teaching and dogma of that religion in a mechanical way. When questioned, these people can become aggressive. This is a defense because, at some level, they are aware that any high thinker can undermine them in seconds. There is little subtlety in the extravert feeler's thinking. It is slow and primitive. The person will tend to stick to generalised, dogmatic statements in order to cover it up.

Introvert Feeling Type

The generally agreed description of the introvert feeling type is: "Still waters run deep". Introvert feeling is a rational function and it judges and values things as an extravert feeler does. It is different to an extravert feeling function in that it puts more value on the subject than on the object. This means that how introvert feelers experience a thing is more important to them than the thing itself. It also means that they are influenced more by the inner world than the outer. Because of the introversion, these people keep things inside rather than express them. This makes introvert feelers often very difficult to understand. Jung writes of them: "They are most silent, inaccessible, hard to understand; often they hide behind a childish or banal mask, and their temperament is inclined to melancholy."[21] Their feelings are intensive rather than extensive. Because everything is going on in the depths, without any access to expression, they can sometimes appear unfeeling or indifferent, even cold.

The relationship of introvert feelers to the outer world is similar to any introvert type. They shrink from the object – their habitual response being 'no' before they can come round to considering a more positive

---

21 *C.W.* Vol. 6, par 639.

response. This shrinking from the object is so that they can protect and fill the depths of the subject. The outer world provides the stimulus for an inner intensity, but that intensity is usually deeply private. The introvert feeler is similar to the introvert thinker in that the world of primordial images is the realm of interest as opposed to the outer world. The primordial images consist of both ideas (for the thinker) and feeling-values (for the feeler). The way of the introvert thinker is somewhat smoother, because it is easier to communicate thinking than feeling, especially in the realm of the inner world of archetypal images and even more especially in Western culture. The introvert feeler is in the difficult position of being receptive to feeling-values of the collective unconscious, often without the temperament or skills to express what he or she perceives.

How this plays out in the lives of introvert feelers is that they set their own standards, which are decided by their skill at picking up the feeling-value in the unconscious, and they live by these standards. This has the effect of exerting a covert influence on their surroundings. Marie-Louise von Franz writes: they "… very often form the ethical backbone of a group: without irritating the others by preaching moral or ethical precepts, they themselves have such correct standards of ethical values that they secretly emanate a positive influence on those around them".[22]

Once the ego of an introvert feeler does not become inflated with the contents of the unconscious that he or she is picking up, the person can remain healthy. If the ego can remain humble in the face of the unconscious contents, then it will be forever aware that there is something higher and greater than it. Jung comments that these people "…neither shine nor reveal themselves".[23] However, they do have

---

22 Marie-Louise von Franz and James Hillman. (1986) *Lectures on Jung's Typology*, Spring Publications, Putnam, C.T., U.S.A. Page 60.
23 *C.W.* Vol. 6, par 639.

amazing depths, they are tuned in to a rich world and are valuable carriers of the contents of that world. Unvalued and misunderstood as they may be, their role in our society is vital.

When studying in Maynooth, a third level college in County Kildare and major Roman Catholic seminary, I attended, with my fellow women theology students, a class on *Humanae Vitae*, the Roman Catholic encyclical on birth control and contraception. We had studied the document well and were eager to hammer out with the professor the flaws in the logic that we found in it. The professor, however, would hear none of it, and we sat through an hour of him deflecting our arguments and finally dismissing us by saying: "You fail to understand". Needless to say, we were all furious. After the class, a smaller group of us went to talk to another professor, a friend and bright light of wit and sanity in the college, to offload our frustration. Unfortunately, he was occupied with someone else and he came out to tell us so. Among us was an articulate thinker who summed up briefly what had happened. However, it was the silent and seething introvert feeler who caught his attention. In picking up the depth of her disturbance, he excused himself from the person he had been with, and brought us to another room to hear us out.

Introvert feelers "… have a highly differentiated scale of values, but they do not express them outwardly: they are affected by them within".[24] The inferior function of the introvert feeling type is extravert thinking. This provides the curious situation where these people are often interested in an immense number of outer facts and have quite a good ability to retain them. The positive side of this inferior thinking is that it is "simple, clear and intelligible".[25] However, like all inferior functions, it is only positive if one remains conscious that it is an

---

24 Marie-Louise von Franz and James Hillman, (1986) *Lectures on Jung's Typology*, Spring Publications, Putnam, C.T., U.S.A. Page 60.
25 ibid., page 61.

inferior function and if one constantly keeps its limitations in mind. Often, the inferiority of this thinking appears as a fascination with one or two thoughts, with which one races through a bizarre amount of material. Jung comments: "… introverted feeling is counterbalanced by a primitive thinking, whose concretism and slavery to facts surpass all bounds".[26]

At the workshop on functions that I mentioned earlier, a woman, a nurse, who was an introvert feeler, had the following story. Her husband came home one evening from a basketball match. He had caught his wedding ring on the basketball loop and had hung from the loop, held only by the ring. His finger was partially severed. The woman, even though she was a trained nurse, simply froze when she saw what had happened to her husband. She just stared at him and said helplessly: "I have no saline here to clean it!" It was the woman's brother, who was with her, who said "For God's sake, get him to the hospital!" The shock of seeing her husband like this had fumbled the woman's dominant function, dismissed years of nursing training, and thrown her headfirst into her inferior extravert thinking function. She accurately, but utterly irrelevantly, stated that there was no saline!

At this workshop, I had asked the group of thirty-three people to divide into their various functions. The group of introvert feelers had, amongst them, a teacher who worked with young children, a psychotherapist and a pastor. The energy of this group was clearly identifiable. It felt peaceful and contained. They were smiling and gentle and I could feel their support for my work, yet they said very little.

Marie-Louise von Franz comments on the fact that Jung always characterised the Freudian system as being extraverted thinking.

---

26 C.W. Vol. 6 par 639.

Her own reflection on the matter was that Freud himself was an introverted feeling type and that his work carried all the signs of inferior extraverted thinking. She claims that as an analyst Freud was a high feeler who had a "hidden gentlemanliness which had a positive influence on his patients and upon his surroundings".[27] What she leaves unsaid is that because the Freudian system sprang from Freud's inferior function, it contained a certain monomania which obsessed over one basic fundamental idea, i.e. sexuality. Be that as it may, it does indicate that even when something springs from an inferior function it can, nonetheless, be brilliant. What supports Marie Louise's theory is the fact that Freud was very reluctant to be put on the spot in defending his material and often sent Jung, his then disciple, to conferences in order to argue the cause. For an introvert feeler, having to think on the spot in a public setting with antagonistic people asking questions and finding fault would be torture. However well Freud's inferior thinking could work in the privacy of his own office, it could not be expected to work well under such pressure.

An introvert feeling type can be confused with an introvert thinking type. Both types share similar responses, especially in areas of social situations and public occasions. Obviously, both types share an introversion, which will have them shy away from the objective world. However, they also share a similar response upon going into a crowded room. Both will hate it! However, there will be a difference. The introvert feeling type will feel into the room and will pick up on the undercurrent, unconscious feeling values in the group. The person will either like it or will not like it. Because of this person's inferior thinking he or she might not have the wherewithal to think the situation through enough to figure out why such undercurrents are there or to simply leave. In this case, the introvert feeler will sit

---

27 Marie-Louise von Franz and James Hillman. (1986) *Lectures on Jung's Typology*, Spring Publications, Putnam, C.T. U.S.A. Page 61.

and suffer it, hating every minute. The introvert thinking type, on the other hand, who may also hate it, will hate it initially because it may not trigger anything for him or her as an introvert thinker. With no positive thinking connection to the event, the person's inferior extravert feeling is triggered. This leaves the person acutely aware of whatever feeling issues the people at the party actually may have with him or her and consequently the person will feel cripplingly self-conscious. However, if no one has any issues with the person, he or she will be fine and will probably enjoy the event thanks to that same inferior extravert feeling.

It is impossible to casually identify any function in a person because of the subtlety of how each function works. One has to consider the influence of both the extravert and introvert attitudes. One also has to consider the workings of the inferior function. Discernment is complicated even more by the fact that people, through the course of their personal growth, will be developing different functions. In developing a function one must live from that function. This will not change one's dominant function, but it does mean that in order to develop another function, one must take energy away from the dominant one for a time. If a person is serious about understanding this material, then all these factors must be taken into consideration. This typology is not for the faint-hearted or casually interested.

The Four Irrational Types
The four irrational types are extravert sensation, introvert sensation, extravert intuition, and introvert intuition.

Extravert Sensation Type
The extravert sensate person is easier to spot than many of the others. These people are realistic, practical, down-to-earth and are often gifted with their hands. Among other things they are the mountain

climbers, engineers, mechanics and craft teachers. The extravert sensation type has a strong relationship with the sensate world, with the material world, with the concrete world. These people have a strong relationship with their bodies and, because of this, often have a strong sexuality. They have a remarkable ability for understanding and handling machinery, or craft materials, and for recognising quality and line and texture. I know one extravert sensate woman who took it upon herself to learn and teach crafts - such as lace-making and tatting - which were dying out.

Extravert sensate types are the best people to report a crime or an accident, because these people have a capacity for picking up factual information and retaining it. In going into a room they will notice every detail, the colour of the walls, the type of furniture, the smells in the room and so forth. Concrete, sensate facts are where they place their value and they are unrivalled in their sense of realism. In a family situation, if the other siblings begin to ask questions about their rearing and about the effect it may have had on them, the extravert sensate will say: just get on with life, why bother asking such questions, what good could it possibly do?

A woman, who was an introvert feeler, was washing her car. As she washed the already cracked headlight, she managed to push her thumb through the glass, through the bulb and onto the wire. Her thumb was bleeding heavily. The top part of it was badly sliced. The woman was at home with her young children and was minding the children of a friend. Shortly after the accident, the friend arrived to collect his children. He was an extravert sensate type. The woman, who was still bleeding, and in shock, held up her damaged thumb and told her friend what had happened. The man, to her amazement, walked past her and began to examine the broken headlight of the car! When he had finished looking at it, he briefly looked at the woman's thumb and muttered something about it not needing a stitch. He then went into the house to collect his children and brought them home. The introvert feeling woman was so amazed by his behaviour that she began to laugh. Later, she heard from this man's wife that he had gone home and had spent a long time phoning around different garages trying to find a replacement headlight. As an extravert sensate, this was his way of showing his concern. Picking up on a woman's distress, panic and shock was quite beyond him, but he did know what to do about the car.

A similar story came from a woman at the workshop mentioned earlier. This woman told how, as a child, she had cut her hand badly when playing outside and had come into the house to find her mother. Blood from the child's hand went onto the carpet. The woman remembers how her mother had soaked the carpet first before turning her attention to the child's hand. As an extravert sensate the mother knew that, if the blood dried on the carpet, she would never get the stain out.

Introvert intuition is the extravert sensate's inferior function and this type will consciously avoid the area of intuition if possible. The intuitions that these people have come up from the deep unconscious. Because of this, they are archaic and often appear in a negative form. These intuitions can be spot-on accurate or they can be completely off the mark. When intuition is the main function in a person, usually either thinking or feeling, as auxiliaries, are fairly well developed and the person will use these to discern whether an intuition is true or not. However, the extravert sensate - because the intuition is coming from an inferior function and seems so unique - tends to take the intuition as it is, without calling in help from an auxiliary function. He or she is unable to test the intuition for elements of truth in it. The person cannot discern what is accurate and what is not. The realm of intuition is, to them, both numinous and unfamiliar.

The gift of the extravert sensate is that this type of person "can quickly and objectively relate to outer facts".[28] These people can be described as people who live life to the full. Whatever objects excite sensations are the ones that are valued. The sensations do not necessarily have to be pleasant but they must be strong. Jung describes the extravert sensate as being a "... lover of tangible reality with little inclination for reflection and no desire to dominate ... To feel the object, to have sensations and if possible enjoy them – that is his constant aim".[29] He goes on to say that this type of person is "... usually a jolly fellow and sometimes a refined aesthete. In the former case, the great problems of life hang on a good or indifferent dinner; in the latter, it's all a question of good taste".[30]

If extravert sensates are healthy they are well adjusted to reality. They dress well, work well in their chosen field and so forth. If, however, the object dominates and the subject disappears behind it, these people become more and more disagreeable. On the one hand they may become mere pleasure seekers, on the other unscrupulous effete aesthetes. The object is squeezed for all it can give, the stimulation of sensation being the only drive. The inferior function, introvert intuition, is forced out of its compensatory role and comes into open opposition to the dominant sensate attitude. This results in intuitions, which up until now have been repressed, being projected outwards. These people experience crazy suspicions and become phobic and compulsive. The easy-going sensation type, who accepts things indiscriminately, becomes a compulsive and neurotic person. Jung points out that, because sensation is not a rational function, reasoning is not the way to reach this type. "Special techniques for bringing

---

28 Ibid., page 28.
29 *C.W.* Vol. 6, par 607.
30 ibid.

emotional pressure to bear are often needed in order to make him at all conscious".[31]

This is in extreme cases, when the person becomes possessed by the object and the sensations it stirs. In more ordinary lives, the inferior function of the extravert sensate plays a less drastic role. For extravert sensates everything has its natural causes. However, because their inferior function is introvert intuition, extravert sensates can be captivated by fairy tales or ghost stories. Through these, primitive intuitive fantasy has a means of expression. Such types can get caught up in esoteric movements because such movements speak to their archaic inferior intuition. Marie-Louise von Franz points out that North America has a high proportion of extravert sensates. This accounts for the success of capitalism there. Extravert sensates do well in the material realm. The down side of this is that North America is also a place where many esoteric and cultic movements thrive. People are caught up by their inferior functions and drawn into these movements.[32]

Introvert Sensation Type

The introvert sensation type is irrational because it is orientated by what happens, as opposed to by rational judgements about what happens. This type, like the introvert feeling type, is hard to fathom and is often misjudged. Unless these people have a well-developed auxiliary function that can help them express themselves they can appear dull. Yet this is because they experience the world in a particular way. Emma Jung, who was an introvert sensation type, said it was like –

---

31 *C.W.* Vol. 6, par 609.
32 Marie-Louise von Franz and James Hillman. (1986) *Lectures on Jung's Typology*, Spring Publications, Putnam, C.T., U.S.A. Page 30.

... a highly sensitised photographic plate. When somebody comes into the room ... every detail is absorbed. The impression comes from the object to the subject; it is as though a stone fell into deep water – the impression falls deeper and deeper and sinks in. Outwardly, the introverted sensation type looks utterly stupid. He just sits and stares, and you do not know what is going on within him.[33]

These people may give the impression of being very slow. Yet what is happening is that the immediate reactions are directed inwards, and the outward reaction is more delayed. If such a person has an ability for artistic expression, either in painting or in writing, the full richness of what he or she has experienced will come forth. If the person does not, he or she is inaccessible both to other people and to himself or herself.

I knew a woman who is an introvert sensate type. At the time of knowing her, I did not know her type. Although I was drawn to her in friendship, I often found the time I spent with her somewhat exhausting. I would say something to her and then there would be a long silence. These were not the long secure silences of easy friendships. For me they were awkward and painful. I judged, at the time, that she was making no effort to respond or to make conversation. My inclination was to try to fill the silences, but this left me feeling exhausted and a bit foolish. It was only years later, when I realised that this woman was an introvert sensate type, that I saw that, in those long awkward silences, the woman most likely simply did not know what to say! My conversational statements were falling into deep water and no response was possible for a long time, if ever. This was simply the woman's type.

33 ibid., page 34.

I have since met other people of this type and I now know that I must relax and allow the silences to be what they are – the person's natural way of taking in information. This type needs to have a time-lapse between listening and speaking. These people move in a different time zone. I know a young boy of this type who is a loner at school but seems perfectly happy to be this. He is contained in his own space, in his own experience of the world. His grandfather is a similar type and was never happier than when he was left alone to cycle his bike around the city. When this young boy gets upset it is disastrous to keep asking him what is wrong. In response he simply gets more and more locked into himself. However, if one of his parents takes him on his or her lap and cuddles him affectionately, over time something in the boy shifts and he recovers from his upset. No reasoning can reach him when he is upset. He must be allowed to process things at his own pace, in his own way. What a person can do for him is to let him know by being physically affectionate that he is loved no matter what. This takes the pressure off him and allows him to take the time to be himself.

The introvert sensation type illustrates most clearly the difference between how an introverted person and an extraverted person experiences the world. The difference is expressed in where the value is placed: either upon the object or the subject. The subject and object plays a role in every interaction in life, but the extravert places most value on the object while the introvert places most value on the subject. The extravert values what he or she experiences, the introvert values how he or she experiences it. Therefore, if you were to put an extravert sensate artist beside an introvert sensate artist and were to ask them both to paint the same landscape, their paintings would be dynamically different. The extravert sensation type will stay true to what is seen and will put very little personal, subjective flavour to it. This person's painting is likely to resemble quite closely paintings of the same landscape by other extravert sensation types. I knew of such an artist, who had a remarkable ability to paint the most wonderful paintings, completely true to what was seen, like a photograph.

The introvert's painting of the same scene will, most likely, be full of subjective factors and influences. If put beside paintings of other introvert sensation types, none of them will bear much resemblance to each other. Jung describes the subjective factor as "... an unconscious disposition which alters the sense perception at its source, thus depriving it of the character of a purely objective influence".[34] What is important for the introvert sensation type is not the reality of the object but rather the reality of the subjective factor. This subjective factor is full of the primordial images of the unconscious world, and makes up a kind of psychic mirror-world of the actual world.

This, therefore, is how the introvert sensation types experience the world. Not only do they pick up all the sensate details of the objective world with photographic detail, but these details sink down into the unconscious and stir up a "... mythological world, where men, animals, locomotives, houses, rivers and mountains appear either as benevolent deities or as malevolent demons. That they appear thus to him never enters his head, though that is just the effect they have on his judgements and actions".[35] Little wonder that such people are hard to fathom.

One of the peculiar aspects of the sensate type in general is that this type can get stuck in concrete reality. Only the here and now exist. Because intuition, which deals in future possibilities, is inferior, such future possibilities are not acknowledged. Sensation types tend to behave in life as though things will always be as they now are. They

---

34 *C.W.* Vol. 6, par 647
35 ibid., par 652.

cannot see how things could be different. Introvert sensation types tend to do nothing impulsively and will have a systematic and hard-working attention to detail and routine.

It was, I think, no coincidence that, at the workshop I gave on functions, of the thirty-three people attending, there were no sensate types whatsoever, either extravert or introvert. The group was a North American group who had travelled to Ireland on a tour which had been advertised as being both Jungian and Celtic in content. Obviously, such an agenda was not very attractive to sensate types.

The inferior function of the introvert sensation type is extravert intuition. At first glance it is easy to confuse introvert sensation with intuition. Many people consider that intuition is about the unconscious and that it deals with an archaic and primordial world. But this is not the case, unless it is introverted. I will deal with this in more detail later when speaking of intuition. Intuition is about perceiving what is beneath the surface. This can be beneath the surface in the unconscious. It can also mean hidden possibilities in the outer world. When it is introverted, it deals with the possibilities of the collective unconscious, when extraverted it looks to the possibilities in the outside world. When an introvert sensation type begins to grapple with their inferior function of extravert intuition they come into a conflict. Intuition comes as a flash. When you try to catch it, it is gone. If your dominant function is sensation then you are gifted at working slowly, with painstaking detail. These two functions are clearly poles apart.

Marie-Louise von Franz speaks of a woman, an artist, who was an introvert sensation type. For many years, she painted the contents of her unconscious. Her paintings were detailed and beautiful. But Marie-Louise von Franz learned from the woman that she corrected and improved upon the images that came to her. Because her sensation was introverted, the material she used was inner world material. But her introversion also meant that the subject was more important to her than the object. Therefore, she allowed herself to subjectively doctor the 'objective' material of her unconscious. Now, this woman's inferior function was extraverted intuition. Marie Louise began to encourage her to put the images down exactly as they came from her intuition, so that she could look at them in their rawness and learn from them. The woman could not! She felt it was impossible. To do so, she would have to loosen the hold that her introvert sensation had on her and give up her love of detail and her subjective value.[36]

Introvert sensation types have been known to get symptoms of giddiness or sea-sickness when they have been forced to assimilate intuition too quickly. As a type, this person is stuck in concrete reality, albeit an introverted inner world reality. To be called to let go of this reality and take on flash-like intuitions can seem simply to be too much.

Extravert Intuitive Type

Both sensation and intuition are irrational functions. Their operation is based on perception rather than rational judgement. "Their perception is directed simply and solely to events as they happen, no selection being made by judgement".[37] This does not mean that sensation and intuition are contrary to reason, rather they are beyond reason. They are not grounded on reason. Extraverted intuition is a function of unconscious perception directed towards the outer world. Because intuition is non-rational and can appear almost magical, it can be mistakenly seen as something that is naturally introverted and belonging to the inner world. This is not the case. The extravert

36 Marie-Louise von Franz and James Hillman. (1986) *Lectures on Jung's Typology*, Spring Publications, Putnam, C.T., U.S.A. Page 35.
37 *C.W.* Vol. 6, par 615.

intuitive picks up the unseen relationships in the outer world and uses this knowledge in the outer world. This is a way of perceiving that is as valid as the sensate way of picking up information. Extraverted intuition is a tool, just as the other functions are tools. Unfortunately, unlike sensation, one only knows if one's intuition is right when what one has intuited has actually happened. It is this uncertainty around intuition that leaves people feeling that it is, perhaps, not as valid a tool as the other functions. An extravert intuitive friend once said to me despairingly, "What is the point of having these intuitions? What good are they when I do not even know if they are real until something actually happens?"

Jung said: "The intuitive function is represented in consciousness by an attitude of expectancy, by vision and penetration; but only from the subsequent result can it be established how much of what was 'seen' was actually in the object, and how much was 'read into' it."[38] The function of intuition transmits images, or perceptions, of how things relate to each other, below the surface as it were. These things cannot be transmitted by any of the other functions. In the same way that the extravert sensate experiences life at the fullest when there is an intensity of sensation, intuition attempts to take in the widest range of possibilities. It is in envisioning possibilities that intuition is satisfied. The extravert intuitive applies these intuitions to the outer world.

There were three extraverted intuitive types present at the workshop on functions. Interestingly, none of the three were altogether convinced that this was what they were. They could see all the other possibilities and were reluctant to tie themselves down. I happened to know these three people personally, so I was confident that they were sitting in with the right group. They were, all three, highly creative people. A tell-tale sign for one of these people was that she drove her car long

---

38 ibid., par 610.

distances with a dog lying across her lap! This is an indication of inferior sensation. Another of these people moved from one exciting job to another, reluctant to be tied down. He did, however, maintain a healthy relationship with his inferior function by building a small hermitage for himself in a country wilderness, where he would live for short periods of time very simply, taking care of his introverted sensate needs.

There is a constant desire in the extravert intuitive person to seek out new possibilities. Stable conditions can suffocate these people. Unfortunately, this can mean that they will often not reap what they have sown. A project, for example, once it is up and running, loses its attraction and the extravert intuitive is off sniffing out the next possible thing to do. If the type is extreme, the person may not even get around to sowing anything at all. He or she may simply move from one thing to another, never actually applying what has been learned in any sensate or concrete way. These people are caught up in newness and possibilities and are phobic about seeing something through to a reality-locked conclusion. Intuition is what drives them and their inferior function, sensation, is something they run from. Commitment can be anathema to them as it involves sticking with something when the rush received from intuition has run out.

People of this type benefit greatly if they have the back up of a well-developed auxiliary function of either thinking or feeling. From either of these, they have access to the judgement that is lacking in their dominant function. When a business woman begins an enterprise and experiences the initial problems that will affect any new project, it is thinking or feeling that will enable her to hold on and ride the problems out. It is only then that she can benefit from the project and make money. If a person is too identified with the dominant function of extraverted intuition, he or she will tend to sell out as soon as the project hits problems, lose money on it and move on to something else.

When an intuitive has found something new, it is common to hear from this person that this is it, this is the thing to end all things, the final turning point, from now on he or she can think of nothing else. Extravert intuitives have amazing enthusiasm. The stronger the intuition the more they become one with the vision. It consumes them. That is, until they have had enough of it and want to move on, to change it or to drop it. "No matter how reasonable and suitable it may be, a day will come when nothing will deter him from regarding as a prison the very situation that seemed to promise him freedom and deliverance and from acting accordingly".[39]

Many business tycoons, entrepreneurs, speculators, stockbrokers, politicians, journalists and publishers belong to this type. They are important people for society both economically and culturally because they are always on the cutting edge of what is new. When Michael D. Higgins, as Minister for Arts and Culture, set up TG4, the Irish language television channel, in 1997, he was working from a deep and true intuition. He saw new possibilities for the language in Irish society. Renewed interest in the Irish language has continued to grow in recent years, and the Irish language channel TG4 has played a big part in that renewal.

For intuition to work, a person needs to look at things with eyes partially closed. The sensate world will tend to distract the workings of intuition, because intuition is trying to see around and beyond these things. However, extravert intuitives use sensate reality as the starting point for their perceptions. They see what is, yet their focus is on what is possible. Because of the nature of intuition, at the time of

---

39 ibid., par 613.

intuiting, they have no way of knowing whether what they intuit is real. It is only when something actually happens in the world can they know that the intuition is actually right.

Extravert intuitive types will not generally pay any attention to their physical needs. They will not know when they are tired, it will not register for them. Nor will they know when they are hungry. Often, if they are extreme types, it will take some kind of physical breakdown before they will pay attention to their bodies. Jung says that if an extreme conscious position of extraverted intuition is reached then "… sooner or later the object takes revenge in the form of compulsive hypochondriacal ideas, phobias, and every imaginable kind of absurd bodily sensation".[40]

Introverted sensation is the inferior function of the extravert intuitive. Such sensation is "slow, heavy and loaded with emotion. Because it is introverted, it is turned away from the outer world and its affairs. It has, like all inferior functions, a mystical quality about it".[41] Marie-Louise von Franz tells a story about a businessman that demonstrates how the inferior function can help an extravert intuitive type reconnect with their instinctual and physical side. She knew a man, a very successful businessman, who developed symptoms from over-work and over-emphasis on his dominant function. He went to meet von Franz and they discussed a dream he had, where a tramp appeared. When he began to dialogue with the tramp, the tramp said that the man should dress like a tramp once a week and go out into the country into nature. The man did this in real life and during his time as a 'tramp' he had profound experiences simply observing nature – a sunset, a tree. He began to experience the divine through his inferior function, introvert sensation. He, however, did not keep up with his

---

40 ibid., par 615.
41 Marie-Louise von Franz and James Hillman. (1986) *Lectures on Jung's Typology*, Spring Publications, Putnam, C.T., U.S.A. Page 39.

walks and fell back into old habits. His symptoms reappeared. As Marie-Louise von Franz says, "That taught him". He began to walk regularly and eventually bought a small farm and a horse. From then on, he religiously cared for the horse one afternoon a week. The horse was symbolic, of course, for his own physical and instinctive body. He had to tend to it slowly, however, and in the real world. It had to be a concrete reality because the man was intuitive.[42]

Introvert Intuitive Type

Like all introverts, the intuitive introvert places value not on outer events but rather on what the outer events, or outer objects, stir within them. Like extravert intuitives, people of this type will be able to perceive the background relationship between things. They will be able to smell out future possibilities. However, this intuition is turned within and thus introvert intuitives know about the slow processes of the collective unconscious. This intuition applies to the archetypes of the inner world, as opposed to the goings on of the outer world. While extraverted intuition produces the business people of the outer world, introverted intuition produces prophets, obscure artists, poets or cranks.

Jung writes: "The peculiar nature of introverted intuition … produces a peculiar type of man: the mystical dreamer and seer on the one hand, the artist and the crank on the other."[43] He describes the crank as someone who "…is content with a visionary idea by which he himself is shaped and determined".[44] It takes judgement, which one has access to through thinking and feeling, "…to shift intuitive perception from the purely aesthetic into the moral sphere". It is this judgement that allows the introvert intuitives to use their perception and gift for the benefit of the world as opposed to being aloof and self-absorbed by it.

---

42 ibid., page 39 - 40.
43 *C.W.* Vol. 6, par 661.
44 ibid.

It is with such judgement that this type is pushed to ask: "What does this mean for me or the world? What emerges from this vision in the way of a duty or a task, for me or the world?"[45]

This function can appear to the outside world the strangest function of all. It is the most obscure and ungraspable. People of this type can appear aloof and strange. Sometimes they appear as the wise-idiot, with a wholly different internal vista to that of the rest of the world.

If they are religious, introvert intuitives will be drawn to the aspects of their religion that echo their inner intuitions. They will believe, for example, in angels and energies and the power of prayer. These people crave solitude and can appear prickly and cold, even unfriendly, if they feel encroached upon. This they share with all the other introvert types. Yet the introvert intuitives have an edge that the others do not. One sometimes feels that anything may erupt from these people. If they have not had enough time alone, there is an uneasiness that is palpable from them, a sense of things bubbling below the surface. Because this function is unseen intuition, that values the inner world as opposed to the outer, it is not obvious what this type can offer the world. The extreme need for solitude can appear to be indulgent. These people will take that solitude with a ferocity that portrays how desperate is their need for it. It is this solitude that connects these people to the unseen inner world that feeds them. They may come back with nothing but a more balanced personality (which in itself is of value), or they may come back with visions significant for all of us.

Such types are indispensable to human kind. They keep us plugged into the newness in the unconscious. In the general scheme of things, the inferior function acts in the psyche as the root into the unconscious, which prevents the conscious world from becoming closed off onto

---

45 *C.W.* Vol. 6, par 662.

itself and therefore drying up. By making links also into the collective unconscious, introvert intuitives create a lifeline for humankind as a whole. The prophets of Israel were such people who told the Jews what their God wanted them to do. These people are the shamans who can tune into what the gods and the ancestor spirits are planning. If introvert intuitives can somehow find a way to articulate or express the perception they have of the collective unconscious world for the benefit of all, they offer a valuable service to the world. Ironically, the art or writings of these people is very often only understood by later generations.

Nietzsche was one such type. His book *Thus Spake Zarathustra* is full of fantastic and archetypal material. If, however, introvert intuitives remain locked in perception without any concrete expression, they remain self-absorbed and aloof, not aware of the effect they have on other people. In the same way that extravert intuitives can flitter from one possibility to the next, introvert intuitives can move from one image to the next, "… chasing after every possibility in the teeming womb of the unconscious, without establishing any connection between them and himself."[46] Or without creating any real connection between themselves and the outer world.

The inferior function of this type is extravert sensation. This manifests as introvert intuitives having, for example, very little ability to notice the needs of the body. They will ignore feelings of cold or hunger, and will not look after themselves when they are sick. People of this type also have great difficulty controlling the appetites of the body. They can fall into alcoholism, drug addiction, or uninhibited gluttony. "Instinctuality and intemperance are the hallmarks of this sensation, combined with an extraordinary dependence on sense-impressions".[47]

---

46 ibid., par 658.
47 ibid., par 663.

Because of inferior sensation, they are also very vague about sensate facts. Like all inferior functions, inferior sensation appears in consciousness only occasionally. It comes and then goes again, like islands in consciousness. An introvert intuitive can be oblivious to a sensate fact for a long time and then can suddenly be struck by it. He or she can then make completely wrong deductions about what is happening!

For example, an introvert intuitive woman walks into a room that has candles burning. She does not notice the candles. It then suddenly strikes her that she can smell smoke and she declares that something is on fire in the room! Marie-Louise von Franz writes that this type can experience great difficulty in relation to sex, because it involves one's inferior function of extraverted sensation.

It is, however, disastrous to try to escape the inferior function. Marie-Louise von Franz says that when one avoids or is 'saved' from the tension of the inferior function "… the creative core of their personality is destroyed".[48] She gives the wonderful example of a German mystic, Jakob Boehme.[49] This man was an introvert intuitive. He had a wife and six children, whom he could not support very well because he was forever writing. One day he saw a ray of light reflected on a tin plate and had an ecstatic inner spiritual experience. What he had experienced in a few seconds, he went on to write about for years. When he had his first book published, a rich German baron, who saw that Boehme was a great seer, promised to relieve him of his financial problems. Amazingly, when Boehme was let off the hook like this, his work lost all its creativity. Boehme needed the tension between his dominant intuition, expressed through his writing, and his inferior sensation, expressed through his financial difficulties. Without that

---

48 Marie-Louise von Franz and James Hillman. (1986) *Lectures on Jung's Typology*, Spring Publications, Putnam, C.T., U.S.A. Page 46.

49 ibid., page 45.

tension, he became sterile and resentful. Having escaped the unease and difficulty of making ends meet in the world (his inferior sensate function), he lost the creative edge of his dominant function (his intuition). Both were intimately related. This principle applies for all the functions and their relationship to the inferior function. For introvert intuitives, if they manage to escape being in the world in a responsible, committed way, they lose the vitality gained by this very struggle and their dominant function becomes sterile for them.

It is a great temptation for the introvert intuitive type to avoid any committed engaging with the material sensate world. It feels anathema to commit to place or relationship. Yet it is this very commitment to sensate reality that enables the introvert intuitive to function more healthily in the world. As with any of the functions, to live in a one-dimensional way, ignoring the inferior functions is, at best, to live an uninspiring and one-dimensional life. At worst, it will lead to some compensating catastrophe – the psyche will try to right itself and may cause a catastrophe as a way of pushing us towards greater health and wholeness.

This typology is neither simple nor black and white. There is much nuance in it and it takes great familiarity with the typology before one can confidently discern what another person's dominant function is. This is so because we must factor in the fact that sometimes people can feel 'most real' when they are expressing their inferior function as opposed to their dominant one. This can be especially the case when people are moving towards midlife and their dominant function is getting worn down. The functions play out differently at each stage of a person's life. In the earlier part of one's life the dominant function is most pure and clear-cut. However, as one moves towards middle age the inferior function needs to be addressed. This will change how one behaves in the world and it may be more difficult to discern what the dominant function is. Jung called this natural progression through life 'The Path of Individuation'. In it he recognised that there is a pattern to psychic growth. This is what we will turn to next.

CHAPTER SIX

The Process of Individuation

The Pattern of Psychic Growth

Impossible Dream

Was it whispered in the heavens,
in the deep dark earth
at the birthing of each soul –
"Dream your impossible dream".

For in the hue of the deep blue sea,
sun at my back,
moon rising before me,
I walk the limestone rock
and know –
mine to create
an impossible dream
and everything depends on it.

Is it how
by dreaming one's own heart
and creating that dream,
we save the world all over again,
from itself.

Having covered complexes, psychic energy, dreams, and the various functions, it is time now to consider what Jung called the process of individuation and to look at some of the archetypes that one encounters during this process. The path or process of individuation is something that seems to happen naturally over one's lifetime, though many people remain unaware of it. Many people obliviously allow life to bump them along. As Jung said, what we refuse to look at, we experience as fate. However, unless we become seriously stuck and disconnected from our unconscious life sources, we usually progress along a path, gradually developing a more mature personality. This psychic growth is not the result of conscious planning. Something else seems to be behind it, regulating it. Jung writes:

> Normally the unconscious collaborates with the conscious without friction or disturbance, so that one is not even aware of its existence. But when an individual or a social group deviates too far from their instinctual foundations, they then experience the full impact of unconscious forces. The collaboration of the unconscious is intelligent and purposive, and, even when it acts in opposition to consciousness, its expression is still compensatory in an intelligent way, as if it were trying to restore the lost balance.[1]

On interpreting some 80,000 dreams, Jung noticed that there was a pattern, an arrangement within the dreams. The organising principle, the 'intelligent and purposive' guiding force behind this pattern, Jung named the Self.

Marie-Louise von Franz addresses the question of whether this process happens regardless of our participation in it.

---

1   *C.W.* Vol. 9(i), par 505.

From one point of view this process takes place in man (as well as in every other living being) by itself and in the unconscious; it is a process by which man lives out his innate human nature. Strictly speaking, however, the process of individuation is real only if the individual is aware of it and consciously makes a living connection with it."[2]

Thus, there is within all living things an internal guiding energy which enables them to become what they are. Within humans, there is this inner guiding factor, but it may remain as a germ, emerging only slightly in one's life, or it may develop more completely. How far it develops depends on the relationship between the ego – the centre of the conscious personality – and the Self; the centre of the entire psyche.

Jung held firmly to the belief that one spends the first part of one's life fulfilling one's obligations. This involves establishing oneself in the world. The primary task here is adaptation.[3] This part of one's life is exemplified by the Myth of the Hero. The task is to conquer the world, to overcome the infantile ties with the parents, to win a mate, to have children. These tasks are often all-consuming for the young person. The actual achieving of these aims is meaningful and satisfying for them. They have enough on their plate to be getting on with.

There are, however, young people, even children, who have experienced a wounding. The normal unfolding of their lives has been disturbed. These children, or young people, can then go inwards seeking some solace or sense, or even distance, from the outward difficulties in their lives. The dreams of these people can often reveal symbols that

---

2 Conceived and edited by Carl Jung. (1978) *Man and His Symbols.* Pan Books Ltd., London. Page 163/4.
3 *C.W.* Vol. 8, *The Stages of Life*, par 749ff.

are circular, or quadrangular (a four-sided figure, especially square or rectangular). These are motifs that have been associated with the Self. In learning how to cope with their lives, these young people or children go further down the path of individuation earlier than most. Marie-Louise von Franz points out: "The actual processes of individuation – the conscious coming-to-terms with one's own inner centre (psychic nucleus) or Self – generally begins with a wounding of the personality and the suffering that accompanies it".[4]

In the more general run of things, this wounding happens more often in mid-life. Jung himself experienced a crisis in mid-life. During this time, he painted mythological symbols and built small cities of clay by the lakeside and recorded his dreams. Later he noticed that many of his clients, who were also at midlife, were experiencing a similar crisis of meaning. Jung saw this mid-life crisis represented in the myths that contained the death of the hero. Myths, such as the myth of Osiris and the story of Christ, involved sacrifice. Myths and stories such as these represent a time when the ego has to give up being in the driving seat and acknowledge a power greater than itself. The ego, having been so long in apparent control of the personality, now must begin to cooperate with a power beyond itself. This greater power, or centre, is the Self. For Jung, the Self is a self-regulating principle that communicates through dreams, fantasies and sometimes through neurotic symptoms. It is the centre of the psyche, conscious and unconscious.[5]

If the process of individuation is a coming to terms with one's own inner centre, then what shape and form does this take? Each person is unique and there are no hard and fast guidelines. Yet there is a common pattern. This process cannot be orchestrated, forced or manipulated. It

---

4   Conceived and edited by Carl Jung. (1978) *Man and His Symbols*. Pan Books Ltd., London. Page 169.
5   *C.W.* Vol. 6, par 789 - 791.

cannot be made to happen. Nor is it wise even to anticipate it. Patrick Kavanagh writes of this in his poem *Having Confessed*:

> Having confessed, he feels
> That he should go down on his knees and pray
> For forgiveness for his pride, for having
> Dared to view his soul from the outside.
> Lie at the heart of the emotion, time
> Has its own work to do. We must not anticipate
> Or awaken for a moment. God cannot catch us
> Unless we stay in the unconscious room
> Of our hearts. We must be nothing,
> Nothing that God may make us something.
> We must not touch the immortal material,
> We must not daydream to-morrow's judgement –
> God must be allowed to surprise us.
> We have sinned, sinned like Lucifer
> By this anticipation. Let us lie down again
> Deep in anonymous humility and God
> May find us worthy material for His hand.[6]

Like a rose bud that will grow full in its own time, one's psychic growth cannot be pulled apart and survive. It can, however, be fed and watered, cared for and nurtured. In order to assist the process of individuation, we can pay attention to our dreams, acknowledge our fantasies, and take note of the physical symptoms we experience. However, we must live it and not just think it. Our lives must be lived in the world. If we pay close attention to the messages from within, our lives can be lived to their fullest potential.

The first 'approach of the unconscious', as Marie-Louise von Franz

---

6   From *Collected Poems*, edited by Antoinette Quinn, 'Allen Lane, 2004.

puts it,[7] is this initial wounding, or this collapse of meaning. When one turns to the unconscious for solace, for meaning, for answers, often what one initially finds is what is wrong with one's conscious attitude. One has come up against one's shadow. If shadow is the first up then this is what must be dealt with. Shadow is an archetype that we find in our personal unconscious. It is in everyone. The task of psychic growth is to individuate the archetypes one finds in one's psyche. This means that one must become conscious of them and cease to be unconsciously identified with them. In the upcoming chapter on shadow, we will see how we project unconscious material out onto the world. The aspects of our own psyche that do not sit well with our conscious ego we put out onto other people. This is projection. It is a mechanism that allows us to discover what is in our unconscious psyche that we are unaware of. If I am a tidy person I may be very irritated by untidy people. If my tidiness is extreme and obsessional I will hate untidy people. This is because in my unconscious psyche there is a compensating shadow element that is hellishly untidy! This untidy character I project out onto the world. It is only when we take the projection back that we can claim the shadow that is ours and somehow make room for it in our conscious personality. By doing this, it ceases to have power over us. This is what is called individuating the archetype.

Once an archetype is individuated, the character of one's unconscious adjusts and changes. After the chapter on shadow, I will look at two other archetypes, animus and anima. Once again, in assisting our psychic growth, we deal with these archetypes through reclaiming projections, working with dreams, and using active imagination. Active imagination is a skill that was developed by Jung. It enables us to go into unconscious material and explore it, without consciously

---

7   Conceived and edited by Carl Jung. (1978) *Man and His Symbols*. Pan Books Ltd., London. Page 168.

manipulating it. Marie-Louise von Franz writes: "If an individual has wrestled seriously enough and long enough with the anima (or animus) problem so that he, or she, is no longer partially identified with it, the unconscious again changes its dominant character and appears in a new symbolic form, representing the Self, the innermost nucleus of the psyche".[8]

The following chapters look at shadow, animus and anima – the first three major archetypes one normally encounters on life's psychic journey. I have approached these chapters from the point of view of how one can individuate these archetypes. How one can work with these tremendous energies in one's life and not be ridden by them or driven by them. It is no mean task, but for those with the necessary commitment and know-how, it is a glorious challenge.

---

8 Conceived and edited by Carl Jung. (1978) *Man and His Symbols*. Pan Books Ltd., London. Page 207.

CHAPTER SEVEN

Shadow and Evil

The Heart of Darkness

The Coward's Wish

I have a coward's wish
stored away in the back pocket
of my Levi blue jeans.

Somedays I take it out
and have a peek.

Most days
I just know it's there
and I shake my ass.

We are all aware that we have one kind of shadow. That is the shadow that is cast behind us when the light is in front of us. As children we played games of stepping on each other's shadows. I remember making shadow figures on the wall at night, as a child, using my hands. We each have, however, another kind of shadow. We sometimes use the word in common language. We can say that people can be 'caught up in their shadow'. The phrase implies that someone can be caught up in behaviour that is not usual for the person. This is shadow behaviour and it refers to the kind of shadow I will discuss here.

Shadow consists of the things in our psyche that we are not conscious of, either because they are not acceptable to our conscious attitude or because they are underdeveloped. Shadow and evil are not the same thing. Shadow is not necessarily bad. It is something that is necessary for our psychic health. We cannot live without shadow and when we attempt to repress it, it can become truly demonic. In order for it not to become extreme, shadow needs to be acknowledged and dealt with consciously. Shadow compensates for our conscious attitude. We need it. We cannot live wholly in the light, however much a misguided Christian idealism would attempt to convince us otherwise.

To try to live exclusively in the light is an illusion and the attempt merely pushes the shadow deeper into the darkness, where it becomes monstrous. When the conscious attitude pulls too much in one direction, the shadow creates a compensatory pull in order to get us back onto a middle line. If the conscious pull is extreme, the shadow's effort at compensation will be equally extreme. When we become aware of shadow, it is possible to give it an airing and thereby avoid allowing our conscious attitude to become entrenched or one-sided. However, as we will see, we have to be careful in dealing with shadow. It is not to be taken lightly.

What is Shadow?

Shadow, as the word implies, is related to light. Without light, there is no shadow. Therefore, shadow is defined in terms of light. It is a contrast to the light. In psychological terms, the light is the conscious ego, and shadow is its opposite. If a person has a highly developed conscience and is very careful about right and wrong, that person's shadow can manifest as a shadow character who would deliberately do the wrong thing. A man who works as a police officer may dream of a shady character who steals or worse, the man may feel compelled to partake in some illegal activity in reality. A highly rational person could have a shadow aspect that is earthy and physical. An earthy person's shadow will be more cerebral and abstract.

The psyche works ideally to create balance as opposed to purity or perfection. It does a person no good to deny, ignore or sit on one's shadow, because, in doing so one merely drives the shadow to more drastic extremes. Whatever the dominant conscious attitude is, there will be a compensatory attitude in the unconscious. The psyche operates according to the laws of nature, which are cyclical and circular, rather than linear. A good depiction of this is Yin-Yang. A full circle is divided into two halves, black and white, by a curved line. Each half contains a smaller circle of the opposite colour. Perfect balance – neither all white nor all black. One cannot persist with a strong attitude in the conscious world without that persistence causing a counter-attitude, which is the complete opposite, in the unconscious world. This is the shadow, and it will express itself, either by projection or by unconscious behaviour. The sorry fact of the matter is that one cannot get away from one's shadow. It is also a sorry fact that most of us desperately want to!

The problem with engaging with the shadow is that it consists precisely of that which we do not want to face. Shadow is the stuff we have put behind us, because we don't want to see it. If we were happy to face it, it would be part of our conscious attitude. Yet even this is not entirely accurate. The shadow is not necessarily negative – its definition is more subtle than that. The shadow is that part of the personal unconscious. It is that which we are not facing or that which we are not aware of. It is the other end of the pole to our conscious attitude. It is material that lies just below consciousness and we can access it without too much difficulty. The shadow consists not only of the things that we like to hide but also our underdeveloped functions and the other contents of the personal unconscious. Jung writes: "By 'shadow' I mean the inferior personality, the lowest levels of which are indistinguishable from the instinctuality of an animal…"[1]

Jung claims that in order for the human psyche to develop at all, the conscious mind has to resist the pull of the unconscious. Without this resistance, the conscious mind could never differentiate itself and separate itself from the unconscious. People who cannot stay separate from the unconscious are seen as being insane. They are constantly being 'visited' by unconscious contents and they cannot distinguish their ego from the unconscious contents. Psychological health requires one to have a clear sense of one's ego and a good boundary between it and the unconscious world.

Robert Bly describes the creation of the shadow in this way: "When we were one or two years old we had what we might visualise as a 360-degree personality. Energy radiated out from all parts of our body and all parts of our psyche. A child running is a living globe of energy. We had a ball of energy, alright; but one day we noticed that our parents didn't like certain parts of that ball […] Behind us we have an invisible bag, and the part of us our parents don't like, we, to keep

---

1   *C.W.* Vol. 9ii, par 370.

our parents love, put in the bag".[2] Bly goes on to describe how, when we go to school, there are further aspects of our personality that are unacceptable. Teachers and other children tell us so. So, more parts of ourselves go into the bag. This process continues throughout our years of growing up. He claims that: "We spend our life until we're twenty deciding what parts of ourself to put into the bag, and we spend the rest of our lives trying to get them out again."[3]

The image that Bly gives us is a poignant one. It demonstrates how, in order to get by, in order to be accepted, in order to be loved and to survive, we need to cut off whole chunks of ourselves and put them into our personal unconscious. The benefit of this is that we are more accepted, more loved and we have more friends. The down side is that an enormous amount of our life-energy is tied up in the personal unconscious. It will not be available to us until we are ready to face into this shadow bag.

Edward C. Whitmont says that ego formation, and the subsequent creation of the shadow, represents the clash between collectivity and individuality.[4] In pushing so much of our personality into the shadow we make ourselves acceptable to the collective. We are willing to compromise our uniqueness, our individuality for the sake of the collective. We are collective beings. We do not wish to live alone. Yet there is a strong thrust in our nature that also pushes us towards individuality. This is what Jung calls the Individuation Process. It is a journey towards the Self, the divine centre of both the unconscious and conscious. In order to make that journey towards the inner core

---

2 Ed. by Connie Zweig and Jeremiah Abrams, (1991) *Meeting the Shadow*, G.P.Putnam's Sons, N.Y. Page 6, in Robert Bly's essay entitled: 'The Long Bag We Drag Behind us'.
3 ibid., page 7.
4 Ed. by Connie Zweig and Jeremiah Abrams, (1991) *Meeting the Shadow*, G.P.Putnam's Sons, N.Y. In C. Whitmont's essay, 'The Evolution of Shadow'. Page12 - 19.

of our psyche, the Self, we must look to our shadow. It is the first step.

To stay with Bly's image, when we decide to open the bag after years of keeping it sealed, we can get a nasty shock. When items are stuffed into our shadow bag and repressed, they regress and become hostile. Robert Louis Stevenson one night had a shocking dream. When he awoke from it he told his wife and she suggested that he write it into a story. This became the famous story of Doctor Jekyll and Mr. Hyde.

In the story, a doctor who is becoming increasingly one-sided, full of altruism and good works, has a shadow side, which takes on a life of its own. The good doctor drinks a medicine he himself has invented which enables him to turn into his opposite. This inferior character is ape-like and savage, and, when given a chance, indulges in all kinds of depravities. The story tells of the tension between the two. It comes to a climax when Hyde, the inferior personality, murders a man for no other reason than the perverse pleasure of it. Jekyll, so shocked by this event, vows to never let the beast out again. But the beastly side of his personality, by being held in for so long, and because of the doctor's extreme one-sidedness, is frighteningly strong. Where once the doctor, in a naive experiment, took medicine to release the monster in his psyche, now he needed medicine in order to keep his shadow contained. Doctor Jekyll finally dies in the effort. Inevitably, Mr. Hyde dies with him, as they were both the one person. The two extremes were so disparate from each other that they effectively killed each other off.

The story shows us how much the shadow is an intimate part of us. When our conscious personality is too one-sided and we repress the shadow, it becomes something monstrous and destructive. Other insights can also be gleaned from this story. Although Dr. Jekyll's shadow personality was personal to him, before long, it took on a depth and awfulness that made it more monstrous than a mere man. Mr. Hyde, as the story played out, became more than Dr. Jekyll's mere shadow. He became identified with the collective archetype of evil. The contents of Dr. Jekyll's personal shadow connected with, and became inhabited by, a more collective archetype, the archetype of evil. So much so that in the story Jekyll perceived Mr. Hyde as being pure evil. The story illustrates that a deliberate decision to do evil – Dr. Jekyll's naive decision to actually live out his shadow, Mr. Hyde – can lead one to actually become evil.[5]

Thus we can see that living out the dark desires of the shadow is not the solution to the shadow problem. To do this can lead us into an evil that far surpasses the limits of our own personal shadow. Jung says of such an experience:

> One can only alter one's attitude and thus save oneself from naively falling into an archetype and being forced to act a part at the expense of one's humanity. Possession by an archetype turns a man into a flat collective figure, a mask behind which he can no longer develop as a human being, but becomes increasingly stunted.[6]

Hyde, as the story develops, appears more and more stunted.

Jung also claims that it is relatively easy to face into the shadow elements of one's own nature, but it is quite another matter to look pure evil in the face. He writes: "… the contents of the personal unconscious (i.e. the shadow) are indistinguishably merged with the archetypal contents of the collective unconscious and drag the latter with them

---

5   Robert Louis Stevenson. (First published 1886/ 1994). *Strange Case of Dr Jekyll and Mr Hyde* . Penguin Books, London.
6   C.W. Vol. 7, par 390

when the shadow is brought to consciousness ..."[7] This is where the utmost caution is called for in taking on the shadow. *Strange Case of Dr. Jekyll and Mr. Hyde* clearly shows us that choosing to actually live out the shadow is not the solution. Nor is it wise to repress the shadow, for that leaves the personality split into two polar opposites. J.A. Sanford, in his piece on Stevenson's story, writes: "Henry Jekyll's fundamental mistake was his desire to escape the tension of the opposites within him".[8] The solution is to carry the tension of the opposites rather than avoid it. It is a hard place to stand and a difficult thing to do, but it is the only solution to the problem of the shadow. We cannot look to the ego for a resolution of this tension. The resolution must come from somewhere deeper, from what Jung called the transcendent function. If a person can contain two irreconcilable opposites in consciousness, the conscious attitude and the shadow aspect, for long enough, something happens. Something new is constructed "that governs the whole attitude, putting an end to the division and forcing the energy of the opposites into a common channel. The standstill is overcome and life can flow on with renewed power towards new goals"[9]. This is work of the transcendent function. However, the first step in dealing with the shadow is to recognise it.

Recognising the Shadow

There are different ways of recognising one's shadow. These are: watching one's behaviour when under pressure; through observing humour; through noticing impulsive acts; slips of the tongue; through projections; through finding out how other people see us and through our dreams and fantasies.

---

7   C.W. Vol. 12, par 38.
8   Ed. by Connie Zweig and Jeremiah Abrams, (1991) *Meeting the Shadow*, G.P.Putnam's Sons, N.Y. Page 29
9   *C.W.* Jung, Vol. 6, par.827

When Under Pressure: People behave very differently to their normal behaviour when they are under pressure. Their shadow which, when they are in top form they can keep a hold of, will come out and show itself. In these situations, sensitive well-meaning people can become selfish and unbearable. Friendly, attentive people can become rude and focused. We are all aware of how different we behave ourselves when we are sick or tired. It strikes me, as a mother of young children, that the children in the world see more of their parents' shadows in one week than any of their parents' friends would see in a lifetime!

Humour: Humour is one good way to find out what your shadow looks like. What makes you laugh? Do you have a sense of humour? What type of humour disgusts you? John Sanford believes that people who do not have a sense of humour most likely have a very repressed shadow.[10] It is usually the shadow that laughs at jokes or at funny, or sometimes even awful, happenings. Most young children find the shadow things hilarious – bums, farts, burps. Their shadows are close to the surface and easy to access. What your shadow finds funny tells you something about the shadow. Paul Rebillot, an original and creative American teacher in the field of Gestalt work, myth and archetypes ran a series of workshops. One of them was on the Shadow. He put everyone attending sitting down in one big circle and he then went around each person. Everyone had to tell three jokes. It did not matter how rude, insulting, stupid or ridiculous they were. Rebillot asked everyone to pay careful attention to how they responded to each joke told. He wanted them to pay special attention to the jokes that caused a strong reaction, whether of laughter or of disgust or of anger. It was in this way that the people at the workshop took a crash course in what they found funny and what they found disgusting. They uncovered their shadow areas.

---

10 Ed. by Connie Zweig and Jeremiah Abrams, (1991) *Meeting the Shadow*, G.P.Putnam's Sons, N.Y. Page 29.

A rather prudish man had a very bawdy wife. She loved to curse and found smutty jokes hilarious. He, on the other hand, would be offended at such things. Over the years that they were together, he loosened up and even began to curse himself occasionally. Being with this woman helped him to befriend his own shadow and become less rigid in his conscious attitude. Interestingly, when asked about his relationship to his wife, he said that it was her laughter and sense of humour that had drawn him to her in the first place. The man was unconsciously drawn to this woman because she lived freely an aspect of his own psyche (her bawdy sense of humour) that he himself had repressed. In living with her over the years he gradually began to accept this aspect of himself.

Impulsive Acts: Impulsive acts are another way of locating the shadow. Shadow can be spotted when we behave in a way that surprises us. I came across an example of this with a young couple who had a small baby. They were to travel to a work engagement and thought perhaps that they would ask the woman's mother to come with them and look after the baby. The mother agreed and quite a bit of organising went on. Everything was arranged but then, out of the blue, the woman wrote to her mother saying she need not come and help out at all! The mother was furious, feeling used and dumped and hurt. When the woman tried to explain herself, she could not do so very well. The woman did not know why she had written such a dismissive and hurtful letter to her mother. She did know, however, that she did not want her mother to come on the trip but simply could not explain why. This behaviour puzzled the woman for quite some time. It was not like her at all. She was usually sensitive to other people's feelings and had a good relationship with her mother. After this incident, the mother, who had been hurt, became less engaged in the life of the couple.

Almost a year later, the woman, on hearing about the idea of shadow, realised that it was her shadow that had written the letter. Her shadow did not care that her mother was upset. But more interestingly, her shadow felt that the woman had been letting her mother come too close into the new family circle. The shadow, which represented instinct in this case for the woman, felt that the mother was, albeit invited, crossing a boundary that was around the woman and her husband and child. The woman's instinct, like all instinct when threatened, lashed out. Upon realising this, the woman, although she still regretted the hurt she had inflicted upon her mother, felt relieved that her mother had, in fact, backed off and left the family more space.

Slips of the Tongue: A slip of the tongue is when we say things that come out differently to how we intended to say them. This is the famous Freudian slip. Observing this is the classic way of tracking shadow. Sometimes we can discover simply an impish shadow, who will make us say at a funeral, when shaking a mourner's hand, "Congratulations", instead of "Sorry for your loss". Or other times we can hear ourselves say something ambivalent about someone we had intended to praise.

A man was telling some people about the solstices in the yearly cycle. He explained that the summer solstice was marked in Christian terms as John the Baptist's birthday. The Winter solstice was marked as Jesus Christ's birthday. John would decrease just like the sun would decrease and Christ would increase just like the sun would increase. "So", said the man, "Christmas falls on the 24th of March, very close to the winter solstice and six months after the summer solstice". There was a puzzled silence. The man had put his own birth date in the place of Jesus Christ's! The man's slip was betraying that although he was a modest man in his conscious attitude, his shadow aspect identified with the charismatic and prophetic personality of Jesus Christ.

Shadow looks for ways to come out. It can reveal itself through the language we use. When we consciously intend to say one thing we sometimes find ourselves saying something quite different. Shadow catches us unawares. When this happens we are forced to exclaim, "why ever did I say that?" A woman upon seeing the new dress her friend has bought intends to say that it is elegant. However, the word elephant comes out of her mouth instead. She is mortified as her friend struggles with weight issues. Once again it is not possible to say what the shadow intended. Did it intend to mortify the woman or to hurt her friend? It is only when the woman confronts this mischievous shadow in active imagination will she find out what the shadow intended. Perhaps it simply was looking for attention.

I have sometimes found myself in the position where I have been introduced to someone. Seconds later I cannot remember their name. Even when it has been repeated for me a few times I still cannot remember it. This can often happen to people when they are not perhaps concentrating on the introduction. However, in the instances I am referring to I was concentrating. But the name would not be remembered. I believe it could well be my shadow aspect that probably does not want to meet the person at all. It wants me to be doing something else, somewhere else. Sometimes it even plays tricks on me and puts another name in place of the correct name. In these instances I will persistently call the person by the wrong name thinking it is the right one.

Projections: We discover our shadow when we become aware of whom we are projecting it onto. Projection is the mechanism that the psyche uses in order to show us our shadow. Without this mechanism we could never know what is in the unconscious. Projection is where we put onto another person something that is, in fact, an aspect of our own psyche. For example I may be a mild, up-tight person who stays in every night and has not got many friends. If I meet another woman who is a party-animal with many friends it is very likely that I will either adore her or I will hate her. This woman, because she is so opposite to my conscious attitude, holds a hook for my shadow projection. I project onto her the contents of my own unconscious shadow and I relate to her with either love or hate as I would relate to these shadow contents.

Projection happens all the time. It is, as I have said, the way that we get to know our own unconscious psyche. For a projection to occur, there must be an appropriate hook. There is no way that I can project something onto another person if there is not at least some aspect of what I am projecting in that person already. This is why it is sometimes so difficult to see what it is we are actually projecting. Often the people we project onto perfectly match the projection.

We can become alerted to the fact that we are projecting our shadow onto another person by the fact that we have strong feelings about that person. We can project positive and negative material onto another, so the feelings can be positive or negative. If we are projecting, the feelings will be intense. Shadow will almost always be projected onto a person of the same gender as yourself. Men will project their shadow onto other men and likewise women will put their shadow onto other women. Think of one person of the same gender as yourself who irritates you. Even better, think of a person that you cannot abide. Write a list of the characteristics you hate in that person. With a little honesty, the chances are that you will see many of these characteristics in your own behaviour that you would rather not admit to. You are projecting these characteristics of yours outwards because you have not yet accepted them and owned them. The same applies to positive projections. Try to think of someone you admire, adore, love. Again, write the characteristics down. These are your unexplored or unacknowledged positive aspects.

In mythology, there are many stories of two male opposites – Cain and Abel, Jesus and Judas, King Arthur and Lancelot. Similarly, there are many stories of two women who are polar opposites, Eve and Lilith, Psyche and Orual, Gwenhwyfar and Morgan le Fay. Within families, siblings often project unlived aspects of themselves onto each other. Same gender siblings can set each other up unconsciously as polar opposites. Each carries for the other the unlived shadow. More often than not, these siblings hate each other. Their relationship is constantly torn apart by intense jealousy, misunderstanding, and competition. These intense feelings can continue into adulthood.

The bonds of family ties and of blood keep these rival siblings together. Otherwise it would be much easier to ignore each other. Oftentimes that is, however, the choice they make, albeit unconsciously. Each tries to have nothing whatsoever to do with the other. Yet, ironically, this is the least wise course of action. At least when the two have to face each other, each is dealing with the real other person and not just his or her shadow projection. However, if one has no real contact with the other, then the projection thrives un-arrested and unchallenged. Unless a person is tremendously conscious, it is difficult to discern where the other sibling begins and where the shadow projection ends. This is made all the more impossible when there is no contact between the two siblings.

Same gender siblings do not always put these projections onto each other. It is more likely to happen when two sisters or two brothers, by nature, are very different. For example, one might be more interested in matter, in the body, in the material world, while the other is more drawn to the spirit world, to mind, culture, ideas. When two siblings carry such opposite traits, they are bound to project their inferior shadow onto each other. Sadly, a sibling in this case experiences his or her opposite through the negative lens of his or her inferior shadow. He or she does not experience the other sibling as another person might. The experience and the perception are contaminated. In the case of two sisters, if the first sister is a high thinker/intuitive type, her feeling/sensation functions are inferior and in the unconscious. She will see her sister, who, let us say, is a high feeling/sensation type, through the lens of her own inferior feeling and sensation, thus perceiving her as selfish and stupid. She will also be sensitive to, and critical of, her sister's actual inferior aspects – her bad intuition and even worse thinking. These, of course, are the thinking/intuitive's strengths.

It is complicated. But it illustrates how difficult it is to actually see people for who they are, separate from who we are and what shadow aspects of ourselves we put onto them. The irony is that the people we do not project onto are the ones we have no interest in meeting or in having anything to do with. Thus, the people we want to know, and the people we actually know, whether we want to or not, are the ones we are meant to be dealing with. There is no getting away from the work of learning to recognise and withdraw our shadow projections. Jung writes of projection: "The effect of projection is to isolate the subject from his environment, since instead of a real relation to it there is now only an illusory one. Projections change the world into the replica of one's own unknown face".[11]

Two male friends once had an argument. The actual topic of the argument was not really the issue. Previously an incident had occurred which had undermined the relationship for one of the men. This left the relationship vulnerable. In the course of the argument, one man was not hearing what the other was saying, because he was reminded

---

11 *C.W.* Vol. 9ii, par 16.

of his father and how his father used to treat him. Neither could the man who had started the discussion be open to his friend's response, because he was triggered into a complex about how his brother used to behave towards him! It took a long time for them to clear the way and get back to talking to each other without the projected baggage.

How Other People See Us: How many of us are prepared to take on board how other people see us? How many of us would be surprised at the discrepancy between how we are seen and how we see ourselves, i.e. how we want to appear, and how people actually see us? If you have the patience and the courage to ask, then this is a good way to discover your blind spots. Of course, how other people see us will tell us a lot about them too. They will be projecting their shadow onto us as much as they will be telling us anything about our own shadow.

Dreams, Fantasies and Literature: How our shadow appears in our dreams depends upon how primitive or repressed it is. Von Franz writes: "If a person represses or suppresses instinctive emotional responses, a hostile animal may occur in the dreams".[12] People who repress bad tempers may dream of large wild animals. Sometimes people who have repressed their sexuality will dream of galloping horses.

Our shadow will also appear as figures of the same gender as ourselves. Women or men, depending upon our own gender, with whom we have difficulty, can be reoccurring characters in our dreams. Often when we are afraid of these aspects in ourselves, they can appear sinister or menacing. In *The Way of the Dream*, Fraser Boa, in conversation with Marie-Louise von Franz, quotes the dream of a social worker who comes from Toronto.[13] In the dream the man is approached by a hairy

---

12 Marie-Louise von Franz in dialogue with Fraser Boa. (1988) *The Way of the Dream*. Windrose Films Ltd., Toronto, Canada. Page 121.
13 ibid., page 123.

ape-man who begins making a pass at his girlfriend. The dreamer is about to lunge at the ape-man when a friend, an earthy type, suggests that they deal with this together. But the dreamer says that he will deal with it himself. He started talking to the ape-man and was amazed when he became very reasonable and eventually turned away and left them. The shadow, when confronted, loses its hostility. When it is avoided and denied, it gains in power and viciousness.

Our spontaneous fantasies also reveal to us our shadow. A young woman disliked another woman intensely. Upon hearing that this woman was thinking about aborting a pregnancy, she went into this long and convoluted spontaneous fantasy. She described to me how in the fantasy she confronted the other woman and let loose her long-held resentment and anger against her. She shouted at her: "When will you ever take the higher ground? For once could you not rise to the occasion of life?" The emotion in the fantasy was so intense that the woman became aware that this had little to do with the other woman in question. She did not even know if the woman would abort or not, but regardless of that, her mind had immediately run away with this fantasy.

It was obvious that the other woman carried her shadow for her. The selfishness that she spoke of to the other woman was, in fact, an aspect of her own shadow. It lurked in her own psyche, unlived and unexpressed, and had turned negative. Consciously she had always tried to take the higher ground. She had carried this role in her family and among her friends for her whole life. What she realised from this spontaneous fantasy was that she needed to let the shadow aspect of herself live itself out a little. While she spent a lot of time helping others out in their lives, she rarely focused on her own interests. This woman had a lot of untapped creativity that could not be lived because she spent most of her energy doing the 'right thing' for others. She badly needed to access a bit of her shadow energy that would allow her to be 'selfish', and focus upon herself and her untapped abilities.

In literature over the centuries there have been explorations of shadow. In Faust, as in the *Strange Case of Doctor Jekyll and Mr Hyde*, the person becomes possessed by the shadow to the detriment of one's life. Both Faust and Doctor Jekyll are one-sided intellectuals. Faust is bored with his virtuous life and enters into a pact with the devil, Mephistophles. By living the shadow to this degree, he becomes a drunk and a libertine. Jekyll, likewise, surrenders himself to the shadow and he becomes the horrific Hyde. Bram Stoker's *Dracula* and Mary Shelley's *Frankenstein* are other enactments of possession by the shadow.

In *The Picture of Dorian Gray*, written by Oscar Wilde, we see another way of dealing with our shadow. In the story, Dorian Gray is a beautifully handsome young man. An artist captures this beauty in a portrait, and Dorian becomes infatuated by the image. He realises that his beauty will fade with time and so he wishes that the painting will absorb these changes and that he will remain always youthful and handsome. His wish is granted. As he indulges himself in various kinds of debauchery, the effects appear on the painting but not on him in real life. He puts on an innocent and beautiful front for the world (his persona) while his shadow (his portrait in the attic) is hidden in the unconscious, with the hope that it will never be discovered. As time goes by it becomes more and more ugly and distorted.[14]

More recent works of literature also portray the shadow for us. In J.R.R. Tolkien's classic work *The Lord of the Rings*,[15] a world inhabited by creatures of light and creatures of darkness, is brilliantly depicted. From a ghastly perversion of the beauty of the Elves, the Dark Lord,

---

14 Oscar Wilde. *A Selection of Stories and Plays*. (2006)   Abbeydale Press, Leicestershire, England. Page 4 ff. The Picture of Dorian Gray.
15 J.R.R. Tolkien. (1968/78/83) *The Lord of the Rings*. Unwin Hyman Ltd., London.

Sauron, has created the Orcs, creatures as ugly and evil as the Elves are beautiful and good. When Sauron created the Trolls, he again perverted the image of something wholesome, in this case the solid and wise Ents. In this epic tale good and evil do battle. Ironically, Tolkien was asked if he, when writing the story, had consciously been trying to tackle the great issues of Good and Evil. He replied, wryly, that, no, he was just writing a story! This, to me, is the power in Tolkien's work. In not attempting to consciously deal with these great questions, he kept his ego out of the way and managed to write a story that did describe the reality of good and evil. He somehow managed to channel the archetypal energies with true precision.

J. K. Rowling also, in her series of books on the boy wizard Harry Potter,[16] has introduced younger people, and older ones too, to the world of shadow, both personal and collective. By allowing a character like Voldemort such prominence in her books, she bravely exposes the nature of shadow and evil. Little wonder that the books are so popular, for even young people somehow know that these things are realities in the world and we need to find our own place in relation to them. In a way, Rowling is counteracting the more modern tendency to sweeten the end of fairytales for small children in order to protect them from ugliness and evil. The nasty endings in the original fairy tales, where grandmother did get eaten by the wolf, were psychological lessons for the children, where they learn that evil exists in the world and that they need to be prepared for it.

We have attempted to sanitise our lives of shadow and this has the effect of making the shadow hostile and enormous. Robert Bly mentions that, in a visit to Bali, he noticed: "their ancient Hindu culture works through mythology to bring shadow elements up into

---

16 J.K. Rowling. (1997ff) The Harry Potter Series. Books 1- 6. Bloomsbury, London.

daily view".[17] He refers to the frightening plays that are acted out daily in the temples. He also mentions how almost every house "has standing outside it a fierce, toothy, aggressive, hostile figure carved in stone".[18] These figures are evil and do not intend to do good. By carving them and expressing them in an art form, these people are taking their aggressive energies and are bringing them upward into art. This, according to Bly, is the ideal. He found that the Balinese, although ferocious in war, were a serene people in daily life. In contrast, Westerners, who put leprechauns and gnomes on their lawns, tend to have an unacknowledged shadow that can lash out in daily life and cause great damage.

Confronting the Shadow – The Conflict

What then do we do with this shadow that we find in ourselves? Marie-Louise von Franz says: "We need a shadow. The shadow keeps us down to earth, reminds us of our incompleteness, and provides us with complementary traits. We would be very poor indeed if we were only what we imagined ourselves to be".[19] Yet we have seen that to live out the shadow, to become possessed by it, is not a healthy way forward. Neither is it wise to repress the shadow. Jung wrote: "The educated man tries to repress the inferior man in himself, not realising that by doing so he forces the latter into revolt".[20] He also says: "Good does not become better by being exaggerated, but worse, and a small evil becomes a big one through being disregarded and repressed".[21]

The shadow can neither be denied nor indulged. Yet it must be lived in some way. This is the shadow problem. How can one live the shadow

17 Ed. by Connie Zweig and Jeremiah Abrams. (1991) *Meeting the Shadow*, G.P.Putnam's Sons, N.Y. Page 8.
18 ibid.
19 Marie-Louise von Franz in dialogue with Fraser Boa. (1988) *The Way of the Dream*. Windrose Films Ltd., Toronto, Canada. Page 119.
20 *C.W.* Vol. 11, par 136.
21 ibid., par 286.

when it stands at polar opposites to the conscious attitude? How does a person entertain a shadow without losing their conscious integrity? "Mere suppression of the shadow is as little of a remedy as beheading would be for a headache. To destroy a man's morality does not help either, because it would kill his better self, without which even the shadow makes no sense. The reconciliation of these opposites is a major problem ..."[22]

Reconciling these opposites may be difficult. It is, however, the very thing that we must do. The first step is to recognise what the shadow is in ourselves. Marie-Louise von Franz describes this:

> ... the pain and lengthy work of self-education begins – a work, we might say, that is the psychological equivalent of the labours of Hercules. This unfortunate hero's first task, you will remember, was to clean up in one day the Augean Stables, in which hundreds of cattle had dropped their dung for many decades – a task so enormous that the ordinary mortal would be overcome by discouragement at the mere thought of it.[23]

The fact that there are aspects to each one of us that are utterly unacceptable to our conscious way of perceiving ourselves is a difficult idea for many people to grasp. We like to think that we are in control. It is hard to accept that large parts of our psyche are not only outside our control, but they are beyond our very awareness. When the prudent, money-efficient man discovers that he has a shadow aspect that would be wasteful and flamboyant with his hard-earned income, he is shocked to the core. It is harder still for him to recognise

---

22 ibid., par 133

23 Ed. by Connie Zweig and Jeremiah Abrams. (1991) *Meeting the Shadow*. G.P.Putnam's Sons, N.Y. Page 35, in Marie-Louise von Franz's essay entitled: 'The Realisation of the Shadow in Dreams'.

and accept that what he thought was a ridiculous 'once-off' gamble of his week's wages on a horse in the betting office was the work of this self-same shadow aspect. To look back over one's life and actions with the knowledge of shadow and its life and actions is comparable to the labours of Hercules. There is a mountain of dung that we must recognise. This means that there are patterns of behaviour that we must own. There are resentments that we must acknowledge. Much that we have shoved into the unconscious in order to maintain our conscious ego needs to be explored and claimed. We need to accept the fact that we are not as nice or well-intentioned or good as we considered ourselves to be.

The next step is to figure out a way of living the shadow that neither compromises ourselves or represses it. Von Franz points out that the shadow conflict for many of us does not become too intense because we instinctively have a type of shifting attitude by which we live. She says: "We try to be good and commit all sorts of bad things which we do not notice, or if we notice them, we have an excuse, a headache, or it was the other person's fault … One has a shadow, a strong instinctive power, and if one does not want to get stuck in an insoluble problem one must ignore some things so as to be able to get through life!" [24]

According to von Franz, however, Christianity has interfered with this practical and earthy way of dealing with shadow. Christianity has tended to polarise good and evil, light and shadow, and it challenges believers to go towards the light and to renounce the shadow. Such a one-sided attitude leaves one in a quandary. "If we go too far with the shadow problem we get stuck or we are martyrs, or we have to cheat a little and live the shadow and not look at it too closely in order to keep up a healthy defense". [25] Von Franz describes how many people she

---

24 Marie-Louise von Franz. (1974) *Shadow and Evil in Fairytales.* Spring Publications Inc., Dallas, Texas. Page 56.
25 ibid., page 57.

has met in the analytical hour try so hard to be decent and in doing so get "cut off from their roots and then don't know how to go on".[26]

A classic example of someone caught in a shadow conflict is a married man who wants to have an affair. He is damned if he does and damned if he doesn't. If he has the affair, he risks losing his wife. Yet even if he does not have the affair, he loses vital libido by rejecting the shadow in him that wants to have the affair. This repressed shadow will then get him sideways. What is he to do? It seems that what must be done is to somehow hold the tension of the two opposites in consciousness. So one must attempt to understand everything that the shadow (unconscious) produces during the conflict and at the same time one must do the right thing with all one's might. When one manages to hold such conflicting thoughts in consciousness, one begins to stand in a new place. One steps outside the set conscious attitude and allows an airing of the unconscious shadow. One begins to acquire substance. If the tension is held truly, the transcendent function in the unconscious will produce an all-encompassing symbol, which will allow the person to move beyond the conflict. The conflict is not resolved in a rational and conscious way, rather reality shifts for the person. One moves on, gains a different landscape, takes on another perspective. The symbol produced by the transcendent function enables the person to move beyond the conflict.

How this manifests in reality is unknown until it is lived. There is no formula. The man who wants to have an affair but does not, if he can hold the tension of conscious attitude and shadow desire, who knows what will happen to him? Who knows what he will or will not do. Von Franz warns against actually setting out to expect a symbol from the unconscious. If you do this the ego can speculate what the symbol might be and can attempt to preempt the transcendent function. This

---

26 ibid., page 59.

is disastrous. The ego must follow through its side of the equation with integrity, never abandoning for one moment its perspective on things. If it attempts to anticipate the solution, without letting the conflict develop fully, then the person will go nowhere with the conflict.

One of the most useful tools in such a conflict is active imagination.[27] Active imagination is something developed by Jung that enables us to pursue images, whether dream images or images that arise spontaneously from the unconscious. It is a process by which we relax our conscious direction and thought functions and allow the image to take on a life of its own. We then converse with the images or characters in the unconscious. When this is attempted, it is often surprising the direction it takes. We often learn things that are new and helpful.

The man above, for instance, who wishes for an affair with a certain woman, can use active imagination to explore what exactly is going on in him. He can set up a meeting, in his imagination, with this woman and let his imagination take it from there. What is it about this woman that fascinates him? If he speaks to her in active imagination, she will reveal herself and her desires. Psychologically the woman in the outer world is a hook for some aspect of the man's psyche. She is his gateway into hidden aspects of himself. In active imagination, she can tell him what newness he needs in his life.

Von Franz, however, cautions that using active imagination like this, without actually dis-identifying oneself from one's emotion, in this case lust/love/desire/passion, can lead to what she calls black magic. To imagine himself like this with the woman, without separating out the factors of himself involved, can have an effect on the real outer world. The man, rather than containing the situation

---

27 See Chapter 4 of this work for more on Active Imagination.

in his imagination, is dabbling with reality in the outer world. But if the man can dis-identify himself from his emotions, if he can stand apart objectively from the active imagination, letting the emotion become personified as something separate from himself, then he is constellating his own unconscious and can discover a transcendent symbol which will release him from the conflict. We are not speaking here of a rational solution to a problem. It will be something other, a third factor, an enriching treasure that will free him from the conflict and allow him to move on with his life.

What is described above is ideal in a sense. For a person to hold the tension between conscious attitude and shadow, until a transcendent symbol emerges, is quite an achievement. It also presumes that there is no wrong attitude in consciousness. Marie-Louise von Franz writes:

> It is easy to believe that the unconscious cannot manifest itself when evil comes from a wrong attitude in consciousness: that is what we tell people all the time – that they have a wrong attitude in their conscious and that therefore the unconscious cannot involve itself in helpful ways and is reduced to inactivity; the unconscious, reduced to complete inactivity, can only produce feelings of guilt and neurotic symptoms.[28]

If this is the case, then the wrong attitude in consciousness needs to be challenged before the unconscious is released to produce its transcendent symbol.

Going back to the man who still wants to have an affair, what does this mean in practical terms? To have a wrong attitude in consciousness

---

28 Marie-Louise von Franz. (1974) *Shadow and Evil in Fairytales*. Spring Publications Inc., Dallas, Texas. Page 104.

could mean that the man believes that he can have the affair on the quiet and that there will be no ghastly consequences. In believing this, he is masking the true conflict and is paralysing the unconscious, which could help him. Instead of discovering any transcendent symbol, he merely becomes insomniac and develops some other neurotic symptoms. He is not totally giving in to the shadow desire, for he does not become openly lustful, neither is he repressing it, for he does have the affair. He is merely indulging a wrong attitude in consciousness and is therefore handicapping the natural healing mechanism of the unconscious.

A disruption of the transcendent function can come not just from a wrong attitude of consciousness but also from a neglected archetype of the unconscious. Every archetype has two sides, light and dark. When both sides are held together in the one image or symbol, everything is fine. When they are split, and the negative repressed, problems arise. This has happened historically with the archetype of the Great Mother. Her shadow aspect became separated from the overly pure Virgin Mary. Jung points out that the figure of the Virgin Mary became more important at the time when the witch hunts and persecutions were at their strongest. The Great Mother archetype which has, in its wholeness, a light side and a dark side, became split into the positive mother and the destructive witch. This destructive witch aspect can avenge its neglect by attacking, not the conscious mind of a person, but the transcendent function. Jung says that: "The shadow of the madonna became the devil's grandmother".[29] This devil's grandmother undermines the process of becoming more conscious, the process of individuation.

How this plays out in a person's life can be seen in a man who has a negative mother complex. Von Franz writes: "A man with a negative

---

29 *C.W.* Vol 9i, par 189.

mother complex is caught by a tremendous but half unconscious ambition and power drive which apparently makes him very successful in life – but he has a dim feeling that something is wrong, especially in his relationship to women. In analysis you discover that the power drive sits like an evil animal on his sex; within the unconscious it harms the sex instinct but does not directly harm consciousness".[30] Von Franz claims that: "... the neglected archetype of the mother in Christian civilization destroys the whole process of individuation, and the whole problem has to be rediscussed from those angles".[31]

In the fairy tale *Sleeping Beauty*, the parents of the infant forget to invite the thirteenth fairy to the child's blessing party. This fairy, described as a bad fairy (she has been neglected and has thus become negative) arrives at the party and curses the child. When the child reaches sixteen she will prick her finger with a spinning needle and will die. The curse is weakened by the twelfth fairy, and at the age of sixteen when the curse kicks in, Briar Rose, or Sleeping Beauty, falls into a deep sleep, along with the entire castle, for one hundred years. This sleep symbolises the sleep of the unconscious, or the inability of the unconscious to produce transcending symbols which will heal the psyche and move the person onwards. The curse was activated through the neglect of the parents to face the thirteenth fairy or the shadow.

Confronting one's shadow is everyone's responsibility. If we shirk this responsibility then it is most likely that someone else will suffer for our neglect. There are many other fairytales where the parents of a child want something, or they are in a fix, and some ugly witch appears. The witch says that she will give the parents what they want, she will fix the problem, but the parents must promise that they will

---

30 Marie-Louise von Franz. (1974) *Shadow and Evil in Fairytales*. Spring Publications Inc., Dallas, Texas. Page 106.
31 ibid., page 107.

give up to her their first child. The parents promise and are delighted to be out of a fix. The years go by, they forget their promise, but on the birth of their first child, lo and behold, the witch appears to claim the prize. This is an important motif in fairytales and one we would do well to pay heed to. This dynamic can be seen in day to day living. Parents get themselves into some psychological fix and, rather than confronting it head on (and they may not have the skills to do this), they make an unconscious pact with their shadow to bail them out if they (again unconsciously) promise their children to their shadow. And hence you have many people living their lives today battling the shadows of their parents, and their parent's parents. A woman who has been physically abused as a child by her step-father marries a gentle and loving man and they have children. One of the daughters, even though she is her father's favourite, grows up and attracts an abusive and violent partner. What has gone underground in the mother is being lived out by the daughter.

These fairy tales (*Rumpelstiltskin, Rapunzel, Beauty and the Beast*) depict the origin of the generational baggage that most people discover when they begin to look to their unconscious. Some are forced to look at it because they carry destructive patterns in their lives that simply prevent their lives from working fruitfully. Others discover these skeletons through tragedies in their families. Still others become aware of them by paying heed to their dreams.

This reality is a lesson for all parents – to attempt to deal with their own shadows and not pass on, wholesale, to their children their unacceptable aspects, and untapped potentialities. Children will have enough work to do with their own shadows without inheriting those of their parents.

Irene Claremont de Castillejo very eloquently writes about this point:

"Life insists on being lived, and anything that belongs to one's life which is allowed to lie dormant has to be lived by someone else. If we do not accept our shadow we force our children to carry the burden of our undeveloped capacities. They may become mediocre scientists or artists because we denied our own talents. They may become doctors, which they are not suited to be, because we failed to use our innate capacity for healing, or inept politicians to fulfil our unlived ambitions".[32]

In the process of individuation, a process which, I believe, happens organically in one's life, but which one can accelerate significantly by becoming conscious of it and by working with the unconscious material which emerges, the challenge is to assimilate the shadow. This does not mean that we become, like Dr. Jekyll, taken over by shadow. Nor does it mean that once shadow rears its ugly head we expend a lot of energy trying to shove it down again. It means that we acknowledge it as being a part of us. It also means that we do not try to be too perfect and that we allow the shadow aspects of ourselves to breathe. The ideal in our lives is to be whole rather than to be perfect. This wholeness means that we are both light and darkness. If, in our conscious attitude, we refuse to acknowledge shadow then we force it into the unconscious and risk it becoming unmanageable. If, however, we say to ourselves: 'I am not perfect, I do not try to be perfect, I have shadow aspects where I am nasty and angry and unfair,' then we claim the darkness and are more likely to integrate these aspects into our lives in a non-destructive way. It is, however, our responsibility to not let these aspects outweigh our brighter aspects.

Not to acknowledge the shadow that is within us is to invite the darker aspects of our psyche to take control of us in moments of stress.

---

32 Irene Claremont de Castillejo. (1973) *Knowing Woman*. Harper and Row, N.Y. Page 41.

What we do not acknowledge is what drives us. I think Christianity, as a system of belief, has done humankind a dis-service with regards to shadow. Christianity (as opposed to Christ and his teachings) has encouraged people to strive for moral perfection. It has taught that people must forgive, without at the same time recognising the need for a person to express outrage, even pure and righteous hatred. It has not allowed for the process of healing from hurt; the process that requires a person to experience the full gamut of their emotions, shadowed and negative as they may be. Many people, as a result of this Christian teaching, short-circuit the healing process and try to jump straight away to forgiveness. What they are left with is a false forgiveness and a lot of repressed shadow.

Robert Bly gives us some novel ways of, what he calls, eating our shadow. He suggests: "... making holes in your habits, visiting primitive tribes, playing music, creating frightening figures in clay ... regarding yourself as a genial criminal ..."[33] He also suggests going to someone whom you know to be holding your shadow and try asking for it back! Bly believes that people who are irresponsible about their projected shadow are contributing to the collective shadow. He says: "... every bit of energy that we don't actively engage in language or art is floating somewhere in the air above the United States, and Reagan can use it". Then it was George Bush. He went to war in Afghanistan and Iraq with all of the collective shadow energy that was available to him. And on it goes.

One final word from Jung on the tension of opposites:

> It has become abundantly clear to me that life can flow
> forwards only along the path of the gradient. But there

---

33 Ed. by Connie Zweig and Jeremiah Abrams. (1991) *Meeting the Shadow.* G.P.Putnam's Sons, N.Y. Page 279, in his essay entitled Eating the Shadow.

is no energy unless there is a tension of opposites: hence it is necessary to discover the opposite to the attitude of the conscious mind. [...] Seen from the one-sided point of view of the conscious attitude, the shadow is an inferior component of the personality and is consequently repressed through intensive resistance. But the repressed content must be made conscious so as to produce a tension of opposites, without which no forward movement is possible. The conscious mind is on top, the shadow underneath, and just as high always longs for low and hot for cold, so all consciousness, perhaps without being aware of it, seeks its unconscious opposite, lacking which it is doomed to stagnation, congestion, and ossification. Life is born only of the spark of opposites.[34]

Evil

During the weeks that I was working on this chapter on shadow and evil, I had a dream. In the dream I am led to a special chamber where some very important words are written. Even in the dream I was aware that the chances of being able to read the words were slim, as I never have been able to read text in dreams. I tried to read it anyway and I squinted and concentrated and there I read: "In the light is the dark". When I awoke I felt it was significant.

All of my life I have been spooked by anything that seemed to point to an evil force or energy. As a small child, even the music of *Ironside*, the detective programme, sent me scurrying upstairs terrified. Devil worship, Satanism, the occult, unnerved me altogether. Several years ago I remember being in Minnesota, staying with wonderfully hospitable friends by a lakeside. One day at dusk I decided to go for

---

34 *C.W.* Vol. 7, par 78.

a walk by the lake. It was winter and there was a lot of snow. I got to the lake walk, which was surrounded by huge trees, and, for some reason, I looked up at one of the nearby trees. I noticed high up there, tied by a string, or nailed to the trunk, was the skull of a small animal, perhaps a goat. On it were painted symbols and signs. It struck me as something of an occult nature. I immediately turned back with heart racing, waiting for the devil himself to appear from a nearby house to pursue me. It was only when I was working on this chapter that I felt the anxiety around evil and Satan ease and I began to understand why it had been so acute all my life.

It is well established in Jungian thinking that every archetype has two aspects, a light and a dark side. (The archetype of the Self seems to be the one exception to this. The Self has no opposite. I will explore this later in the Chapter on the Self). What this dual aspect of each archetype implies is that even the archetype of the God as Father, light and perfect as he is supposed to be, has a dark side. This concept has not filtered into common thinking and it would be good if it did. Archetypes deal with wholeness, for they are a natural phenomenon. They do not deal with perfection. Yet for centuries, God the Father has been presented as perfect. In monotheistic theologies God the Father has no opposite, no dark side. He is all good, all powerful. He has, basically, been split off from his shadow. In psychology, what applies to humans also applies to the gods. When someone is split off from their shadow, that shadow becomes hostile and uncontrollable and comes out sideways. When God the Father became split off from his shadow, his shadow became evil and satanic.

Since the development of monotheism in the past four thousand years, the relationships between the archetypes have become estranged. It begs the question, does human consciousness produce the archetypes, or do the archetypes produce human consciousness? Perhaps this is a chicken and egg question. I do not know the answer. One way or the other, with the arrival of a patriarchal consciousness – of monotheism and a father god who claimed to be the one and only true god – two things happened. One was the undermining and degrading of the Great Mother, the Feminine archetype, expressed as Goddess, Earth, Nature. The dominant masculine archetype, Father God, fell out of right relationship with the feminine archetype. The second thing that happened was that the dominant masculine archetype, Father God, became split off from its shadow. I believe that the second consequence was an effect of the first. Had the dominant masculine archetype stayed in good relationship with the feminine, it would not so easily have become split off from its shadow.

The Irish comedian Tommy Tiernan brilliantly and comically illustrated this split-off attitude from the feminine in his retelling of the story of Abraham, when he almost sacrificed his son, Isaac. In Tommy's recounting of the story, he tells it exactly as it is told in the bible until the last moment. Then, on coming down the mountain, Abraham says to Isaac: "Do me a big favour, son. Don't tell your mother".

The same reality is reflected in religious institutions that demand celibacy from their male priests. The recent exposure of case after case of child sexual abuse among the clergy demonstrates how terrible this shadow is when cut-off from the feminine. In Greek mythology, Dionysius represents the shadow of the masculine archetype in relationship with the feminine archetype. Dionysius is pleasure seeking, indulgent, trickster-like and sensual. In Greek society, such shadow was allowed expression. However the shadow of a male god that is both out of relationship with the feminine and also split off and alienated, is absolutely satanic. The world has experienced hundreds of years of this satanic energy, an energy that is evil and wholly destructive, an energy that preys on the innocent.

We are all too familiar with this energy – this evil. It is the evil of the Inquisition, and the burning of the 'witches'. It is the evil of World War II and the concentration camps. It is the evil of Bosnia and ethnic cleansing. It is the evil of torture. It is the evil of fathers who sexually abuse their daughters, of priests who sexually abuse the children entrusted to their care. Split off, voracious and destructive, it comes out from the cracks and pollutes our lives. We all know the feel and taste of this evil.

I spoke earlier in this chapter about the shadow side of the Great Mother archetype – the witch. When the witch is not acknowledged, or when she is cut off and driven underground, her destructiveness manifests in a particular way. The failure to acknowledge the witch cuts a person off from the healing powers of the unconscious, from the transcendent function. When this happens, a person becomes stuck, they stagnate. There is no new life or new growth. However, when the shadow of the masculine archetype, the Father God, is split off, the evil of Satan emerges to corrupt, destroy, and prey on the innocent.

I want to explore the idea of a Divine Quaternity as opposed to a Divine Trinity. The masculine Divine Trinity consists of Father, Son and Holy Spirit. This allows no room whatsoever for the shadow in the divine masculine archetype. The shadow is split off from the archetype and is therefore uncontained. In being repressed, unacknowledged and denied, it is dangerous and demonic. If we were to conceive of a divine masculine Quaternity, there would be the Shadow alongside the Father, Son and Holy Spirit. The shadow of the divine would be acknowledged and contained within the archetype. Satan would be embraced as an aspect of the divinity.

It was this insight that dispelled the spooked experience that I have felt throughout my life with all things occult. The shadow of the divine masculine, when it is not contained within the archetype of the divine masculine, takes on a wild, uncontained character, and it was this uncontained character that unnerved me. When God's shadow is contained within the masculine divine archetype, it is counterbalanced by the positive aspects of the divine masculine. It is part of a continuum. This does not mean that it is not shadow, or that it does not allow for the possibility of evil. It does, however, allow for some relationship between the different aspects of the divine masculine.

This healthier relationship between God and the Devil is seen in the Old Testament. We see where the Devil talks to God about Job and prods him to test the man who is faithful. God and the Devil seem like old pals on different sides of the fence. The Old Testament writings reflect a time where, in terms of consciousness, the Great Feminine archetype was being repressed, yet the splitting off of the shadow of the Father God had not yet become fully established. This split becomes total in later Christian teaching.

It is also more wholesome to consider a feminine Divine Quaternity as opposed to a feminine Trinity. In the Celtic tradition, the feminine Divine Trinity consists of the Mother, the Maiden and the Crone. It does not, however, allow for the dark side of the Goddess, her Shadow. If we include the Shadow aspect we have a Quaternity. If we do not acknowledge the shadow aspect of the Great Goddess, then that shadow lurks outside of the archetype, split off and doing untold damage wherever it can.

The above consideration of a Holy Quaternity to replace a Holy Trinity raises a further question. Is the archetype of evil a split off aspect of the God and Goddess archetypes? Jung notes in Volume 7 of his *COLLECTED WORKS* that: "The image of the demon forms one of the lowest and most ancient stages in the conception of God".[35] Is it possible for us humans to consciously change the archetypes we have inherited? Can we add a fourth divinity, the Shadow, to the Holy Trinity and get away with it? We are back to the chicken and egg question. Does our perception of the archetypes change the archetypes, or is it that our perception is changing because the archetypes themselves are changing? If we begin to perceive the divine archetypes as having their shadow integrated, would our experience of evil change? Or is the archetype of evil shifting? Is the archetype of evil beginning to reconnect with the divine archetypes?

Certainly, many people perceive that the feminine archetype is changing – there seems to be a new conscious feminine archetype emerging. Is it this, within the collective realm, that is influencing the divine archetypes to reintegrate their shadow aspects? It seems that, in history, it was a reneging on the divine feminine archetype that led to the splitting off of the Divine Shadow. So, therefore, is this new emerging conscious feminine archetype again shifting things in the heavens? These questions I cannot answer. I can only bat them about and see what insights emerge from the questioning.

There is no doubt that, if we were to perceive the divine archetypes as having their shadows integrated, it would greatly change our experience of ourselves. Jung comments that the concept of the Trinity allows humans to believe that they are bad and that God is good. He writes:

> As I have said, it makes a great and vital difference to
> man whether or not he considers himself as the source

---

of evil, while maintaining that all good stems from God. Whether he knows it or not, this fills him with satanic pride and hubris on the one side and with an abysmal feeling of inferiority on the other. But when he ascribes the immense power of the opposites to the Deity, he falls into his modest place as a small image of the Deity, not of Yahweh, in whom the opposites are unconscious, but of a quaternity consisting of the main opposites: male and female, good and evil, and reflected in human consciousness as confirmed by psychological experience and by the historical evidence.[36]

Different Types of Evil

Some evil simply devours light and goodness. Any attempt to understand it, to address it or to acknowledge it, seems to merely feed it. This kind of evil must be starved because it cannot be redeemed. Marie-Louise von Franz cites a case she once had where she was working with a woman and was getting absolutely nowhere with her. The woman was obsessed by the negative animus. Jung, who was von Franz's control analyst at the time, had one session with the woman. After the session, the woman went home and phoned a medical doctor, telling him everything Dr. Jung had said and more besides, stirring trouble from the whole encounter.

Jung's comment was that one must watch what a person does with the psychic energy that one gives them. Is it used for constructive purposes or destructive purposes? In the case of this woman, Marie-Louise von Franz comments: "… it was as if her evil animus was sitting in front of her mouth and whenever one gave her a good bit, he got it. In effect the demon got fatter and she got thinner".[37] Jung's advice was to

---

36 *C.W.* Vol. 18, par 1617.
37 Marie-Louise von Franz. (1974) *Shadow and Evil in Fairytales.* Spring Publications Inc., Dallas, Texas. Page 172.

throw the woman out of analysis, telling her on the way that she was a cheating, lying, devil! This was von Franz's first case and she was loath to do so. However, she did it and the woman improved so much so that in a number of years she wrote a letter of thanks to von Franz. This is an evil that works merely for destruction. Marie von Franz called it "a psychological death atmosphere".[38] It can manifest in the simple form of a spoilsport – and it can also manifest in events as evil as ethnic cleansing, cold-blooded murder and paedophilia.

Jung, however, made the point in his book *Aion*,[39] that, before Christianity, evil was not quite as evil. Marie-Louise von Franz agrees and comments: "The rise of Christianity added a kind of spirit of evil to the principle of evil, which it did not have before. The sharpening or differentiation of ethical reactions into too clear-cut black and white lines is not favorable to life".[40] This implies that, when a person is immersed within the flow of life, within the flow of nature itself, the experience of evil is different than that of a person who is cut off from instincts and from the natural life. Contemporary Western society, with its rational, cerebral culture, and its roots in a split-off Christianity, has exacerbated the human experience of evil.

There is a kind of evil that is evil because it is split off and neglected. Christianity split off the shadow from the divine and in so doing intensified its potential for evil by driving it into the unconscious and the darkness. There are no hard and fast guidelines in dealing with this type of evil. A natural life does not run along the straight lines of black and white ethical distinctions. There are many fairy tales where there is no one way to deal with the evil encountered in the story. Each story represents a whole new set of ingredients and whereas, in one story, it

38 ibid., page 173
39 *C.W.* Vol 9(i).
40 Marie-Louise von Franz. (1974) *Shadow and Evil in Fairytales*. Spring Publications Inc., Dallas, Texas. page 174.

is appropriate to confront evil, in another, to do this is disastrous and it is better to hide. If one is connected with wisdom as opposed to a one-sided ethical morality one can use one's wits and one's instinct to counteract this split off evil. Basically, "it means walking on the razor's edge to be able to say the right thing, or have the right reaction at the crucial moment, for that turns the whole problem".[41]

Marie-Louise von Franz talks of a natural evil as seen in stories and fairytales. She speaks of evil experienced by people who are not cut off from nature. This experience of evil is of an overpowering natural phenomenon, which does not pose any ethical problem. The natural phenomenon is experienced as spirits, evil spirits. Evil for the primitive peasant in man is highly numinous, fascinating, terrifying. It is nature but it has something divine about it. "Wherever man has lived in nature there are such ... ghosts around which, though slightly different, all have the same feature of being unnatural, super-human, gruesome and overwhelming".[42] When a person encounters these ghosts or spirits they deal with them or they escape them. There is no question of it being a moral issue.

This type of evil is projected evil. The question must be asked – is there evil in the natural world? Is an earthquake evil, or a volcano, or a tsunami? Are tribal peoples projecting the contents of their collective unconscious onto nature when they see these phenomena as super-human, daemonic entities? When people experience natural phenomena that are overwhelming, archetypal contents are stirred in their psyche. These archetypal images are then projected onto nature. There is a danger of becoming possessed by these archetypes.

---

41 ibid., page 169.
42 bid., page 125.

"Possession means being assimilated by these numinous archetypal images".[43] In studying various indigenous stories and fairytales Marie-Louise von Franz notes that there is a process of possession. It begins when a person demonstrates no instinctual warning. The person then displays a lack of judgement. Thirdly he or she loses the instinct for self-preservation. Finally, by falling into evil, he or she receives supernatural powers, gifts or qualities. This final endowment is a power that a person finds hard to give up. It makes that person resistant to exorcism. This process of possession does not merely apply to the 'primitive' person. A similar process happens in our everyday life. Marie-Louise von Franz comments: "Analysed psychologically, this is exactly what happens if a human being identifies with an archetypal figure. He gets the life energy and even certain parapsychological gifts, clairvoyance and so on, connected with the archetype".[44]

The conditions under which people fall into this evil possession include, according to von Franz, the drinking of alcohol, loneliness in nature, being in a foreign country, and, finally and perhaps most significantly, an infantile and naive curiosity combined with a lack of respect for the powers of evil. This last she describes as: "Stepping over the border, going beyond a respectful attitude towards the numinous powers".[45]

Finally, there is a type of evil that is welcomed in by a person being carried away by one-sidedness, by "only one single pattern of behaviour".[46] When one is carried away by one-sidedness one is in danger. We can see in nature where a mother cat will attack a huge dog in order to protect her kittens. She can die protecting her young. She is carried away by the instinct to protect her young, which has

---

43 ibid., page 128.
44 ibid., page 129.
45 ibid., page 143.
46 ibid., page147.

overridden her instinct to protect herself. The same is true of a broody hen which will peck at a huge invader (a human) rather than flee her nest. This is perhaps the natural root of this behaviour in humans.

Humans can be swept away by certain patterns of behaviour. These patterns of behaviour are archetypal patterns. If, for instance, one becomes enraged with another person and begins to shout at them and hit them, one is being carried away by an archetypical rage that has possessed them. One is no longer aware of any other aspects of their personality. It is a dangerous thing to happen because it is the way for evil to enter. When a person becomes habitually one-sided, single-minded, or closed-minded, there is a much more imminent danger of evil.

Jung states:

> Indeed, from the psychological point of view demons are nothing other than intruders from the unconscious, spontaneous irruptions of unconscious complexes into the continuity of the conscious process. Complexes are comparable to demons which fitfully harass our thoughts and actions; hence in antiquity and the Middle Ages acute neurotic disturbances were conceived as possession.[47]

To sum up the different types of evil, there is a type of evil that is insatiable and that must be cut off and starved. There is nothing to be gained by indulging this evil. Secondly, there is evil that comes from psychic contents that have been split off and ignored. How we deal with this evil depends upon each unique situation. To handle it healthily, we must be rooted in our instinct and in a natural wisdom

---

47 *C.W.* Vol. 6, par 175.

that does not pay heed to moral ethical teachings. There is a third type of evil that can be seen as natural evil but is a projection of our psychic contents onto nature. This occurs when overwhelming natural physical events happen to us and as a result archetypal images are stirred in our psyches. We are in danger of becoming possessed by the archetypes that are activated. Finally, evil can enter our lives when we are habitually one-sided in our patterns of behaviour. The patterns of behaviour are archetypal patterns and we can be at their mercy.

Shadow is a very important part of our lives. We are foolish to either deny it or to indulge it. When we learn to recognise it we are left with the task of knowing what to do with it. It is difficult to hold in consciousness that which is unacceptable to consciousness. For this is partly what shadow is; the very parts of ourselves that must be kept in the darkness to allow us to be our ego selves. However, these very aspects of ourselves also make up who we are in the broader sense. It is our right relationship to them that allows us to be whole people. In acknowledging them we know that we will never be perfect people. But better to be whole than to be perfect. Evil is very different to shadow. It is true that some evil is merely shadow that has been pushed too far into the unconscious until it has become truly demonic. However there is evil that must be starved and there is evil that can only be dealt with if a person stays in tune with their instincts and with the natural world. When dealing with any archetype it is wise to stay connected, connected to one's physical body and connected to a clear sense of one's conscious identity (ego). The next archetype that I will explore is the Animus.

CHAPTER EIGHT

Anímus

The Lover Within

Amergin

The tall man stood
at the helm of the ship
watching,
waiting,
pained as he played
with word and vision,
seeking the new land.

Poet,
harper,
word-weaver,
discerning a world
in the mist,
discovering the soul's passion.

From the ninth wave
he comes to land,
bowing to the goddess,
he secures her name
to his shaping.

Amergin – Druid,
dreams a new tomorrow.

"The primary business of the animus is to be a creative tool. Its secondary role is to give the necessary stamina to all endeavours". [1]

What is the animus? Where does the idea come from? Does it really exist? How do we experience it? Edward C. Whitmont writes "... both sexes have what are called male and female sex hormones. Jung was the first to demonstrate an analogous situation psychologically".[2] Jung himself writes:

> It is a well-known fact that sex is determined by a majority of male or female genes, as the case may be. But the minority of genes belonging to the other sex does not simply disappear. A man therefore has in him a feminine side, an unconscious feminine figure – a fact of which he is generally quite unaware. [...] I have called this figure the 'anima', and its counterpart in a woman the 'animus'.[3]

I will look at the animus in this chapter. In the following chapter I will deal with the anima. For Jung the animus was 'the personification of everything masculine in a woman".[4] He describes it as 'the archetype of man in woman.'[5] Every woman has within her psyche a masculine element, which balances or compliments her conscious feminine personae. Jung stated that the animus and anima were contra-sexual elements – the animus was to be found in a woman, the anima was to be found in the man. He claimed that the animus was peculiar to the

---

1 Jane Wheelwright. (1984) *For Women Growing Older.* C.G. Jung Educational Centre, Houston. Page 53.
2 Edward C. Whitmont. (1982) *Return of the Goddess.* Routledge and Kegan Paul plc. London. Introduction page x.
3 *C.W.* Vol.9(I), par.512.
4 *C.W.* Vol.9(I), par. 525.
5 *C.W.* Vol.18, par. 1262.

feminine psychology.[6] Jung noticed that the consciousness of women was different to that of men. If this was so he had to conclude that the unconscious of women was also different to that of men.[7] He noted that personal relations were more important to women than to men. Politics, technology, science and commerce were not captivating to a woman according to Jung, yet "she develops a minute consciousness of personal relationships, the infinite nuances of which usually escape the man entirely".[8] I will speak later about how some of what Jung wrote about women and the animus is coloured by his time and culture. What I wish to outline here is the kernel of Jung's teachings about animus.

Jung says of the animus and the anima that they are "empirical concepts"[9]. Empirical means "relying on observation and experiment, not on theory".[10] It is possible to experience the animus, either in ourselves or in others. It is most obvious in the negative, when it is obnoxious. However, the animus has a vital role to play in our psyche. It is in learning what it is and how it functions that enables us to make maximum use of it. This is not an easy task. It is easy to lose sight of what the animus really is and there are many traps into which one could fall on this difficult venture of exploring it.

Even though the animus is masculine energy, I prefer to use the term 'it' rather than 'he' to refer to it. This is because the animus is an archetype. It has tremendous energy and a life of its own. We can become possessed by it or we can learn to work with it creatively. We must constantly be awake to its presence. Even though it is a 'he', at the same time it is not a 'he', because it is 'many'. It is much more than

---

6   *C.W.* Vol.18, par.1158.
7   *C.W.* Vol. 7, par. 330.
8   ibid.
9   *C.W.* Vol. 7, par 36.
10 *The Pocket Oxford English Dictionary.* (1969,1978, 1984) Oxford University Press.

one. It is as many and as diverse as all the men in the world. This is the potential diversity that lies within each woman. So to call it 'he' is to be seduced into the idea that it is graspable and manageable. Jung writes:

> The animus does not appear as one person, but as a plurality of persons. The animus is rather like an assembly of fathers or dignitaries of some kind who lay down incontestable, 'rational' *ex cathedra* judgements. On closer examination these exacting judgements turn out to be largely sayings and opinions scraped together more or less unconsciously from childhood on, and compressed into a canon of average truth, justice and reasonableness, a compendium of preconceptions which, whenever a conscious and competent judgement is lacking (as not infrequently happens), instantly obliges with an opinion.[11]

One woman, who communicated with her various animus figures through active imagination, decided to get them all into one room. Each animus figure was represented in her imagination by a different personality. The assembled power had her quivering. As the story in her imagination unfolded, she had to humbly call on a grandfather animus to protect her. She ended by promising never to deal with all her animus figures *en masse* again.[12]

We discover the animus the same way as we do any contents of the unconscious – through dreams, active imagination and through projection. Projection is when we put outside of ourselves, onto the world around us, the contents of the unconscious. Whatever we

---

11 *C.W.* Vol. 7, par. 332.
12 Irene Claremont de Castillejo. (1973) *Knowing Woman.* Harper and Row, N.Y.
    Page 75.

project onto must have a hook for the particular contents that we are projecting, otherwise the projection does not work. Let us say, for example, that there is an aspect of a woman's psyche that she is not conscious of. This is her heroic animus, the part of her that wants to make a difference in the world, but she is not aware of it. Because of it, this woman is attracted to a man who is making a difference in the world. The connection with the man is very powerful because it carries the projection of an aspect of the woman's own inner animus. On the negative side, if a woman has an inner animus that is devilish and cynical she can be either attracted or repulsed by men who have a similar characteristic. If she is attracted, it could lead to a demon lover relationship. If she is repulsed she could demonize men who carry a hook for this projection and judge the men in her life more severely than they may in fact deserve. By looking at the male figures in their dreams, women can get a picture of the state of the animus in their psyches and its level of development. Is the main male figure in the dream an infant boy, a four-year-old, a young student, an older man? Is the dream about a devil or a bishop, a gang of robbers or a group of monks?

A woman dreamed one night that she was pursued by a soldier with a rifle. He came closer and closer until he had the rifle in her face. She was terrified that he was going to shoot her. However, she managed to somehow overcome him and she tied him up. She put him into an upstairs room in a house, and left, with him still tied up. In the end of the dream, the woman felt guilty about him somehow. On working with this dream in active imagination, she went back to the soldier in the upstairs room and she untied him and spoke to him. He did not seem a bit threatening. He pleaded with her that he just wanted to write! A rifle can be a phallic masculine symbol. As such, it represents goal orientation, wanting something out there, accuracy in one's mind as to what one wants, and a desire to shoot, to let fly, to go for it. The soldier, when the woman dialogued with him, revealed himself as a positive energy within her that she had been ignoring.

The animus is well known among women for making them feel bad about themselves. One can use active imagination to track this negative impression. A woman found herself feeling very depressed about herself all day. That evening, she decided to try to get to the bottom of it. She focused on the feelings she had experienced during the day and allowed some image to surface from her unconscious. What appeared was an overweight, sweaty, self-flagellating monk. She was horrified! When she began to speak with him, he told her that he represented the collective male energy in her family. He was oppressed and ineffective, overweight and useless. In dialoguing with this character, the woman gained insight into the feelings she experienced of lack of self-worth and an inability to act in the world. This is the value of active imagination. It is a way of taking images from our unconscious and using them to learn about ourselves.

Frieda Fordham[13] writes that the animus (as with the anima) seems to derive from three roots. Knowing these roots is important because it gives us a sense of the magnitude of what we are dealing with. The animus is not a simple reality, neither is it simple to deal with it. The three roots are as follows:

1. The collective image of man which a woman inherits both through her culture and her genes.
2. A woman's own experience of masculinity, coming through her contacts with the men in her life, starting with the father, or some other dominant male figure.

---

13 Frieda Fordham. (1953) *An Introduction to Jung's Psychology*. Penguin Books, England. Page 55

3. The latent masculine principle in herself – peculiar
to her own psyche and personality.

The animus is an archetype that is in every woman, shaped and tempered by each particular woman's contact and experience of men in the world, and further tempered and formed by the unique personality of the woman herself, something which is her own.

When Jung describes the animus as it manifests in the world in women's behaviour it appears as opinionated, it proclaims universal truths arrogantly, it announces that it is 'always right'. This is so because when it appears in women like this it is playing a role in the world where it does not belong. He says:

> ... all these traits, as familiar as they are unsavoury, are
> simply and solely due to the extraversion of the animus.
> The animus does not belong to the function of conscious
> relationship; his function is rather to facilitate relations
> with the unconscious. Instead of the woman merely
> associating opinions with external situations – situations
> which she ought to think about consciously – the animus,
> as an associative function, should be directed inwards,
> where it could associate the contents of the unconscious.[14]

The role of the animus is to filter the contents of the collective unconscious through to the conscious mind. Because of our ignorance in relation to the animus, it often interferes in places it should not. The animus belongs to the inner realms and works there as a light-bearer, shining up the contents of the deep unconscious. If the animus begins to interface the outer world for a woman it is going somewhere that it does not belong.

---

14 *C.W.* Vol. 7, par. 336.

The ego is the part of the psyche that interfaces with the outer world and it uses personae and the dominant functions to do this. Each person has different personae for different situations. If we are healthy we do not become over-identified with our personae. We can put them on and take them off with ease as each situation in our lives arises. If the animus in a woman's psyche moves from the inner realm to interface the outer world in the place of personae the woman can get into serious trouble psychologically. She becomes animus possessed. It is this animus possession that has gotten the animus a bad name in the world. Jung writes:

> A woman possessed by the animus is always in danger of losing her femininity, her adapted feminine persona [...] These psychic changes of sex are due entirely to the fact that a function which belongs inside has been turned outside. The reason for this perversion is clearly the failure to give adequate recognition to an inner world which stands autonomously opposed to the outer world, and makes just as serious demands on our capacity for adaptation.[15]

If the animus remains in the inner realm it has a very positive and vital role to play in the psyche. Jung notes: "Not all contents of the… animus are projected… Many of them appear spontaneously in dreams and so on, and many more can be made conscious through active imagination. In this way we find that thoughts, feelings and affects are alive in us which we would never have believed possible".[16]

Animus as an Archetype Accessible to Both Genders

I now come upon a point of disagreement with Jung on the animus. As I have stated above, Jung believed that the animus was peculiar to

---

15 *C.W.* Vol. 7, par. 337.
16 *C.W.* Vol. 9(ii), par. 39.

the psychology of women. This implies that the man does not have an animus, nor does he have access to the animus as an archetype. The question I have is this – does the animus have to be exclusive to the woman's psyche? As an archetype should it not be available to both genders even though it has a specific role to play in the woman's psyche since it is the counter-sexual element?

What prevents Jung allowing for this is that he equated the entire collective unconscious of a woman with the animus. Or rather he said this about the anima and then concluded that it is the same for the animus. He writes: "The collective unconscious as a whole presents itself to a man in feminine form. To a woman it appears in masculine form, and then I call it the animus".[17] When he speaks of the collective unconscious here he means the collective unconscious that lies beyond the personal unconscious where the shadow lies. He is, in effect, saying that while one finds the shadow in the personal unconscious where it is fairly easy to access, the animus and anima inhabit the collective unconscious. In experiencing them we are going deeper into the unconscious. While the shadow elements take on the gender of the conscious personality, the animus and anima take on the gender of the unconscious personality.

However, it seems to be an enormous claim to make that the entire collective unconscious appears to a woman in masculine form (hence the animus) and to a man in feminine form (hence the anima). I would rather subscribe to the idea that, for a woman, parts of the collective unconscious are experienced as masculine. This includes the part that compensates for the conscious ego and biological gender of a person, which, it must be remembered, is a tiny part of the whole picture when you are speaking of the entire collective unconscious. The woman does indeed experience the animus as a counter-sexual element. It

---

17   *C.W.* Vol. 18, par. 187.

has a role to play in filtering the unconscious to the consciousness. However, it is not the entire collective unconscious, nor does the collective unconscious of a woman necessarily appear as masculine. For example, the archetype of the wise old woman arises from the collective unconscious and is available to the woman. Also, the witch archetype, the goddess archetype, the virgin archetype and so many more. This allows for the archetype of animus to be more than a mere counter-sexual element for the female psyche. It is a freestanding archetype in its own right. This means that it is relevant to men as an archetype. I will explore this later in the chapter.

Separating Animus Out from the Function Types

It seems to me that in reading both Carl Jung and Emma Jung on the animus two things need to be considered. The first is the time in which these thoughts were written. The role of women in the world in the Jung's day was radically different to what it is now. Even now we have, to date, mere glimpses of what women are capable of when freed from the terrible restrictions and limitations, which still affect them today in the Western world. These restrictions are being lifted to some extent in a practical sense in so far as equal opportunities are somewhat more available to women. But restrictions still exist in our thinking and our prejudices and much of what we see that women are capable of is at the cost of them staying connected to their feminine instincts as they find themselves competing and functioning in still very masculine dominated domains. We are only at the beginning of a very long journey towards discovering what women can truly do and be, when freed from the current limiting mindsets and prejudices. It could similarly be said about men, that they too have yet to blossom and realise their full capabilities, and that this will not happen until they are freed from the present cultural patriarchal expectations. If we have only come so far, we can get a sense of where thinkers were at in the time of the Jungs.

It is clear to me that in reading both Carl Jung and Emma Jung, on the animus, they describe women in ways that are unacceptable today. Emma Jung writes: "It is well known that a really creative faculty of mind is a rare thing in woman. There are many women who have developed their powers of thinking, discrimination, and criticism to a high degree, but there are very few who are mentally creative in the way a man is".[18] It is offensive in the extreme to be told that there are few women who are as mentally creative as men.

The second point to be considered is this. Because in the past women have been generalised as being predominantly feelers and men thinkers, the animus then is seen as the capacity in women to think – the anima as the man's ability to feel. This is a mistake. The animus must never be identified with one of the four functions, i.e. thinking, feeling, sensation, intuition. The animus is a function in itself that filters the unconscious contents to the conscious mind. It is also an archetype in the collective unconscious. The animus is neither the capacity to think nor the capacity to do. What lends to this misjudgment is the fact that, if a woman is a high feeler, then her thinking function is in the unconscious and it is something that this woman's animus will carry to consciousness. If enough women are seen to be high feelers, then what one sees is women using the animus to carry a thinking function, which is unconscious, undifferentiated and basically dreadful. One can then be led to believe that this is what the animus is and does. One can conclude that animus carries the bad thinking ability of women. This is demonstrated very clearly in Jung's writing. He says:

> When the animus breaks out in a woman, it is not
> feelings that appear, as in a man, but she begins to argue
> and to rationalise. And just as his anima-feelings are

---

18 Emma Jung. (1985). *Animus and Anima*. Spring Publ. Dallas, Texas. Page 21. Emma Jung having raised five children immersed herself in intellectual and analytical work. She wrote on the Animus, the Anima, the Grail legend and became an analyst.

arbitrary and capricious, so these feminine arguments are illogical and irrational. One can speak of an animus-thinking that is always right and must have the last word, and always ends up with "That's just the reason!" If the anima is irrational feeling, the animus is irrational thinking".[19]

To be fair, Jung was speaking of when the animus is extraverting in the world and not in its rightful place in the inner realm. However, it is clear that he believes generally that the animus would be inferior thinking in a woman and the anima would be a man's inferior feeling.

But this is not so. Even if every woman in the entire world were a dominant feeler, whose animus carried the inferior thinking function to consciousness, this would still not define what the animus was. The animus is not one of the four functions, which help us to live in the world – thinking, feeling, sensation and intuition. It is an independent archetype of masculinity and in the woman's psyche it connects her to her unconscious realm. It is not limited to the contents it carries. It is not solely a channel for inferior thinking.

Emma Jung goes on to say: "The creativity of woman finds its expression in the sphere of living, not only in her biological functions as mother but in shaping of life generally, be it in her activity as educator, in her role as companion to man, a mother in the home, or in some other form".[20] Here, if we can resist the apron and kitchen bias, I find that we are perhaps coming closer to some helpful truth. If there is to be no difference between men and women, then what is the point of thinking in terms of opposite and complimentary aspects of the psyche. There is a difference between men and women. There

---

19 *C.W.* Vol. 10, par. 80.
20 Emma Jung. (1985). *Animus and Anima.* Spring Publ. Dallas, Texas. Page 21.

is a difference between the masculine and the feminine. The point is, what is it? The answer does not lie in one gender hijacking two of the four functions of thinking, feeling, sensation or intuition. It does, perhaps, lie closer to the above, trying to describe what is peculiar to a woman's way of being in the world as opposed to a man's.

I believe that what is peculiarly feminine is connectedness and relatedness. Thus if women do work which, traditionally, has been done by men, they will, if they are deeply connected to their feminine soul, do it in a radically different way to the way men have done the same work. Unfortunately, in today's world, it is often the case that women are expected to do the work in exactly the same way as men. Where a woman tries to do this, she will become animus possessed – that is, her animus will invade the realm of the outer world. The place for the animus is within, interfacing the unconscious and the conscious mind. It is not its place to act in the outer world. When it does, we see animus possession at play and it is never a pretty sight.

Here again, the distinction between the four functions, as the tools that are at our disposal for living in the outer world, and the animus, as the filtering tool that connects us to our inner world, is worth repeating. To steer clear of confusion we must constantly disengage the animus from that which it is communicating. If it is appropriate to use one's sensation function in a task in the outer world, and if this function is usually unconscious (i.e. not a dominant one), then we need the animus to communicate this function to us. This is its task. What can happen is that the animus becomes identified with that which it is communicating. Where a woman must use her inferior sensate function and the animus becomes identified with that function, then her animus appears in her behaviour as a swaggering, arrogant yet badly skilled labourer. We are, perhaps more familiar with the animus as channelling the inferior thinking function. In this case, the animus appears in the woman's behaviour as a dogmatic, unbending voice, which pronounces generalised, yet irrelevant, statements and is often judgmental and scathing.

When the animus does not become identified with the function it is channeling, and when it is operating healthily, it makes the woman conscious that in this area she is less skilled than in her strong areas and that she must take more time and recognise her limits. It makes her aware of the fact that she can use her inferior function (and must, if she is to become fully rounded and mature) but that only by taking it slowly and with humility can she succeed. So, for example, when using the inferior sensate function, she will ask advice, have patience and approach the problem calmly. Unlike a friend of mine who, while trying to fix a problem underneath the stairs, got disorientated and instead of hammering upwards managed to hammer herself on the head!

In the case of needing to use an inferior thinking function, a woman must resist the temptation of jumping on the bandwagon and coming out with the typical powerfully fueled righteous negative animus statements. She must look carefully at what ideas are being presented to her, acknowledging that, while at first she perhaps cannot make head nor tail of them, she can slowly disentangle the threads and make sense of them, in time, for herself.

The key to working with an inferior function is to acknowledge that it is, indeed, inferior. There is nothing to be gained by ignoring this fact and pushing on regardless. As I have said already, but it is worth repeating, you can discover your inferior function by looking at the disastrous areas in your life, by looking at what you are really bad at. I have also said that evil creeps in through the inferior function. If the animus is filtering the unconscious contents to the woman's conscious mind, while at the same time staying separate from these and helping the woman to work within the limits of her inferior function, it is working in an ideal manner. The animus rarely does, however, in reality, work in an ideal manner! When I speak of the animus problem in this chapter it will become clearer what happens for a woman when the animus does not keep its place and she becomes possessed by the animus.

The whole area of trying to establish what belongs to the masculine and what belongs to the feminine, in this day and age, when gender roles are in such flux, is extremely difficult. If I say that relatedness and connectedness are to do with femininity, then am I saying that it is the feminine in a man that allows him to relate and be connected? What about his feeling function or his intuitive one? Surely these enable him to be related and connected? In the same way, if I claim that the ability to focus and to differentiate is an attribute of the masculine animus in a woman then what is the difference between differentiating / focusing and the thinking function, which a woman can have, independent of the masculine side of her psyche?

We have established that there is a masculine element in a woman's psyche and that this is called the animus. We have also established that the role and purpose of the animus is different and separate from that of any of the four functions. So now let us ask the hard questions: Is focusing different from thinking? Is relatedness different from feeling? Is it a young girl's animus, her masculine element, that gets her the highest Leaving Certificate results in her school or that has her studying chemical engineering in college? My answer is 'no'. It is her thinking function. Thinking is her dominant function, and she is a gifted thinker. Because thinking is her dominant function her animus was not involved.

In the same way, I do not think it is a man's anima, his feminine element, that enables him to discern right and wrong. It is his feeling function. I cannot say to a woman that it is the masculine element, her animus, in her psyche that allows her to think well, or, even worse, that her thinking, because it is her animus, will be inferior to a man's. Nor can I tell a man that it is his feminine element, his anima, that allows him to feel deeply. What I can say is that it is the masculine element, the animus, in a woman's psyche that enables her to access her thinking function if, and only if, it happens to be an inferior function. And I can say to a man, that it is the feminine element, the anima, within his psyche that will enable him to access deep feeling, if, and only if, it is an inferior function.

This allows for women who have brilliant thinking functions and men who have a capacity for deep feeling. In these instances, the woman with the brilliant thinking will need her animus to filter her inferior feeling function to her, and the man with deep feeling will need his anima to filter his inferior thinking function to him.

If this is the case, then the idea that men are better thinkers than women, and that women are better feelers than men, is nonsense. It also puts paid to the idea that the domain of the animus is in thinking and sensation, and that the domain of the anima is in feeling and intuition. Until now, these ideas have been dominant, but in the next hundred years or so, with each gender exploring areas, up until now not seen as readily available to it, who is to know how things will change? Up until this century and some would say well into this century there has been a cultural bias in the West. This bias has been in favour of women who are high feelers and high intuitives and of men who are high thinkers and high sensates. The roles that men and women were expected to play backed up this bias. It is not far-fetched to consider that many women and men spent their lives living out of their lower functions in order to fulfill this collective cultural bias. Today the gender roles are undergoing a change, albeit slowly. Women are able to enter professions that up until now were the domain of men only. The young girl mentioned earlier who got the highest Leaving Certificate in her class and studied chemical engineering in college was one of four women in a class of thirty. Forty years ago she would perhaps have married young and attempted to live out of her lower functions.

If it is the case that people in the west are now more free to live out of their dominant functions than in the past, then it is fair to assume that there will be more women who are dominant thinkers and sensates and more men who are dominant feelers and intuitives. In time this will have an enormous influence on western culture. Already women are working in fields previously exclusive to men. However, there is a long way to go before there are enough women involved in these areas for things to change structurally. It is not hard to imagine that if there were the same number of women in government as there are men that the nature of the government would be changed significantly. It is the same when men are drawn to work in professions previously exclusive to women. A friend working in speech therapy in Ireland once commented to me that if there were more men working in this area working conditions would be improved and pay would increase.

The belief here is that women do work in the world, even in the same professional fields as men, differently. Two things need to happen if this is to be observed more clearly. We need a culture where men and women chose lifestyles and careers according to their dominant functions and not the old gender cultural bias. We also need women to stay connected to their feminine selves and resist becoming animus driven. Only then can we look at what is peculiarly feminine. We would see how a woman with a dominant sensate function is different in the world to a man with a dominant sensate function; how a high thinking woman behaves differently to a high thinking man. I believe they are different, profoundly different. But how so, and in what way, I can only intuit.

I do not believe that the animus and anima are genderless tools that merely filter the unconscious contents, whatever they may be, to the conscious mind. I believe that they appear as masculine and feminine and that they are as different from each other as the physical man is from the physical woman. What is important is that we must not let the animus become identified with what it 'lights' up in the unconscious. The animus must not become identified with any of the functions. In the past, the tendency has been to identify the animus with thinking and sensation. The energy of the animus, separate from thinking and sensation, is the energy of the animus archetype. It is the energy of focused-ness, of spirit and differentiation, and of meaning.

According to Irene Claremont de Castillejo, the animus offers a focused type of consciousness that makes it a 'torch bearer'.[21] It is not human or moral and so it will shine its light on the unconscious in a haphazard and arbitrary way, unless it is otherwise directed. This is the root of many of our troubles with the animus. If we are conscious, we can direct the animus to shine up unconscious material that is relevant to our lives. If we are not conscious, the animus energy in our psyche can shine up, at best, irrelevant material, at worst, destructive material. I will speak more of this when dealing with what Emma Jung called "the animus problem". It is possible to look at the different stages in the development of consciousness and in doing so to observe how the animus manifests at each stage.

---

21 Irene Claremont de Castillejo. (1973) *Knowing Woman*. Harper and Row, N.Y. Page 78.

Stages of Psychological Development and Relationship to the Animus at Each Stage

In Neumann's *The Origins and History of Consciousness*[22] there is a description of the different stages in the development of consciousness. These apply not only to the individual but also to the history of humankind, as seen in mythology and culture. There are six stages. Some of the stages are common to both men and women. However, others are peculiar to women. Neumann has allowed for the fact that women's psychological development is different from mens' and that patriarchal culture, to date, has not helpfully reflected this.

Looking at these stages is helpful. It gives us a framework for the development of the consciousness of a woman, and her relationship to her animus at each stage. It therefore enables us to understand how we often are stuck at one stage or another and need to grow up from that stage and move on. A tragic example of someone who was stuck at a stage and did not have the perspective to see further than that stage to the next one, is the life and death of poet Sylvia Plath. She committed suicide. Paula Bennett wrote of her: "For Plath to achieve autonomy meant that she had to destroy the dependent-prone side of herself. Once that self was destroyed, however, all that remained was a woman too wicked to live".[23] Deldon Anne McNeely comments "It is tragic that she felt she had to destroy the dependent part of herself rather than help it grow up".[24] In situations like this, perspective is everything. Neumann's framework gives us perspective.

The first stage, which applies to both men and women, is psychic unity. All is one. The infant at the breast feels no distinction between himself or herself and the breast or the face that he or she can barely

---

22 E. Neumann. (1971) *The Origins and History of Consciousness*. Bollingen Series XLII. Princeton: Princeton University Press, N.J., U.S.A.
23 Paula Bennett. (1986). *My Life is a Loaded Gun*. Beacon Press, Boston. Page 159.
24 Deldon Anne McNeely. (1991). *Animus Aeternus*. Inner City Books, Toronto, Canada. Page 100.

see beyond the breast. Jung claimed that some remote native tribes in Africa were still at that stage, even in adulthood. He called it 'the primitive mind'. For these people, there was no distinction between the person's body and the tree or the river or any other part of the natural world. All is one. Jung called this *participation mystique* [25]and saw that it was the bottom line for every case of unconscious identity or projection. Jung referred to this stage as the *Unus Mundus*. Neumann called it the Unitary Reality. Edward C. Whitmont in his book *Return of the Goddess* calls this stage the Magical Phase.

Neumann points out that it is at this stage of identification with the mother that men and women's experience of being in the world are different. For a boy child to preserve his masculine identity, he must see himself as different, separate from this primary relationship. Therefore he must be able to be detached and objective in relation to it. A girl child, however, is the same as the mother. She can hold on to that identification with mother without her experience as feminine ever being undermined. Neumann thus held that woman's first and natural way of relating is by identification and relatedness, while the man's way is objectivity and separateness. The boy child had to distinguish himself from the mother in order to experience himself as male.

The second stage, Neumann calls the Self-Conserving Stage. Whitmont calls it the Mythological or Imaginal Phase. It is the bridge from the magical to mental functioning. He describes it as "a… step into a first sense of inwardness and personal separateness from what is now conceived as an outer, objective world".[26] For the woman it

---

25 '*Participation mystique* is a term derived from Lévy-Bruhl. It denotes a peculiar kind of psychological connection with objects, and consists in the fact that the subject cannot clearly distinguish himself from the object but is bound to it by a direct relationship which amounts to partial identity.' *C.W.* Vol.6. par 781.

26 Edward C. Whitmont. (1982) *Return of the Goddess*. Routledge and Kegan Paul plc. London. Page 50.

happens when the feminine ego recognises its separateness from the unconscious. The focus is on remaining safe within familiar feminine limits. Men are experienced as alien and strange.

In the third stage, the feminine ego is invaded by the Paternal Uroboros. This is experienced as a capturing of the woman's consciousness by a numinous, transforming power. Neumann suggested that it would be like being taken and ravaged by a male divinity, as Persephone was by Hades, Lord of the Dead and as the Virgin Mary, in the Christian faith, was by the Holy Spirit. The power of this capture is enough to take the feminine ego away from the attachment to the exclusively feminine world but it holds her enthralled and submissive. Whitmont describes it as the mental, patriarchal ego phase. "The transition from the mythological to the mental stage of consciousness involves a transition from animism and soul to the three-dimensionality of the outer spatial world, of things perceived by the five senses".[27] Reality equals that which is visible.

The next few stages are peculiar to feminine conscious development. The fourth stage is called the Patriarchal Partner. The feminine ego moves to become free of the father's captivity. This may happen in a woman's life by forming a relationship with a man, which shifts the woman away from the father. It could also take the form of some activity spurred on by her inner masculine (animus) which distances her from the father world and allows her some independence. The activity, however, remains in the realm of the patriarchy, as does her male partner. So, even though she has shifted out of the father's grasp, she still remains in the patriarchal world, in activity, relationship or mentality, or all three. Her inner push for psychic health, or the circumstances of her life (I believe the two things are connected) will push her on to the next stage.

---

27 ibid page 70.

The fifth stage is called True Confrontation. This is where the woman can see herself as equal to the masculine. She can recognise other people as separate from her projections onto them. Jung described this stage as involving an "unusual loneliness". He goes on to say: "This is because a *participation mystique* is created by not controlling them (the animus and anima); when one allows a piece of one's self to wander about and be projected into other people, it gives one a feeling of being connected".[28]

The sixth stage is Experience of the Female Self. This involves integration and renewal and a fruitfulness of mind and soul that is uniquely feminine. It is the true *conjunctio*.

There are many models on offer for human psychological development. This one I find useful because from it we can trace where a woman is in terms of the psychological journey to wholeness. There is no time frame for this journey and everyone is at a different point along the way. If we were to look at the animus in relation to these stages of development it would be different at each stage. Emma Jung describes four animus stages: Power, deed, word, and meaning. "Power corresponds very well to the first stage, the deed follows, then the word, and finally, as the last stage, meaning".[29] The inner reflects the outer all the time. Therefore as men are in the world, so the masculine is in the woman's psyche.

The Mother-Influenced or Mother-Bound Woman and her Animus
Very early on in their lives, women psychologically align themselves, unconsciously, either with their mother or their father. Until such time as they move on to stage five, true confrontation, when they begin to take back projections and confront reality with an independent

---

28 C.G.Jung. (1930-1934) *The Visions Seminars: Notes of the Seminars.* Spring Publications, Zurich. 1976.
29 Emma Jung. (1985) *Animus and Anima.* Spring Publ. Dallas, Texas. Page 3.

psychological stance, they are bound to their unconscious choice of parent. They remain either mother-bound or father-bound.

A mother-bound woman has not yet established a separate identity from her mother. She lives in an unconscious symbiosis with the mother. A woman can remain fused with the mother for an entire lifetime. In the outer world, she may have made all the separations. She can marry, have children and run a very efficient home. Yet, unconsciously, she is fused with her mother, she has no separate ego identity, and she has not cut the unconscious cord between them.

In psychological development, little girls from the ages of two to five will ordinarily be enthralled with their father or the Father archetype. At the age of two, they will shift out of the exclusive mother world and experience the otherness of the father world. This is especially so when there is a loving father present to mirror this stage for the child. If such a father is not present, then the child will pick up on the masculine traits in her mother or others nearby. When a child's father is either absent or is a weak, negative or ineffective presence in the child's life, then the girl child could be more inclined to remain orientated towards the mother. This is not necessarily so. Although I know of no mother-bound women who had negative or absent mothers there are women who are father-bound even though their fathers were absent or were a negative presence.

It is impossible to define what makes one girl-child orientate towards one parent, while another girl-child will unconsciously choose the other. Circumstances can influence the child's unconscious choice of parent-influence. Yet how they influence cannot be defined. However, it is probably safe to say that a woman who has remained psychologically bound to her mother did not have a positive father influence in her life.

Psychologists, who have studied family systems and issues of co-dependence, have discovered patterns that occur in all families. Each member of a family unconsciously carries a role in the family. John Friel was one of the pioneers in this field, as was John Bradshaw.[30] The first child was seen to be connected to the father, the second to the mother, the third was sensitive to the relationship between the parents, the fourth was the scapegoat, and the fifth and any after that repeated the pattern again. In this schema, for reasons to do with the very structure of the family, a first daughter would be connected to the father, as would a fifth daughter. A daughter, if a second child, would be connected to the mother. This is not a hard and fast scheme to be rigidly applied to everyone. Rather it is a scheme that has been observed to be often the case and as such is helpful.

I have also come across some families where the collective in the family supported either the masculine or the feminine principles. For example, the father is idolised by all the female members of the family. He is set up as the hero and all his faults are fondly overlooked. Members of the family may not be aware that this is what is happening but woe betide anyone within the family who might challenge this basic unconscious belief. In families like this, often it is the mother who is perpetuating the myth of male superiority. She is dependent on her husband, and she needs her children to endorse this dependency.

In other families, the mother is the dominant psychic force in the family. She keeps each child tightly bound to her and the penalty is high for anyone in the family who disturbs her comfort zones. As one woman said of her mother: "She was great when we were little. It's just she wanted to keep us that way!" In both cases, it is difficult

---

30 For some idea of the work of these people see: *Bradshaw on the Family*, John Bradshaw. (1990) Health Communications Inc. Florida, U.S.A. Revised edition and John Friel and Linda D. Friel (1991) *Adult Children: The Secrets of Dysfunctional Families*. Health Communications Inc. Florida, U.S.A.

for the members of the family to see outside of the collective family complex, be it a father complex or a mother complex. The family is dominated by an archetype, either the Father archetype or the Mother Archetype.

In the case of the mother-bound woman, an unconscious fusion with mother can play itself out in her life in many ways. It can be difficult for her to focus, especially to focus on her own needs. A woman can get the kids ready for school, organise the house, be highly successful in her chosen career and yet find it impossible to walk out the door to go for a walk for herself, or go for a massage, or take a holiday. She can find it difficult to discipline herself in areas of health, body-weight and soul-time. There may be a constant underlying longing for oblivion. This can take the form of over-eating, or bad eating habits, other substance addictions or simply wanting to sleep all the time. There can be a feeling of being drained all the time, of people feeding off you, of having to serve others.

If a woman is challenged by life to take care of herself, if she leaves the home and gets a flat of her own, or if her partner on whom she has been dependent leaves, or dies, then she can shift out of this fusion with her mother. If she does, she will begin to forge her own ego identity. She will become a definable separate entity from the mother. She will begin to know who she is. However, it is difficult to shift entirely from the mother-influence. The problem is more than a fusion with her own personal mother, it is an immersion in the Mother archetype. Even if a woman has achieved a degree of separation and psychological independence, she may continue to notice the influence her mother has on her. She may continue to struggle with weight-issues or discipline issues or simply issues around minding herself. However, the more established her ego identity becomes, the more she will relate to her own positive masculine side (her animus) and the less she will be prey to her mother's and her own negative animus.

I believe that a mother-influenced woman with a strong ego identity, who has separated out from her mother, will continue to see the world and everything in it in a different way than a father-influenced woman. It is not better or worse but simply different. The instinctive priorities may be different or there is a subtle energy that is different. For instance, a woman who is a dominant feeler and who has done significant work on her inferior function – thinking - and can use it very well, will still use it in a noticeably unique and different way to a dominant thinker. The same applies in the case of a mother-influenced woman, who has a strong separate ego and a good relationship with her animus and with men in the world. She will still relate to the world and to men differently than a father-influenced woman. And a father-influenced woman who has re-aligned herself with the deep feminine and the archetypal mother, will forever be shaped by her original connection with the father and the masculine.

A woman, who is psychologically mother-influenced, is likely to give less weight to her relationships with men and more to her women friends. Her orientation is towards women. This has nothing to do with sexual orientation, rather it is her primary reference of value. She has a deeper-felt connection with women than with men because of her connection with her mother. She may have good relationships with men, and even a particular man, yet it is her women friends who anchor her and make her feel safe in the world. This is a mother-influenced woman at her best. She has a strong ego identity.

A woman who is capable of healthy friendships with men, and one man in particular, is a woman who is not so mother-bound as to be like Persephone in Greek mythology. Persephone was so connected to her mother, Demeter, that it took the rape by Hades, the god of the underworld, to separate Persephone from her mother. Such women, like Persephone, behave in a belittling manner towards men. This can be simply a cover for their fear of men. Men are experienced as alien and strange. They are 'other' in a threatening way.

The animus for a mother-bound woman can be experienced as a weak, ineffective, sometimes diseased man, or a sickly boy child. On an even more negative scale, it can appear in dreams as abusive or abandoning. Again, it may appear as a monster or a rabid animal. If a woman is very unconsciously mother-bound her animus can be split off. Any aspect of the psyche that is split off will become negative in order to gain a reconnection.

To say a woman is mother-influenced or father-influenced is not necessarily a negative thing. It merely describes an unconsciously chosen orientation – towards the mother or towards the father. The orientation will colour a woman's perception of the world around her, it will influence how she will experience both men and women and it will also influence how she will be in the world as a woman. None of this is necessarily negative or positive. The degree to which one is influenced by either will determine whether it is a positive or a negative thing, whether the influence has become a bondage. A mother-influenced woman can journey through her growing up, being bound to her mother and the Mother archetype, and still emerge in the world as a person who can healthily relate to men and who can appreciate the otherness of men. She can also have a well-developed animus and be innovative and dynamic in her life and in the world. She will always perhaps have a special love for women and all things feminine, yet this need not detract from her experience of men and maleness. On the other hand, a mother-influenced woman may also remain mother-bound for her entire life, tortured with eating problems and self-disgust, fearing and distrusting men and being crushed by her actual mother's disapproval, manipulation and control.

The presence and strength of an ego identity, separate from the mother, is what makes the difference between the two realities. But truth cannot be painted in black and white. We each slide up and down along a scale of psychological health every day, spiraling in and out of issues and attitudes again and again. Gradually we gain more awareness, more consciousness, more knowledge of what drives us, and what comes from our true centre. By continuously looking in the mirror again and again we gradually come to terms with our true reflection and who we really are.[31]

The Father-Influenced or Father-Bound Woman and her Animus

For women who are influenced by, or are bound to, the father, the shift away from the mother world to the father world has happened. The girl-child has separated out from the mother. She accepts a masculine assertiveness and a drive towards separateness and independence. From the age of two to five she 'danced to please her father' (from the song by Dory Previn). Ideally, this stage can be resolved. The patriarchal energy can be translated into something manageable by the girl's ego-identity and she becomes aware of herself as a blossoming

---

31 Some writers (Deldon Anne McNeely in *Animus Aeternus,* 1991, Inner City Books, Toronto, Canada, for one) would imply that a woman goes through, for example, the mother stage and then must go through the father stage and then the path leads to the animus being experienced as brother/hero/patriarchal partner and finally, equal partner. In an ideal schema perhaps that is how it should happen. Yet, it seems to me that women, at some very early stage in their psychological lives, unconsciously choose one or the other, the mother or the father stage and this orientation will stay with them for their whole lives. The stage after the mother or father one, in animus terms, is the brother/hero/patriarchal partner. A woman who is mother-influenced does not have to go through the father-influence in any major way, in order to reach the next stage of animus. I do not believe that a mother-influenced woman will ever experience the world like a father-influenced woman, or vice versa. The orientation runs too long and too deep. And so the animus of a mother-influenced woman will take a different path of development to that of a father-influenced one, in order to get from the mother stage to the brother/hero/patriarchal stage.

girl-woman, rooted in a feminine source, yet having access to the masculine creative energies.

Oh for the ideal world! For as many reasons perhaps as there are women in the world, it sometimes happens that a child will not grow out of this father-fascination and she will spend her life dancing to please her father. (Which is what Dory Previn's song is actually about). It could be that the child has experienced being emotionally abandoned by her mother and she therefore turns psychologically towards the father. It could be that the father is the more emotionally present parent. Or perhaps the child has been born into a line of women who have all opted towards the father and she is, in fact, unconsciously driven/pushed in that direction by her own mother. Unfortunately, it can happen that a child is fascinated by the father, even when he is an abusive figure – alcoholic, violent, compulsive, domineering, or cruel. In situations like this, the mother is often a father-bound daughter herself, who has not managed to free herself from the devil within, the devil outside, nor from the devil which is the dark underside of the cultural patriarchy.

Deldon Anne McNeely writes:

> When a woman persists in this stage beyond her early fascination with the personal father, she lives in an attitude of inflation as the special daughter of the archetypal father, unconsciously identified as his partner. There may be loss of earthiness and an estrangement from the mother-world and from her feminine nature; or, if not an estrangement, a tendency to disparage feminine values except as they are useful to please the father-world.[32]

32 Deldon Anne McNeely. (1991). *Animus Aeternus.* Inner City Books, Toronto,

The very fact of persisting in this father-bondage comes from a weakened relationship with the mother and the Mother archetype. And so it stands to reason that this is the trademark of this way of being in the world. The feminine is looked down upon and the masculine is elevated.

The dynamic can go something like this: A girl child goes through the psychological stage where it is appropriate for her to surrender to the 'good father'. If the good father can receive this surrender with appropriate boundaries, both psychological and physical, then the child can move on. If, however, this surrender is not received by a loving father and is rebuffed (perhaps because the father feels threatened by the sexual nature of this surrender and is not sexually mature enough himself to hold his own in the face of it), the child feels spurned and abandoned and she now must carry this archetypal energy alone. The effects are usually lifelong. She will project the archetypal energy of the good father onto the world and be enthralled and entrapped by it. She will be besotted by male institutions in the world and will be frustrated because, as a woman, her entry into them will be limited. She will be attracted to men, older men, who will patronise her and father her.

This dynamic is played out in the book *Pygmalion* by George Bernard Shaw.[33] Henry Higgins creates this beauty in the world by transforming Eliza from a rough-cut lower-class woman into a high society lady. The book carries this particular psychological dynamic to its fullest when Eliza actually chooses to stay with Henry Higgins rather than marry the young man who falls in love with her. This is the tragic side of the dynamic. A woman who cannot grow beyond this entrapment by the Father archetype remains tied to the father at

---

Canada. Page 117.

33 George Bernard Shaw. (First published 1916) *Pygmalion: A Romance in Five Acts.* Penguin Books Ltd., London. (2000)

the expense of her living an independent life. She is bound within; her young, independent animus is not as attractive as the older father one, and outside in life the same applies; the younger man is spurned for the older one.

On the even darker side of things, if the surrender of the little girl is received by the father but not appropriately received, the damage can be catastrophic for the child. If the father does not have good psychological and emotional boundaries, then he can bind the little girl to himself and she becomes his psychological partner, his little anima. In her life, she will be a projected anima woman. She will not have an identity separate from what her father projects onto her. He will project onto her his inner woman and she will play that out. She may grow up to be very sexualised, yet her way of being a woman in the world will not be sourced in the true deep feminine. It is sourced in her father's fantasies and inner pictures of what it is to be a woman. In time she will carry other men's fantasies also and play them out.

It is from these circumstances that we have the Marilyn Monroes of the world – women who unconsciously played out men's fantasies by being the kind of women men fantasied about, women who were essentially empty of a personal ego-identity. Or a woman may grow up as Daddy's intellectual partner. She may shun her woman's body and think only her mind is important. She knows she cannot be Daddy's sexual partner and therefore she will be his intellectual one. She will value her intellect and academic pursuits and see herself as having a woman's body as opposed to being a woman. She is like the Greek Goddess Athena who sprang full-grown out of the head of her father, Zeus. Although this woman looks very different to her sister-woman who is living out the father's projected anima images, who is like a sex goddess, they are both cut off from the deep true feminine. Both are bound to the father. In a book on this subject of father-daughter relationships, Linda Schierse Leonard writes:

> The father-daughter sacrifice has its roots in the dominance of masculine power over the feminine. When the masculine is cut off from feminine values, when it does not allow the feminine principle to manifest itself *in its own way out of its own centre,* when it does not allow the feminine its manifold number of forms but reduces it only to those which serve masculine ends, it loses its relation to the values of the feminine realm.[34]

The darkest possibility in this dynamic, wherein the girl-child surrenders herself to the father, is when the father has no physical boundaries when he receives the child's surrender. This results in sexual abuse and incest. It is the darkest side of the good father. This is Satan. The Dark Father/Black Magician/Satan side of the Father archetype is constellated for the child and she will be haunted by it for life. "An aura of irresistible horror lurks forever in the mind of every incest victim. The archetypal power of the father is what makes a girls' experience of incest so damaging, unmanageable and enduring".[35]

In all of these cases, save the ideal ones, the woman experiences a wound, for the powerful Father archetype is constellated and not contained for the child. Marion Woodman writes: "… her world of inner uniqueness has been violated to the point where she fears even to look in the mirror for fear she won't be there".[36] She goes on to say that: "The bright side of the father-daughter relationship is

---

34 Linda Schierse Leonard. (1982). *The Wounded Woman*. Shambhala Publications, Boston, Massachusetts, U.S.A. Page 30. Emphasis mine.
35 Deldon Anne McNeely. (1991). *Animus Aeternus*. Inner City Books, Toronto, Canada. Page 129.
36 Marion Woodman. (1990) *Addiction to Perfection*. Inner City Books, Toronto, Canada. Page152.

creativity and spirituality; the dark side is incest".[37] That incest can be psychological/emotional incest or physical incest. All are seriously damaging.

The animus figures of the father-bound woman can be power-driven, judgmental, or perfectionist. The father-bound woman can be plagued by an inner atmosphere of suppressed contempt. She might feel that nothing she does is good enough, that *she* is not good enough. She can be assailed inwardly by at least two different manifestations of animus energy. Marion Woodman calls the first The Bad Witch and the second The Demon Lover.

The Bad Witch is the woman's mother's negative animus, that now lives in the woman's own unconscious. It is highly critical and it is vicious. The 'not good enough' voice comes from the Bad Witch. She is insatiable. Nothing will ever be good enough, or right. Woodman writes: "There is no satisfying a witch because her appetites are not grounded in the instincts and therefore have no natural satiation point. Meanwhile, the real instincts are starving".[38] The mother's animus is negative because her masculine creativity is unlived. It is unlived because of her dependence on her husband/church/institution. This negative animus will play a strong role in a daughter's unconscious. When a woman is living out of this Bad Witch energy, she is driven and unhappy and oftentimes cruel. She is disconnected from any true feminine source or principle within herself and therefore has nothing to nurture her.

The Demon Lover is a more complicated dynamic. Woodman writes:

---

37 ibid., page 168.
38 ibid., page 118.

The girl most vulnerable to the demon lover is the one who adores or fears the idealised father. [...] Having accepted his anima projection from infancy, she has lived to please him, to share his intellectual pursuits and to meet his standards of perfection. In the dynamics of such a relationship, the mother is experienced either as absent or as a rival. While the daughter experiences herself as the beloved of the father, consciously she knows she dare not share his bed, yet instinctively her energies remain incestuous. Thus her love is split off from her sexuality. In fantasy she dreams of her spiritual lover; in reality, she remains unconscious of her sexuality, acts it out without love, or fears it as some explosive power that can destroy her. She tends to 'fall helplessly in love' with a man who cannot marry her and around whom she creates an ideal world in which she is either adored or dramatically rejected. In life, she lives without her body; in dreams, she appears behind glass.[39]

The essential point about The Demon Lover is that he lures the woman away from her own life. He wants the woman to live in a fantasy world and so his is the voice that says the man she is dating or even married to is not good enough for her. The real man in her life can never compare to him. And so the woman will fantasise about the romantic lover, about how a real romance might be, how a 'true' lover might treat her. Her partner has no hope of rivaling this fantasy and the real relationship is often sabotaged. This is the work of the demon lover. The bondage to the Father archetype has remained intact and the relationship to a real man in the real world has been destroyed.

---

39 ibid., page 135.

This is the case if the woman has managed to actually be in a relationship in the real world. Sometimes a woman will remain forever locked in a glass case because no man is good enough for her, no man could ever stir her the way her inner lover does. What is tragic is that this dynamic is most often unconscious. Even though the woman may consciously say she wants a relationship and wishes to marry and have children she will either find no one who is attractive to her or, in some cases, when someone suitable appears on the scene, a wall of invisible unapproachability will surround the woman and the person will pass right along, leaving the woman hurt and baffled.

The dynamic of The Demon Lover can even appear in women who have healthy relationships with men. A woman who was happily married found herself criticising her husband. He was not affectionate enough, not romantic enough. She felt dissatisfied with their relationship. She found herself fantasising about meeting a lover and dreaming of how he would behave towards her – and about just how different he would be to her husband. This went on for a short time until she consciously decided that it was unhealthy. She recognised that her fantasies were undermining her relationship with her husband. That night she had the following short, yet shocking, dream.

> *A young man was about to be executed. Having been captured the dreamer saw him in silhouette. Behind the young man's own shape appeared a shadow of two arms with hands that had claws on them. It was scary, like a horror film. The dreamer knew that this clawed creature was the young man's real self and that this real self would now destroy the young man and thus itself also, because it had been caught. It did. Nothing was left behind.*

The dreamer interpreted the dream to mean that, because she had recognised the damage that The Demon Lover animus was doing to her relationship with her husband (it was caught and about to be executed), it had self-annihilated after revealing its true evil nature.

A father-bound woman who experienced one aspect of her animus as a vicious and cruel voice made a break-through in relation to that animus through active imagination. In her life she was working on breaking out of the father-bond and on becoming independent, ready to explore her own identity in the world, separate from father and partner. She became aware of how irritated she got when her partner criticised something she did. The irritation went deeper than the criticism ever merited. When she followed her feelings they led to a nasty and vicious voice that said, "You're useless, you can do nothing right, there is something wrong with you". She was shocked that she had this voice within. When she thought about it, she noticed that when her partner did criticise something she did – for example, that there was too much salt in the dinner – her pattern was to reply in a sarcastic voice: "Go on, say it, I'm such a dreadful cook".

She realised that she had projected this horrible, nasty, inner voice onto her partner and that his usually mild criticisms were magnified a hundred times by its viciousness. In reaching this awareness, the woman had taken the first step. Step one – she had disentangled the voice within her from the voice of her partner. She had drawn back the projection. Step two was to imagine what her feeling looked like, the feeling she experienced when she was being criticised. She was shocked to discover the image of a young girl, perhaps three or four years old, badly physically beaten. Through active imagination she took the little girl in her arms and held her tightly. The young girl was the aspect of herself that felt beaten and battered by this vicious, negative and critical voice.

This led to step three. Fueled with anger on behalf of her inner child who was battered by these criticisms, she faced the negative voice, asking where it came from and what had made it so cruel. The voice admitted that it was cruel but explained that it was so because it was starving. It represented a starving aspect of the woman's psyche. The only way it had of drawing attention to itself in order to be fed was to be cruel and relentlessly critical. It went on to explain that it was an inheritance from the woman's mother's line. The voice was a collective animus voice from a line of women who were *all cut off from the feminine source* in the psyche. These were women who had pandered to the masculine. The voice said that it was starved of a connection with the soil of the feminine. It urged the woman to connect with the feminine within herself and to let her ego-identity flow from within.

Every time the woman looked to her partner for approval, the voice said it was starved a little more. Every time she looked outside herself, to institutions, to fashions, to other people to define herself, it was starved a little more. Every time her work in the world was defined by masculine principles, it was starved. It urged the woman not only to connect to the feminine source within herself, but also to let her work in the world flow from that source, gestate in that place and organically appear in the world. That would be this voice's food – work in the world that was sourced in the deep feminine within. Only then could it let the negative criticisms go and be a voice of power for the woman.

Development of the Animus Beyond the Father Stage and Mother Stage

A healthy forecast of animus development would move from the father image on to less dominating images. This could be, for example, a brother-type image, or a buddy or a pal image. Women often develop their masculine qualities through friendships with men.

This precedes the intrusion of the hero. The hero is someone who is strong enough to draw the woman away from the father-world or the mother-world. Often women at this stage of animus development are attracted to men who are radically different to their fathers. This helps them to break that bond and to explore a different type of masculine energy. The hero displaces the powerful father and the woman begins to experience an inner steadiness. She begins to think differently, experimenting with new ideas. The hero is still a patriarchal figure but he is not the patriarch.

What is inner is also outer. As the woman relates to the hero in her outer life she is also beginning to experience these qualities within. The hero in outer life is often accompanied with strong romantic and sexual energy. This is necessary to displace the powerful hold the father has on the woman's psyche. Deldon Anne McNeely in *Animus Aeternus* says that:

> The heroic attitude seems to be actualised in several ways: one is an awareness of one's philosophical mind and the capacity to think for oneself, attended by a feeling of righteousness and authority. This indicates the beginning of the introjection of the patriarch which was previously projected. The second heroic attitude involves the recognition and acceptance of one's sexuality. A later development of the heroic attitude is the recognition and acceptance of one's yin-ego, which values being as well as doing. The female is coming to know her own mind, her own body and her own feminine attitudes.[40]

---

40 Deldon Anne McNeely. (1991). *Animus Aeternus*. Inner City Books, Toronto, Canada. Page 139.

This stage is, in the ideal world, seen in women during adolescence. It is my experience, however, that women can experience these stages at any time. Also psychological growth does not seem to be linear. It is more like a spiral where we go through stages and then seem to be repeating them. All the situations are different, yet the pattern is alarmingly similar. Deldon Anne McNeely says "Nothing in the psyche is thoroughly outgrown or killed off – but comes in and out of focus".[41] It has also been my experience that we can project father and brother and hero and eventually equal partner all onto the one person over a period of time.

Jung claims that we can only know the unconscious contents by projecting them out and then taking them back inside and claiming them as our own. It is possible that one person can carry all this for us, if we are on the path of psychological health and are constantly working to claim our inner contents for ourselves, and if the other person is on a similar journey. It is also possible to project the material onto many men and to move from one relationship to another as the material becomes integrated.

The final stage of development of the animus is the equal partner. The hero, although not paternal in nature, is still part of the patriarchal framework. He saves us, we are indebted to him. The relationship is not equal. When a woman comes to the point of the equal partner she has ceased to look outside herself for what she needs. She is not dependent on a man or anything outside of herself for her existence or for sustenance or for rescue. She knows that she has it all within. She begins to experience calm and courage inside. In her relationship with a man in the outer world, she is interested in who he is as 'other' as opposed to what he can do for her. Because she is self-contained, and confident of what she has, she can claim her own mind, her own ideas

---

41 ibid., page 147.

and she can trust her own instincts.

When we speak of the development of the animus, we are talking about stories of female individuation. In fairytales related to female individuation, there is always a period of withdrawal, of ego-surrender and introversion, when "the woman learns to care for and love herself by discovering the deepest core of her feminine being".[42] This is where development of the animus takes us – to the deepest core of our feminine being. The role of the animus is to help the woman in this descent to the feminine core and to bring back the treasures therein to the conscious realm.

When the animus has reached this stage the woman can begin to experience the Self, in Jungian terms. The Self is the Divine Centre within. One does not inhabit the Self, rather one finds a way of accessing it and bringing its wisdom to consciousness. The mature, equal animus is the key to being able to do this. It is the torch bearer *par excellance* when it can walk the way to the Self and back.

These stages of animus development correspond roughly with the stages of psychological growth proposed by Neumann, which I described earlier. They are mere descriptions of patterns of growth. They are neither time bound nor linear. As I say, psychological growth, both my own and what I have observed in others, seems to be more like a spiral. One does not, it seems, go through one stage neatly, tidy up and then move on to the next. However, I find the descriptions of these stages helpful in attempting to track women's experience of the inner masculine.

---

42 ibid., page 155.

The Animus Problem

According to Emma Jung in her book *Animus and Anima*[43] the two myths, The Fall of Man and The Fire stolen by Prometheus deal with the reality of the increase of consciousness in humankind. Any psychic energy in the psyche, which is over and above what is needed for mere survival, leads into new paths. It is this overflow of psychic energy that distinguishes us from the animal world. But having it is fraught with difficulties and acting on it may have the effect of being considered a sin, a misdeed. Consciousness or Logos is what distinguishes human from nature. Because of it the human is driven from the garden of paradise, from being a natural child. However, neither is the human a god, for he or she is still tied to the physical body (as Prometheus was tied to the rock). It is this painful tension between nature and spirit which is at the heart of the animus problem. The harmonisation of the two is the major work to be done.

Where do women experience the spirit principle?[44] A girl-child tends to project the spirit principle outwards. She therefore experiences it in her father or other males in her world. If she continues to project it outwards, as a grown woman, she remains unconscious. She can project it onto her partner. Then there exists "a kind of compulsive tie to the man in question and a dependence on him that often increases to the point of becoming unbearable".[45] Her man is "expected to take over all the functions that have remained undeveloped in the woman in question, whether the thinking function, or the power to act, or

---

43 Emma Jung. (1985) *Animus and Anima*. Spring Publications, Dallas, Texas.

44 Here Emma Jung uses spiritual principle rather than spirit principle, but I find this unhelpful. I believe that the feminine principle is spiritual also. I do not go along with the split between nature and spirituality. Therefore, I use words like masculine and logos and spirit but not spiritual. The first three denote an aspect of the psyche but spiritual is a descriptive judgement which, when set against nature, implies that nature is not spiritual.

45 Emma Jung. (1985) *Animus and Anima*. Spring Publications, Dallas, Texas. Page 10.

responsibility towards the outside world".[46] Carl Jung believed in an inner drive towards wholeness and it is this that usually disturbs such projections. That and the fact that the partner is not the inner archetype, but only a hook that the projected archetype hangs on.

The inner drive towards wholeness sees to it that in time the discrepancy between the man and the archetype becomes apparent. By the time this happens, "a woman is already in the midst of the conflict, and there remains nothing for her to do but to carry through to completion the process of discriminating between the image within and the man outside".[47] It is clear therefore that the first thing a woman must do with this animus issue is to distinguish her inner masculine component from the man or men in her life.[48] A woman may also project her inner masculine onto institutions; onto a work institution, onto the church and so forth. These projections must also be drawn back. "It seems to me that to relate to this component, to know it, and to incorporate it into the rest of the personality, are central elements of this problem..."[49]

If the first step in dealing with the animus problem is to take back our projected animus from the outside, then the second is to try to separate the animus within from ourselves, that is, from our ego-identity. This is because of a phenomenon called possession by the animus. Animus possession happens when the feminine ego-identity is overrun by the masculine. It is indeed ironic that women who are animus-driven have not actually dealt with the animus problem at all. Possession by the animus happens because the woman has not

---

46 ibid.
47 ibid., page 12
48 Once again, here Emma Jung uses the term 'inner masculine-intellectual component'. I don't accept that the masculine has the monopoly on intellectual since I think this relates to the thinking function which a dominant thinking type woman has full and easy access to.
49 *Animus and Anima.* Emma Jung. (Spring Publications. 1985). Page 12.

given the masculine aspect of her own psyche enough attention. It has either not been applied or has been applied in an inappropriate way. The feminine ego-identity has been over-run in animus possession because, on the one hand, the masculine energies have not received the proper attention and are therefore dominant and negative. On the other hand, the masculine principle is dominant and the feminine principle has been left out in the cold. "What is really necessary is that … the logos in the woman should be so fitted into the nature and life of the woman that a harmonious cooperation between the feminine and masculine factors ensues and no part is condemned to a shadowy existence".[50]

Animus possession is not a pretty sight. The woman can suffer from feeling pressured and burnt out. She can be assailed by depression and dissatisfaction and a loss of meaning in life. She can lose interest and yet be forced, because of her driven career or lifestyle, to carry on. The animus can also step in to disturb the woman's relationships with the people in her life. She can be brutish and bullying, ruthless and sometimes cruel. This is because the animus in these instances is not connected with the feminine. It is basically not connected at all. When the animus does not receive the appropriate attention, it begins to interfere in the outer world. This is not its role. Its true role is as a mediator between the inner unconscious realm of the woman's psyche and her ego-consciousness. This role does not extend to the outer world, even though it has a profound effect on the woman's relationship to the outer world.

Yet the task of distinguishing the animus from ego-consciousness is an extremely difficult one. This is mainly because it appears in one's mind as an opinion or a voice. It also brings with it a peculiar authority and aggressiveness. Emma Jung claims that it gains this authority

---

50 ibid., page 13.

from its connection with the universal mind. The negative animus (by this I mean the animus that has not received the appropriate attention and is not functioning properly) can be recognised by its judgmental statements that appear irrefutable and yet are irrelevant. Emma Jung writes:

> As far as I have observed, this voice expresses itself chiefly in two ways. First, we hear from it a critical, usually negative comment on every movement, an exact examination of all motives and intentions which naturally always causes feelings of inferiority, and tends to nip in the bud all initiative and every wish for self-expression. From time to time, this voice may also dispense exaggerated praise, and the result of these extremes of judgement is that one oscillates to and fro between the consciousness of complete futility and a blown-up sense of one's own value and importance. The animus' second way of speaking is confined more or less exclusively to issuing commands or prohibitions, and to pronouncing generally accepted viewpoints. [51]

There are two aspects to animus functioning. The first is discriminating, judging and understanding. The second is abstracting and setting up general laws. The first appears as a single person, the second is a plurality, a kind of council. Emma Jung points out that the animus can cause huge damage in relationships or situations when it inserts itself in the place of genuine human feeling. It has often been observed that the way for a woman to release the power of animus possession over herself is to tap into genuine feeling. Real tears or laughter dissolve its power and the woman can come back to herself. We have all perhaps experienced ourselves or other women pronounce some

---

51 ibid., page 20.

clever opinion, which is factually accurate, yet seems to wreak havoc because it is devoid of any relevance to the actual situation. It is not connected. This is the trademark of the negative animus.

Emma Jung suggests that women make these irrelevant comments, over and against any feminine sense of appropriateness or instinct, because there is a generally held belief (albeit unconscious) that the masculine is somehow superior to the feminine. They/we sell out our feminine ego-identity, which ideally is connected to a deep feminine source, because the masculine has for so long been considered superior. And so that masculine within is allowed to step in in places where our instinct, if heeded, would keep it for the appropriate time. Its rightful place is as consort to the feminine, interfacing the unconscious with the conscious ego. It is not meant to be an interfering and domineering presence in the woman's outer life.

Resolving the 'Animus Problem' is the way to resolving the problem of how one is to be a woman in the world. The first task, as seen earlier, is to detach the animus from figures in the outer world, to withdraw the projections and claim the energy for oneself. The second task is to distinguish the animus voices from our own voice, to avoid animus possession of the ego-identity.

The third task is to personalise the animus energy and to use this personalised and therefore higher animus to connect with the true inner self, the deep inner core. Personalising the animus energy involves a growth in consciousness. When the animus energy is not personalised, not made conscious, it is raw archetypal energy that invades one's life and drives one, without one even being aware of it. When the animus energy is personalised, it creates the bridge between the deep inner core, that is the Self, in a woman and the conscious ego-identity. It has reached its highest place. It is the King in dream images, a higher principle that brings about real transformation as opposed to the Magician, who is concerned with magic and power and illusion. Personalising the animus is the same as individuating the archetype. It involves taking the archetypal energy and, by becoming conscious of it, using its creative power.

The fourth task is to nurture this personalised animus energy, by channeling the excess psychic energy it provides out into the world in a creative and connected way. A woman friend of mine reflected once that a powerful reason for doing all the inner healing work over years is to enable oneself to be truly creative in the world. It is a profound insight. Our various dysfunctions or negative complexes use up a lot of psychic energy. When these complexes come into a better balance then psychic energy is freed up. This psychic energy can be channeled by the animus into our unique creativity in the world. Irene Claremont de Castillejo writes:

> To me it seems that the power to focus is the essential quality which makes man the creative creature that he is. Sparkling ideas or images of incredible loveliness may float through the mind of almost anyone; float through and out again, unused, unavailing and unhoused. But he who has the ability to focus, see and hold the idea as it emerges, can create something with it. He can build a temple or a philosophy. He can build an atom bomb.[52]

Channeling this excess psychic energy into the world creatively may involve one of two entirely different approaches. For some women it will require that they step out of doing for other people and that they begin to tune into their own unique creative centre. They will begin

---

52 Irene Claremont de Castillejo. (1973). *Knowing Woman*. Harper and Row, N.Y. Page 76. "Man" here refers to humans in general.

a project of their own in the world that is not necessarily primarily oriented toward others. In order to do this they will have to organise their lives in such a way that allows for it. If married with children, it may be that they will have to share out and delegate responsibilities that they have until now taken solely onto themselves. If single, they might have to battle the voices within that say their idea is useless, that they don't have time for such nonsense. Basically, these women will have to assert themselves in the world with the gifts they can bring to it.

The second type are women who have already established themselves in the world with careers. Oftentimes, these are the type who are more likely to suffer from burnout. This will be so if their work in the world does not spring from a deep feminine source. Their work is animus driven. Women in this situation need to make a connection with the inner feminine source. They must use their animus energy to do this. They have to take their animus energy away from their career and focus it on their inner needs, on what nourishes their soul. They need to track their dreams and their feelings. They need to reconnect with their instincts.

Unfortunately for such women, it often takes a breakdown of some kind to actually stop them doing what they are doing. It is not that their careers are necessarily wrong in themselves. After a break, it is often possible for them to return to their work with success. However, what often needs to be looked at is what it is that has them doing that work. If a woman can connect inside to her deep feminine source then her desire to do that work could well remain. The benefit is that she can do that work while still nourishing herself from her source. Her desire to do the work comes from within, from a life-giving place, rather than from a power driven place. The animus, when functioning correctly, provides drive, meaning, innovation and enthusiasm to a woman for her being in the world. If it is not functioning correctly, it will drive the woman into the ground. She will be doing work in the world while accessing no connection to her soul needs or sources of soul nourishment.

Emma Jung comments that when the animus problem became acute for women she observed that there was an increased interest in other women and their relationships with them. I believe this is so particularly with women who have been father-bound and are moving out of that bondage towards a connection with their inner feminine core. The inner reflects the outer and vice versa, so it follows that a woman will look at other women with new eyes. They cease to be competition or threat and become sister-women.

The animus archetype spans from Devil to God. It can be a destructive presence in the psyche wounding a woman with negative destructive voices. It can be a torch-bearer and tool for creative endeavours in the world. The true work of the animus is to keep a woman clear of being possessed or overwhelmed by complexes. Yet for it to do this, a woman must accomplish the four tasks outlined earlier.

It is consoling to see that the negative animus energy can be turned around with courage and determination. Just as in the fairytale 'Beauty and the Beast' when the ugly and repulsive beast was faced and loved he transformed into the Handsome Prince. Note how it was the father in the story who landed Beauty into this mess. However, in time she grew to love the Beast. This too is our challenge. To befriend the beast and discover the inner prince.

Animus as the Archetype of Meaning

So far I have dealt with the animus within the psyche of women. As
I have explained earlier, it was Jung's understanding that the animus
was peculiar to women and did not appear in the psyche of men.
The animus was the contra-sexual aspect of the woman's psyche.
It contrasted the gender of the person. Just as a woman has a small
number of male genes in her physical body, so too, psychologically,
she has the animus as the compensatory, albeit inferior, male aspect
of her psyche.

Jung also believed that the entire collective unconscious of a woman
presented itself in masculine form. I have disputed this earlier. The
collective unconscious is far too vast to make it possible to say that
it presents itself only in masculine form to a woman. Far better to
say that the animus is one archetype of the collective unconscious.
Certainly it has a very specific role to play in the psyche of a woman.
However, it can be argued that it also has a role, a different role, to
play in the male psyche.

As an archetype the animus cannot be limited to one gender. It is
accessible to both genders. If the animus can be understood as the
archetype of meaning, then it is senseless to say that only women
have access to it or that men, because they are men, have lives that
are automatically imbued with meaning. Just as the animus must
not be confused with any specific function – thinking and sensation
being the most likely ones – neither can it be exclusive to any specific
gender. It is not even accurate to say that the animus is masculine.
The archetypes are trans-gender, beyond gender. What can be said is
that, although the animus is not masculine, it does however always
manifest as masculine when it takes a human or animal shape.

I suggest that the animus does appear in the male psyche. This throws a different light on the old rule that when a male dreams of a man, that man generally represents his shadow. The man in the dream does represent shadow in so far as it is unconscious and therefore belonging to the shadow realm. However, the occurrence does not automatically indicate shadow in the sense of something inferior and underdeveloped. It could indicate animus, as in the archetype of meaning. If one interprets a man in a male's dream as an archetype of meaning then one looks at the message very differently. A good example of this would be the appearance of the the Wise Old Man archetype in a man's dream.

If we have the archetypes of both meaning (animus) and life (anima) available to us then we can choose between them at any given moment. Women are not destined to be full of the life archetype (anima) with an inferior grasp on meaning (animus). Neither are men destined to be driven with meaning and at a loss when it comes to life as an archetype.

When a male dreams of a man, that dream figure can be carrying a very important element from the unconscious to do with the archetype of meaning. If this is the case, it needs to be looked at as such. Similarly, when a woman dreams of a woman, the dream figure may be anima as much as shadow and as such it would carry the archetype of life. When we acknowledge that both archetypes are available to both genders, then we are free to choose how that archetype plays out in our life. It can be said that, to date, it has been believed that the archetypes do not appear to both genders equally. It is my view that this is because of social and cultural conditioning and a general bias in our understanding of these matters. This is an understanding which says that meaning and women do not go so well together and that life and men also don't fit naturally.

Viktor Frankl wrote an extraordinary book called *Man's Search for Meaning*.[53] In it he looked at the fact that people in concentration camps in Hitler's regime woke up each day in the most awful of circumstances and continued to live meaningfully. He asked what that meaning was. When humanity sinks so low, as it did in that time, where could meaning be found? He himself was an inmate of a camp. He realised that what kept him going was the fantasy that when he was freed, he would lecture to people about the experience and what he had learned from it. He realised that each person had a different spar to cling to and this spar gave meaning to their abysmal life circumstances. It is my view that this spar is provided by the archetype of meaning, the animus. It is available to both men and women. In the concentration camp situation, we see people, men and women, living with meaning where one would imagine none could be found. The archetype is there for us in whatever situation we find ourselves.

The animus gives us access to the deep unconscious where great riches dwell, where dreams are gestated, and where the material is found by which humanity can soar. Once a vision is lit up by the animus and acknowledged, then discipline is needed to make that vision a reality in the world. What keeps us going is the element of meaning that has been translated into the simple things in our lives. It is to be found in the project that excites us. It can be in our daily work or our hobby. It can be in a dream for the future or in an interpretation of things in the here and now. It is the presence of the archetype that makes a situation meaningful to us. This is the animus, the archetype of meaning.

The animus plays a powerful role by allowing people to access unconscious contents and to find meaning in the world. Much that is good has been done with this archetype. However, the animus can also

---

53 Viktor Frankl (First Published 1946) *Man's Search for Meaning*. Beacon Press. Boston, M.A., U.S.A. (2006)

be used to give meaning to activities that are distasteful, inhuman or corrupt. It was the animus, the archetype of meaning, which allowed Hitler to delve into the collective unconscious and find therein the symbols that enabled him to lead a nation to commit the most awful atrocities. Just as there is an endless list of wonderfully meaningful human achievements, so equally is there, unfortunately, an endless list of appalling atrocities that were carried out in the name of something that gave meaning to those who performed them. The animus is amoral. Ethics and morality are not present in the archetypes. They access the depths for us, and what we find there, we can do with what we will.

In trying to understand the animus as the archetype of meaning, it is helpful to observe what happens when it is missing. What is most noticeable about this lack is that one can still function, and will often function quite well, without it. This is in sharp contrast with the anima, which I will look at in more detail in the next chapter.

The anima is the archetype of life. When it is missing one cannot function. It feels as if the plug has been pulled and one simply cannot go on. One experiences depression, lethargy, lifelessness. Not so without the animus. Without the archetype of meaning, the colour has drained away from living, yet one can still carry on. Things have lost their meaning, but one continues to do them automatically. One merely gets by.

When one looks at modern Western society, and the lives that many people live, it is evident that there is a ferocious lack of animus, of meaning, of spirit. Many people have settled for jobs that do not inspire them. They have compromised themselves in their daily employment in order to acquire material things or to have the money to do what they want in their free time. The trend is for their work to become more stress-filled and their free time reduced through longer commuting. So they end up burnt out and exhausted.

It is animus that offers the meaning associated with 'free time' or 'possessions'. These things are meaningful to people today, and it is what most people seem to focus on. But the span of meaning is vastly wider than this. It has also got much greater depth. When we look to anima as an archetype we will see that it is the bringer of soul to our lives. What the animus brings is spirit. How many of us live spirited lives? How many of us are excited by what we are doing every day? Many of us are spending most of our time doing things we do not want to do in order to have a mean-spirited pay-off. The span of meaning is vast, endless. Where do we, each one of us, pitch our meaning? What value do we, each one of us, get from the archetype of meaning, the animus in our psyche?

There is a phenomenon that one might simply call loss of spirit. It is found in situations where we have pitched too low our demands on animus. Where we live lives that are mundane in the extreme, we experience a corresponding meanness of spirit, a colourlessness. A more dramatic version of the same thing occurs where something happens in a person's life that is so shocking, or so traumatic, that one's spirit leaves them. You may know of many stories of people who experienced traumatic events and were left spiritless. When my young daughter fell against a table and severely damaged her front teeth and gum, I was so shocked by the event that for three days I felt that my spirit had left me. For those days I merely functioned and the colour was missing.

The relationship between the animus and the anima is clearly described in the story, told by Clarissa Pinkola Estés, of the old man who, at the dead of night, staggers to the door of the wise old woman and sits in her lap while she rocks him all night. The woman rocks him on and on and, come predawn, he has become younger and younger until just before sunrise he leaps out of her lap and jumps into the sky, the golden boy. He becomes the sun to shine another day.[54] There is a natural rhythm if we would only heed it. When the animus has done its work it is time to turn to the anima, to the life source. It is time to stop, to rock, to simply be. In time the animus will come back to itself. It will leap out of the lap of the anima and shine on for another while. These two archetypes, the animus and the anima, the archetypes of meaning and of life, belong with each other. They are a syzygy, a pair. Where one is, the other is not far away. Ideally, they work together.

The animus is the counter-sexual aspect in a woman's psyche. It is a function in the psyche. It is a tool – the light-bearer in the darkness of the deep unconscious. It is an archetype. It is the archetype of meaning. We cannot access the depths of the unconscious consciously without the animus. We cannot live meaningfully without animus. Jung wrote: "Since we are human we have all functions, and each function has its specific energy which should be applied or it will apply itself".[55] The animus will play a role in our lives whether we are aware of it or not. It may extravert itself and inhabit places in our lives and behaviour where it has no positive role to play. Better for us to befriend it and allow it to do the best it can for us. That is, to interface our conscious ego with the deep unconscious. In playing this role in our psyche the animus can ultimately lead us to glimpse the divine centre within, the Self. This, ideally, is its most glorious purpose.

---

54 Clarissa Pinkola Estés. (1992) *Women Who Run with the Wolves*. Rider, London. This is the story of *The Three Gold Hairs* told on page 328.
55 C.G. Jung. (1984) *Dream Analysis*. Routledge and Kegan Paul, London. Page 11.

CHAPTER NINE

Anima

Giving Back Soul to the World

From Clifden Onwards

Landscape that lies
like a lazy woman
sprawling shamelessly,
unselfconsciously.
Caressed occasionally into ecstasy
by a vivid, vibrant
sunshine.
Blue ocean stretching
out from her thighs
to be lost in the
hazy distance.

With her cunning play of illusions the soul lures into life the inertness of matter that does not want to live... She makes us believe incredible things, that life may be lived. She is full of snares and traps, in order that man should fall, should reach the earth, entangle himself there, and stay caught, so that life should be lived.

Jung, C.W. Vol. 9(i) par 56

There is so much information on anima, as Jung has written profusely on it. The canvas is vast and vague and ungraspable. And this, in fact, is the very nature of anima. She is that wisp of cloud, so definite and beautiful until you try to grasp it and it disappears from your sight altogether, taking another shape or form. Jung confirms this when he says:

I have noticed that people usually have not much difficulty in picturing to themselves what is meant by shadow […] But it costs them enormous difficulties to understand what the anima is. They accept her easily enough when she appears in novels or as a film star, but she is not understood at all when it comes to seeing the role she plays in their own lives, because she sums up everything that a man can never get the better of and never finishes coping with. Therefore it remains in a perpetual state of emotionality which must not be touched. The degree of unconsciousness one meets with in this connection is, to put it mildly, astounding.[1]

In this chapter I want to explore firstly how Jung saw anima. Once that is done, however, I want to move beyond this to describe how anima is even more than what Jung described.

---

1   *C.W.* Vol. 9i, par 485.

How Anima is Traditionally Seen in Jungian Thought

"The anima is presumably a psychic representation of the minority of female genes in a man's body".[2] This is one of the ways that Jung defined anima. She is the contrasexual side of man. The woman in every man's psyche. The so-called inferior female. Jung also spoke of anima being the compensatory and complementary aspect of the male psyche. The persona is the man's interface with the outer world, the anima is his interface with the inner world or the collective unconscious. "I have defined the anima as a personification of the unconscious in general and have taken it as a bridge to the unconscious, in other words, as a function of relationship to the unconscious".[3]

This is an important image. When we remember the structure of the psyche described earlier, we have the ego, which is the centre of the conscious psyche. The persona is the aspect of the ego that interfaces with the outer world. It is the mask we put on and (hopefully) off as we interact with people in our lives. We each have many masks or personae, as different aspects of ourselves are required in different situations and it is not wise to get caught in one persona. Behind the ego, like the part of an iceberg that is submerged below water, is the unconscious, both the personal unconscious and the collective unconscious.

Let us speak here specifically about men – in suggesting that the anima is a man's interface with the inner world or collective unconscious, it would seem that the anima plays a similar role for a man as the animus does for a woman. The animus interfaces the woman's ego with the collective unconscious. The animus is the lightbearer who shines a light on the unconscious. It is important to note that the anima, although she plays a similar role of interfacing the unconscious for a

2 *C.W.* Vol. 11, par 48.
3 *C.W.* Vol. 13, par 62. The anima personifies the total unconscious only so long as the anima remains undifferentiated from other archetypes.

man, is far from being a lightbearer. Rather she brings the unconscious to the man, in the shape of a mood or an affect, or sometimes as symptomatic complaints, obsessive fantasies or dreams. She brings the unconscious to a man but not in an illuminating way, rather in a hazy, dim, dusky way. Although she is for a man an interface with the unconscious, she is very different to the animus.

To continue with the structure of the psyche, the ego is the centre of the conscious psyche but the Self is the centre of both the unconscious and the conscious psyche. The animus and anima, as interfaces or messengers back and forth between the worlds, are extremely important players in our psyche. They can connect us to that sacred centre, the Self. This indeed, ultimately, is their role. Jung refers to this in the opening quote in the chapter. The anima entraps and entangles a person so that they are forced to live life. It is in that living of life that one finds oneself delving into the depths towards the Self.

When a man becomes overly identified with his outer role in the world, with his persona, a strange thing happens. He becomes locked into an unconscious identification with the anima.Jung says that when this happens there is trouble to come: "Anyone who is himself his outward role will infallibly succumb to the inner processes; he will either frustrate his outward role by absolute inner necessity or else reduce it to absurdity, by a process of enantiodromia".[4] Enantiodromia is the phenomenon where everything that goes to one extreme will in time swing back to the opposite extreme. Jung goes on to say that the anima or soul-image that a man becomes identified with can be projected out into the world; "…onto definite persons with the corresponding qualities".[5] If it is not projected outwards then a person becomes preoccupied with the inner processes; one falls into narcissism. When

---

4   *C.W.* Vol. 6, par 807.
5   ibid., par 808.

this happens a person becomes more and more overwhelmed by the unconscious.

Ironic though it may seem, it is by projecting this psychic material outwards that one can get on with developing one's persona. It is only when the projection collapses, that is when the carrier of the projection dares to behave independently and therefore differently, that the person making the projection has to assimilate its contents. Often, even then, the contents simply get projected onto someone else. This whole phenomenon is seen in men (again I speak specifically of men) who become identified with who they are in the world, with their work; in other words, with their persona. Enantiodromia is a natural phenomenon in the world and it is inevitable. Therefore a man cannot maintain this over-identification with his role. What happens in these cases is that his inner processes go into overdrive. The anima, because she is being ignored, will manifest in the world of the man and will lure him to catch his attention. If the over-identification is severe the anima and her lure will be all consuming and dramatic. The man is thrown into chaos because everything he has worked for is now threatened by this new all consuming passion. The new passion, generally for a new woman in his life, is as fervent as was his over-identification. And because of this he cannot see the wood for the trees. If the man is young then he will perhaps have found his wife-to-be. If he is already married then his wife, his family, his work, all seem to pale into insignificance when compared to this new love in his life.

It may take a man years to dissolve the projection of anima from this woman. While the woman holds it for him he can go on living, functioning normally. His persona interfaces with the world and his inner processes, that is, his anima, have an outlet through the projection onto a woman in his life. Basically, libido, or psychic energy, is flowing. It is not being blocked or left swirling around inside, it is flowing out into the world.

Jung speaks of the danger when the anima is not projected. He writes:

> As long as an archetype is not projected, and not loved or hated in an object, it is still wholly identical with the individual, who is thus compelled to act it out himself. We have a word that aptly characterises this attitude; it is 'animosity'. This expression can best be interpreted as 'anima possession', denoting a condition of uncontrolled emotion. The word 'animosity' is used for unpleasant emotions, but actually the anima can induce pleasant ones as well.[6]

However, even though the anima is projected and all seems well (and, please note, all the fairy tales end just there – the prince and princess live happily ever after etc. etc.), that supposed moment of "happily ever after" is often the beginning of the unraveling of the projections, albeit not before the honeymoon is over. Now begins the challenge to recognise that the contents projected actually belong to oneself and that they are a call from the unconscious to explore the unconscious and to assimilate aspects of it into consciousness. Not many people seem to answer this call. Most of us, when the projections collapse and we realise that the other person is not in fact whom we thought he or she was, simply find someone else to carry our unconscious contents. We move right along. Jung says:

> The repression of feminine traits and inclinations naturally causes these contrasexual demands to accumulate in the unconscious. No less naturally, the imago of woman (the soul image) becomes a receptacle

---

6   *C.W.* Vol. 10, par 78.

for those demands, which is why a man, in his love-choice, is strongly tempted to win the woman who best corresponds to his own unconscious femininity – a woman, in short, who can unhesitatingly receive the projection of his soul. Although such a choice is often regarded and felt as altogether ideal, it may turn out that the man has manifestly married his own worst weakness.[7]

Two things are clear in relation to the anima. It is not something that can be intellectually grasped and assimilated in the abstract. It must be lived.

It is no use at all to learn a list of archetypes by heart. Archetypes are complexes of experience that come upon us like fate, and their effects are felt in our most personal life. The anima no longer crosses our path as a goddess, but it may be, as an intimately personal misadventure, or perhaps as our best venture. When, for instance, a highly esteemed professor in his seventies abandons his family and runs off with a young red-headed actress, we know that the gods have claimed another victim. This is how daemonic power reveals itself to us.[8]

The second thing is this, once the anima has you and you are in the throes of the passion she stirs, it is a very difficult thing to reason your way back to 'normality' and hold together life as you once knew it.

Jung however makes an interesting point in relation to the anima and the age of a person. He claims that younger people can experience even the total loss of the anima without a problem. This is because a person's younger life is about establishing oneself in the world and in a man's case this means being a man and disconnecting himself from the anima fascination with the mother. However, at midlife, around the age of thirty-five, "permanent loss of the anima means a diminution of vitality, of flexibility, and of human kindness. The result, as a rule, is premature rigidity, crustiness, stereotyping, fanatical one-sidedness, irresponsibility, and finally a childish 'ramollissement' with a tendency to alcohol".[9] One cannot lose the anima as it is an aspect of the psyche. However, one can lose touch with it or one can lose access to it.

Sources for Anima in a Man

Jung cites the three sources for a man's anima. Firstly there is the influence of women on him in his life, starting presumably with the mother or first primary carer. "The anima can be defined as the image or archetype or deposit of all the experiences of a man with woman".[10] Secondly the man's own inner femininity, that is, his own personal countrasexual personality. And thirdly a man's anima is formed from an inherited collective image of woman, that is, an archetype of woman. This third is a synthesis of what woman has been from the beginning of time.

Origin of the Word Anima

Jung chose the word anima to denote the counter-sexual aspect of a man's psyche, yet he meant the word anima to be distinct from soul as understood in a classical European philosophical sense. It is also distinct from soul in the Christian sense of immortality. Jung means the word anima to be understood in the classical Chinese philosophical sense "where the anima (p'o or kuri) is regarded as the feminine and

---

9 ibid., par 147.
10 *C.W.* Vol. 13, par 58.

chthonic part of the soul".[11] The primitives considered soul as the magic breath of life, as a flame. This is also what Jung meant when he used the word. Anima is also distinct from psyche. The anima is one archetype of the psyche.

It is important to try to distinguish these three entities from each other: Anima, Soul and Psyche. Even Jung himself interchanges them sometimes: "By psyche I understand the totality of all psychic processes, conscious as well as unconscious. By soul, on the other hand, I understand a clearly demarcated functional complex that can best be described as a 'personality'".[12] Jung uses soul here when, in fact, he means anima. When asked to define anima, Jung called it "a semiconscious psychic complex, having partial autonomy of function'."[13]

Marie-Louise von Franz on the Anima

In relation to the process of individuation, the anima is the second symbolic figure that appears behind the shadow. The shadow is the first. Marie-Louise von Franz speaks specifically of men and writes that: "The anima is the personification of all feminine psychological tendencies in a man's psyche, such as vague feelings and moods, prophetic hunches, perceptiveness to the irrational, capacity for personal love, feeling for nature, and – last but not least – his relation to the unconscious".[14] We could get into a discussion here on what the 'feminine' actually is, however, for the sake of moving along, von Franz's statement can be understood to mean that which is generally considered feminine. She goes on to describe how, in Eskimo and other Arctic tribes, the medicine man clearly demonstrates how the

---

11 *C.W.* Vol. 9i, par 119.
12 *C.W.* Vol. 6, par 797.
13 *C.W.* Vol. 9i, par 64.
14 Conceived and Edited by Carl Jung. (1978) *Man and his Symbols*. Pan Books Ltd., London. Page 186. This is in part three of the book, written by Marie-Louise von Franz and entitled *'The Process of Individuation'*.

anima "is experienced as an inner figure in a man's psyche. ... Some of these even wear women's clothes or have breasts depicted on their garments, in order to manifest their inner feminine side – the side that enables them to connect with the 'ghost land' (i.e. what we call the unconscious)".[15]

We have already said that one of the sources for the anima in a man is his mother, or primary carer. Marie-Louise von Franz writes that if a man feels that his mother has had a negative influence on him, his anima:

> ...will often express itself in irritable depressed moods, uncertainty, insecurity, and touchiness. [...] Within the soul of such a man the negative mother – anima figure will endlessly repeat this theme: 'I am nothing. Nothing makes any sense. With others it's different, but for me ... I enjoy nothing". These 'anima moods' cause a sort of dullness, a fear of disease, of impotence, or of accidents. The whole of life takes on a sad and oppressive aspect.[16]

In this aspect the anima is the *femme fatale* who lures a man to his death. This negative anima lures a man away from reality into fantasies that can never be fulfilled. The harsh contrast between dull and oppressive reality and rich fantasies that will never be achieved can drive a man to suicide.

The negative anima can also manifest in a man's personality by "waspish, poisonous, effeminate remarks by which he devalues everything. Remarks of this sort always contain a cheap twisting of the truth and are in a subtle way destructive".[17] Ironically, von Franz

---

15 ibid., page 186.
16 ibid.
17 ibid., page 190.

writes that, even if the experience of the mother has been positive, a negative anima can still be produced. A man can be effeminate or his experience of his mother can have the effect that women prey upon him so that he expects to be pampered and in fact cannot cope with the cut and thrust of life. A more subtle negative anima engages a man in an intellectual game which cuts a man off from life and from his real feelings and from real life decisions. "He reflects about life so much that he cannot live it and loses all his spontaneity and outgoing feeling".[18] The necessity of living life as opposed to getting sucked into fantasy is very real. Von Franz comments that a frequent way for the anima to make herself known is through erotic fantasy. She writes: "Men may be driven to nurse their fantasies by looking at films and strip-tease shows, or by day-dreaming over pornographic material. This is a crude, primitive aspect of the anima, which becomes compulsive only when a man does not sufficiently cultivate his feeling relationships – when his feeling attitude towards life has remained infantile".[19]

It is interesting that in Jung's words, at the very beginning of the chapter, anima leads one towards life yet here we see the negative anima drawing a man away from life, sometimes towards death itself. How is this to be understood? In one of the Celtic tales, Cú Chulainn sees three swans flying by as he is walking by a lake. He takes up his bow and shoots at them. One falls. When he runs to the spot where the bird has fallen he sees a beautiful woman. He falls in love with her. She is Fand of the Otherworld. Cú Chulainn agrees to go with her into the Otherworld. When his companions find him beside the lake, there is but a shadow of a man left behind. Cú Chulainn is diffused and lethargic. They take him home to Emer his wife and she consults a druid. The druid recognises that Cú Chulainn has gone to

---

18 ibid., page 191.
19 ibid.

the Otherworld and he advises Emer to go to a threshold place where the two worlds meet to speak with Fand's husband. Emer does this and somehow manages to get Cú Chulainn back. He is, however, still besotted and cannot focus on his old life. The druid finally gives him a potion of forgetfulness and he is restored to himself, free now of the Otherworld and of Fand.[20]

This seems to be a regular phenomenon with the anima. Unlike the animus, which can bring clarity, the anima tends to lure a man into her realm and wrap him in mists, making him useless in the 'real' world. When she does this, she is not leading a man to life – rather she is pulling him inwards towards some twilight place. Another energy, like Emer, is needed to snap a man out of it. Emer and, of course, the druid.

'Life' can be interpreted two ways. There is the outer world and the life one lives in the outer world. There is also the inner world and the life one lives there. One dovetails into the other all the time. The inner life is projected outwards and one is brought on a merry dance with these projections. This, I believe, is what Jung meant when he said that the anima wants life to be lived. She is perhaps indifferent as to which life is actually lived, the inner or the outer – she can appear in both and be powerful in both. In its positive aspect the anima is responsible for the fact that a man finds a marriage partner. However, if the marriage plays out as Jung earlier intimated; 'the man may have married his own worst weakness'.

Von Franz mentions another function that the anima fulfills: "Whenever a man's logical mind is incapable of discerning facts that are hidden in his unconscious, the anima helps him to dig them out".[21]

20 For a telling of the tale see: T.W. Rolleston. (1986) *Myths and Legends of the Celtic Race*. Constable and Company, London. Page 225 ff, *'Cúchulainn in Fairyland'*.
21 Conceived and Edited by Carl Jung. (1978). *Man and his Symbols*. Pan Books Ltd.,

She continues: "Even more vital is the role that the anima plays in putting a man's mind in tune with the right inner values and thereby opening the way into more profound inner depths".[22] Basically, as said earlier, the anima in her positive role is the mediator between the ego and the unconscious. She is the mediator to the inner world and to the Self. As a positive participant in the psyche, the anima allows a man to access his inner depths but does not trap him there. She allows him back to the outer world with the treasures he has found, new sources of inspiration, a sense of connectedness, a joy in living.

Jung outlines four stages of anima development, similar to the four stages of animus development. For the anima these are:

1. **Eve** – Eve "represents the purely instinctual and biological relations."
2. **Faust's Helen** – Helen represents a romantic aesthetic aspect that is still bound by sexual elements. 3. **Virgin Mary** – Mary raises love or Eros to the spiritual dimension. 4. **Sapientia** – Sapientia, or Sophia or Wisdom transcends purity and leads to wholeness.[23]

In the Middle Ages the fantasy world of individuals was clearly recognised and expressed in religious and cultural ways. However, later on, when the anima became fused with the heavenly Virgin who was all-pure, this effort required by an individual to relate with the anima personally was abandoned. As the Virgin was perceived as all-positive and flawless, the more negative, earthy, real aspects of the anima were disowned and from this spawned a belief in witches.

There are two extremes in relation to the anima, neither of them ideal. The first is when the anima is carried by an officially recognised figure.

London. Page 186. This is in part three of the book, written by Marie-Louise von Franz and entitled *The Process of Individuation*. Page 191.
22 ibid.
23 ibid., page 195.

The disadvantage of this is that she loses her personal, individual aspects. The other extreme is when she is seen as a purely personal entity. The danger in this is that if she is projected onto the outer world (as she surely must be) then it is only there that she can be found. In this case either a man becomes victim to his erotic fantasies or he becomes utterly dependent upon an actual woman in his life.

Von Franz speaks extremely practically about how a man can benefit from the anima and her messages. The anima can only be a positive presence when a man decides to take her very seriously. This means he must take seriously his moods, expectations, and fantasies because these are all sent to him by the anima. This is difficult because most men are trained to ignore their emotions and moods. The next thing is to fix them in some form. This can be done by writing, painting, musical composing, dancing and so on. Once a man begins to fix the material then other unconscious contents surface from the depths and connect with the earlier contents. Von Franz writes: "After a fantasy has been fixed in some specific form, it must be examined both intellectually and ethically, with an evaluating feeling reaction. And it is essential to regard it as being absolutely real: there must be no lurking doubt that this is 'only a fantasy'. If this is practiced with devotion over a long period, the process of individuation gradually becomes the single reality and can unfold in its true form".[24] When a man can do this, the anima helps him to differentiate both his feelings and his behaviour towards women.

Slaying the Dragon

The term 'Slaying the Dragon' is often used in relation to male psychological development. I have heard people react to the saying, believing that it is a product of patriarchal misogynist thought – if you consider that the Dragon, i.e. the Mother, must be slain before

---

24 ibid.

a man can be psychologically free and mature. Why should one slay the mother? Yet it is not the mother who is, in fact, slain, rather it is the influence of the mother complex on a man. This must be slain, or separated from. The Great Mother, as in the archetype the Goddess, need not take any of this personally. Nor need the mothers in the world. If a man remains psychologically bound to the Mother complex, he remains infantile and cannot develop his relationship with his own true personal feminine nature, i.e. his anima.

A man who remains locked within the mother complex is terrified of a relationship with an actual woman, for to him it means being devoured. He will avoid this at all costs either by having relationships with a lot of women, so no one woman can actually 'get her hands on him' or he will simply avoid relationships and will live in a fantasy world. In the former case he is owned by the mother complex in his desperate attempt to be owned by no one. In the latter case he is being devoured by the mother complex. His fantasies suck his life energy away from real living. Not surprisingly, men in this situation have been known to dream of women vampires sucking their blood.

It is important to note here that all men have a mother complex, as do all women. It is impossible not to have one, as all of us have been born from a mother. However, the dragon to be slain is not the mother complex in and of itself, it is rather, when the man has reached the point where he is locked *within* the complex, then it is time to slay the dragon. Slaying the dragon means realising that one is trapped within the complex and then doing the wearying yet necessary work of walking around the walls of the complex. The latter involves finding out where the complex influences one's behaviour and adjusting the behaviour accordingly. For example, a young man who had reached the age of thirty was still living with his mother in her house. Psychologically he was locked within a mother complex. For his own psychological wellbeing, he needed to move out. Simple and all as that might sound, it was nearly impossible for him to do. Facing his actual mother and telling her was not the hardest task. Rather, the thought of doing it made him feel lethargic, and he was haunted by anxiety. When he did eventually move out, he had indeed slain the dragon.

The Roman Catholic Church, by enforcing celibacy on its clergy, effectively blocks men from healthy expression of their sexuality in the real world. It therefore drives them into the clutches of the devouring mother. Mother Church is the devouring mother for these men. At the root of the celibacy rule in the Roman Catholic Church is the need for control. The price of this control is, on the one hand, deviant sexuality or covert sexual relationships, and, on the other, psychological bondage. Many of these men in the clergy are locked into a negative mother complex as big as the Church.

Men who are caught in a mother complex will tend to either idealise women or degrade them. They admire the unapproachable women and satisfy themselves sexually with prostitutes. They suffer from a split anima and cannot bring the two images together. In neither case are they dealing with real women. The fairy tale Rapunzel tells of the mother witch who keeps the two aspects of woman apart so that she can have control. She keeps Rapunzel locked up in the tower (the intellect), separated from the real earthy woman. Rapunzel must be thrown down from the tower. She must be brought down to earth. The prince is blinded (his idealisation of Rapunzel is over). Rapunzel and the prince must wander in a wilderness apart for many years before they can come together finally. This means that there is much growth that needs to take place before the two extreme images of woman can be integrated in a man.

The dragon to be slain is not the negative mother complex, nor the positive mother complex, nor the mother complex itself. Slaying the dragon means freeing oneself from being trapped *within* the mother complex. The dragon is the entrapment. Once one realises that one is within a complex, that is the first step outside of it. Because a man's femininity is sourced within the mother and the experience of the mother, a man must detach from the mother in order to individuate. In doing this he can explore his own uniquely personal feminine nature. Until he does this he is limited in the kind of relationship he has with a real woman in the world. By slaying the dragon, that is, escaping the entrapment of his mother complex, his relationships with women can move beyond either idealisation or degradation, and he gives himself the opportunity to know and love a woman for who she really is.

Jung says again and again that it is not enough to know these things, one must live these things. Some men attempt to escape the battle with the dragon by intellectual means. They build a mental, intellectual, very masculine realm where the mother cannot follow. This is what the Oedipus myth demonstrates. Oedipus very cleverly answers the Sphinx and thinks he is free. But he goes on to marry his mother and the consequences are dire. An intellectual overcoming of the devouring powers of the mother complex is not enough. This battle must be actually lived through, not just thought through. If a man can live out this battle and free himself from the devouring mother complex, he can then access the true riches of the feminine, which are contained in his anima. Mind you, the anima is another archetype, another complex. But the trick there is not to get trapped by that particular face of the feminine either. Von Franz said "We are alive when we feel alive, and what makes us feel alive is the contact with that flow of the unconscious psyche. That's why dreams are so important".[25]

---

25 Marie-Louise von Franz in conversation with Fraser Boa. (1988) *The Way of the*

Jung likes to separate the anima from the mother archetype on the one hand – "Nor is she (the anima) a substitute figure for the mother".[26] And yet, on the other, he says that the anima "...appears equally as maiden and mother..."[27] It seems anima can appear in whatever form she wishes, she can take on the cloak of mother, maiden, nymph and so forth. What I believe Jung is trying to clarify is that conscious relationship with the anima means a movement into adulthood – a growth away from and out of being bound to the mother complex.

Anima is All of the Above and Much More Than

James Hillman,[28] when speaking of the anima, makes the distinction between her description and her definition. In Jung's time, in his culture, the feminine was conceived differently than it is today. I hold that what the feminine actually is, in and of itself, no one can really say. One can, however, speak of that which is perceived as the feminine at a certain time in history. Certainly, how the feminine was perceived in Jung's day is different than how it is perceived today. Jung describes the anima as "... the glamorous, possessive, moody, and sentimental seductress in a man ... She intensifies, exaggerates, falsifies, and mythologises all emotional relationships".[29] And indeed, in his day, anima was seen as an inferior, excessive, feminine entity. The dominant culture at that time had a particular relationship to the feminine which was condescending and repressive. Today, one hopes, the dominant culture is more integrative of the feminine and therefore our description of it will be different to Jung's. Hillman writes: "We should therefore not identify a description of the anima in a rigidly patriarchal, puritanically defensive, extravertedly willful and unsound period of history with her definition."[30] He goes on to

---

Dream. Windrose Films Ltd., Toronto, Canada. Page192.
26 *C.W.* Vol. 9ii, par 26.
27 *C.W.* Vol. 9i, par 356.
28 James Hillman is a psychologist, scholar and international lecturer. See Appendix 1.
29 *C.W.* Vol. 9ii, par 422.
30 James Hillman. (1985). *Anima, An Anatomy of a Personified Notion.* Spring

say: "The task now is to discover what descriptions suit her in this time and how she is mythologising today".

Anima as the Archetype of Life for Both Men and Women

It has been said earlier that the anima is a compensatory contrasexual complex in a man's psyche. But she is not merely compensatory. She cannot be limited to this role. She is much more than a compensatory function of the psyche. In the same vein neither is she merely a contrasexual element. To limit her to these definitions is to imagine her as a one-dimensional black to the conscious mind's white. This is not so. As a contrasexual element in a man's psyche the anima is peculiar to men. However, the anima as an archetype is common to both men and women. She is an archetype of the collective unconscious and therefore is not limited to one gender alone. Women have access to her and she plays a significant role in their lives. To break the anima away from being limited to contrasexuality frees her to be the archetype she is – the archetype of life.[31] As the archetype of life, she is essential to the psychic health of both men and women.

Hillman comments: "… Anima gives each of us a sense of an individualised soul, altogether apart from whatever she might compensate. But this individualised soul is merely an intimation. And just this latency, this pregnancy in her unknownness, ignites the compulsions toward her. Because she bears in her belly our individualised becoming we are drawn into soul-making."[32] Here Hillman contends that anima enables us to make soul. He claims that it is a way of being, a "structural notion" or an "archetypal structure of consciousness".[33] This ties in with the anima as the archetype of life.

Publications, Dallas, Texas. Page13.

31 *C.W.* Vol. 14, par 646 and *C.W.* Vol 9i, par 66.

32 James Hillman. (1985). *Anima, An Anatomy of a Personified Notion.* Spring Publications, Dallas, Texas Page 15

33 ibid., 21.

To be involved with anima is a way of being in the world, a way of behaving, of perceiving that lends soul to the world, that lends soul to life itself.

Before I explore further this idea of soul-making, I would like to continue to state what anima must not be confused with, or limited to, for this might help us in our attempt to grasp the mystery she is. Anima is not to be confused with feeling. The anima has been confused with the feeling function. This is because culturally the dominant function in men has tended to be seen to be thinking, with feeling therefore men's inferior function. The anima has been identified with this contrasexual inferior feeling function. This is a confusion. The inferior function, such as feeling in this situation, is the gateway for shadow and animus and anima. But these latter archetypes should not become identified with any one function. This confusion has happened in the past simply because the inferior function has been considered to be the same for so long for so many people. The archetypes are energies beyond the functions. It is ironic that anima should become identified with feeling since feeling is a rational function and the anima is far from rational!

Part of the reason that anima has been identified with feeling is that anima has been seen as the function of relationship. This may be so if we mean that the anima, as said earlier, is the mediator between the conscious world and the unconscious world. As such she promotes the relationship between unconscious contents and our consciousness. However, if we mean that the anima is helpful in a relationship in the outer world with another person we are seriously mistaken. This is the very place she will wreak havoc. In many classical renditions of anima she is either non-human or half-human. She leads us away from the human situation and reality. She creates moods, illusions. The anima leads out of human feeling not into it. "As the function that relates conscious and unconscious, she occludes conscious feeling, making it unconscious and making the human, inhuman. She puts other things in mind than the human world".[34]

This insight about the anima is essential. She leads away from the human. Therefore she must not be anthropomorphised. Western civilisation has done this. We have humanised everything. In the Disney version of the film Dr. Doolittle, for example, all the animals are presented behaving like little people. There is Mr. and Mrs. Rat, the tiger speaks like a tired professor, and so forth. I cannot think of one Disney film involving animals where these animals are not anthropomorphised. These films, although ostensibly about animals, give the animals human personalities, human speech, and human agendas. No attempt is made to present an understanding of animals, in and of themselves, as being other than us humans.

In contrast, I saw one film that did attempt to leave animals to be themselves. This was a film called *Instinct*. In this film, an anthropologist working on observing Silverback Gorillas in Africa goes missing for two years. When he is found, he appears to have gone insane. He murders two wardens, injures another and refuses to speak. In a high security mental institution for the criminally insane, he has to undergo a thirty-day psychiatric assessment. The psychiatrist who works with him finally gets him to speak. Through listening to the anthropologist during their meetings, the psychiatrist follows him back to the jungle and discovers his life with the gorillas. The gorillas had accepted the presence of a human among them. For those two years, he had shed everything he had carried with him. He began to live as humans did long ago with the exception that he was living as one of a family of gorillas.

---

34 ibid., 47.

When the wardens found the man among the gorillas, they began to shoot and kill all the gorillas. It was the very day that the leader male Silverback gorilla had handed the man a young baby gorilla to hold, the first time such a thing happened, and a sign of his belonging to the group. It was in this context that the man killed the wardens – to protect the group he had become a part of. For two years he had lived with the gorillas and his instinct was shaped by that experience. He could not pull himself back and behave differently, even if he had wanted to. There is no attempt in the script to make the gorillas human. Rather, you have a man molded by the life of the gorillas. The humans come off piteously throughout. Humanity's utter disregard for otherness, for the natural world, is clearly shown throughout. Our insistence on dominance and dominion and control is revealed.

The human tendency is to do the same with the anima. We humanise the anima and in doing so we strip the world of soul, of a content we do not understand and cannot grasp. I believe this is what happens also when we attempt to humanise the animal world. We have refused to meet anything on its own ground, or even halfway there. We simply project human contents onto that which is beyond us. We have done this to the gods, we have done it to the animals, and we do it to the anima. We have lost all sense of humility in the face of the other, in the face of the unknown.

In analysing dreams, the tendency has been to interpret images from a feeling developmental point of view. So, for instance, if one dreams of a cold-blooded creature, like a lizard, the tendency is to think that this indicates the need for it to develop into something warm blooded. Anything that strikes us as primitive is interpreted as indicating the need to develop into something more human and more acceptable. This approach to the interpretation of dreams assumes that images such as these in our dreams indicate that we need to work on our personal relationships. Hillman, however, makes the argument that perhaps these images should be interpreted with feeling values of their own, as they are. He suggests that these images can have meaning in and of themselves, and that there is more to them than just indicators of the need for feeling development in us. Hillman states that the images are depotentiated when "… all the feeling goes to the development, to the transformational progress of the images into something more human". He goes on to say: "It is as if the Christian myth of the incarnation is continually being applied to the images of the anima, that all images must follow the model of the inhuman becoming human (incarnating), and that all psychic factors are to enter human relationships. Ridiculous, of course".[35] When we try to understand anima and animus images in the light of feeling development we simply dismiss all the otherness, all the animals, the daemons, the gods. We turn the numinous into that which we can understand and grasp.

The lessons we can learn from this discussion are, on the one hand, not to allow anima to be involved in our human relationships or she will cause chaos, and, on the other hand, not to try to humanise the anima and reduce her to our human nature. Anima belongs to the realm beyond our humanity. Anima is other, anima is mystery.

Women and Anima
I have presented this chapter the way one might peel through the layers of an onion. I have started with the outer layers, for clarity's sake. Initially, I wanted to begin at the centre, and go straight into writing of anima as the archetype of Life, as being a part of both the woman's and the man's psyche. It is this aspect of the anima that excites me, as it pertains directly to me as a woman. However, anima for so long has been the prerogative of men that I felt to begin with an historical

---

35 ibid.

perspective would enable us to build a new understanding of it block upon block. And so I began with compensation and contrasexuality. These are traditional roles for the anima and they still stand. Yet anima must not be limited to these. They are merely the outer layers of the onion. How anima plays out in male psychology has been described for a long time now. It is time to begin to ponder what effect the anima archetype has on a woman's psyche.

A certain type of woman could be termed an 'anima type'. This woman is like a tabula rasa, she catches the projections of men and lives them out. It has been presumed to date that these women are affected by the anima archetype only through the men who project the archetype onto them. These anima women play out the romantic idealisations of anima. They also play out the more negative side of anima; trite, trivial, cheap, silly, brainless, bimbo etc. Hillman writes: "… this 'anima type' presents us with an archetypal condition of soul that is drowsily nymphic, neither asleep nor awake, neither self-sustainingly virginal nor faithfully conjoined, lost and empty, a tabula rasa".[36]

The question to be asked here is whether or not such women would even exist in this state if there were no men around them to project upon them. If anima was not available to women then this would be impossible. However, because anima is available to women then such women can and do exist, independently of men and their projections. While there are certain women who live out a particular kind of anima-being which is attractive to men, although denigrated by them at the same time – the kind described above – there are also other women who likewise live out a type of anima that does not fall into this category. These women may seem vague and diffused. They float about in a mist and do not seem particularly bothered by their lack of direction or clarity. Both kinds of women can be anima women.

---

36 ibid., page 57.

Not necessarily women upon whom men have projected their anima fantasies but rather women directly linked into the anima archetype of their own nature and accord. Hillman claims that: "Anima, as archetype of life, can be utterly devoid of meaning."[37] Indeed, as stated in the chapter on animus, the animus is the archetype of meaning. This is why both archetypes, animus and anima, go together. I will speak more of this later.

If it is the case that women have access to the anima archetype, we can have a different view of the images that appear in their psyches. Hillman writes: "The roles which Jung assigns to the anima (b)[38] – relation with the mysteries, with the archaic past, enactment of the good fairy, witch, whore, saint, and animal associations with bird, tiger, and serpent (to mention only those he there mentions) – all appear frequently and validly in the psychology of women". [39] How the anima effects a man is also how it effects a woman. Women are equally drawn into the unconscious world. They experience an interiority that balances their outer personae in the world. "Women are as salty in their weeping and resentments, as bitchy in their gossip, as abysmal in their dour brooding as men. ... Here the anima, archetype of life and archetype of the feminine, influences the psychic process regardless of sex, and we are freed from the masculine-feminine fantasy of anima."[40]

It was generally thought by Jung that a woman did not have an anima; that by biology, by the fact of being a woman, she somehow was anima. Anima and femininity and woman and soul were all one. Thus a woman did not have anima, she did not have soul. By the very fact of being a woman she was soul. Jung wrote: "... I find the scholastic

---

37 ibid.
38 (b) indicates this reference in Hillman's text: C.W. Vol. 9i, par 356.
39 James Hillman. (1985). *Anima, An Anatomy of a Personified Notion*. Spring Publications, Dallas, Texas. Page 57.
40 ibid., page 59.

question *Habet mulier animam?* especially interesting, since in my view it is an intelligent one inasmuch as the doubt seems justified. Woman has no anima, no soul, but she has an *animus*. The anima has an erotic, emotional character, the animus a rationalising one" [41] I can imagine Jung chuckling as he makes this controversial statement. He was a man surrounded by highly creative and intelligent women, his wife, Emma, not the least of them. He makes it on the basis that the animus is the compensating element in a woman's psyche. However, it is not valid to say that women need not grapple with the nature of soul, with the nature of life; that their only challenge is to grapple with meaning. It is hardly acceptable to claim that somehow, because they are women, the perception of soul and the reality of life come naturally to them. Nor is it valid to imply that men do not need to tackle meaning; that a man, because he is a man, will never wonder about meaning, will never lose track and focus. It is surely true that women need anima / soul as much as they need meaning in their lives, and men need meaning and animus as much as they need soul in their lives.

In the interpretation of dreams, it has been the practice to interpret the appearance of a person in the dream, who is the same gender as the dreamer, as the dreamer's shadow. According to this approach, the character of the same gender as the dreamer represents an unconscious and underdeveloped aspect of their psyche. This, however, must now be refined. If a woman dreams of another woman, this character may well represent an unconscious shadow aspect of herself[42], but it may

---

41 *C.W.* Vol. 17, par 338.

42 Hillman suggests that the idea of shadow can now perhaps become more refined, that something is not shadow merely because it is feminine in a woman or masculine in a man. He says that perhaps the shadow could be reserved for that which is morally repressed. Personally, I do not agree with this. To allow the archetype of shadow to be reduced to the moral realm is tricky ground to say the least. Same gender characters in our dreams can be shadow in the sense of being unconscious and can be animus and anima also. This sounds confusing, I know. How can the archetype of shadow be one and the same time the archetype of animus or anima?

also represent anima, soul, life, a way of being. It could be that the archetype of anima is taking on a shape and sending a message about soul.

This new understanding of anima allows us to interpret our dream figures differently. It also gives a new slant to the understanding of the daughter/father dynamic. Previously the thinking has been that a daughter is like that empty page on which her father projects his anima contents, she then acts these out. This thinking comes from believing that the anima archetype can only get to the daughter through the father's psychic projections. It also comes from the belief that the emptiness in the daughter is there for the very purpose of being projected upon.

However, seeing now, as we do, that the daughter has access to the anima archetype from the very beginning of her life, father or no father, a different picture is created. The daughter is not merely a screen to be projected upon, without soul or independence or individuality herself. She is not merely a blank slate waiting for the father to create upon. The daughter, in carrying this emptiness, is actually living out "an authentic archetypal manifestation of the anima in one of her classical forms, maiden, nymph, Kore ..."[43]

We need to question who creates whom when it comes to fathers and daughters. It is true that fathers shape daughters but it is also true that daughters shape fathers. "The enactment of the maiden-daughter in all her receptive charm, shy availability, and masochistic wiliness draws down a fathering spirit. But its appearance and her

---

How indeed. Yet it seems to me that the archetypes are not cut and dried. They are energies that flow into each other. They are not concrete statues. In fairness what they are and how they interrelate will remain a mystery to us. We can only attempt to describe them knowing that we can never truly know their nature.

43 James Hillman. (1985). *Anima, An Anatomy of a Personified Notion.* Spring Publ., Dallas, Texas. Page 63.

victimisation are her creation. Even the idea that she is all a result of the father (or absent or bad father) is part of the father-fantasy of the anima archetype."[44]

When we begin to grapple with the anima archetype at this level, we must call into question the very femininity of the archetype. Jung himself questioned this. "When projected, the anima always has a feminine form with definite characteristics. This empirical finding does not mean that the archetype is constituted like that *in itself.*"[45] This means that we cannot know what the archetype is in and of itself, we can only see how it is projected. Thus we cannot say that the anima archetype is feminine, nor can we say that soul is feminine or that life is feminine. All we can say is that the forms upon which the archetype projects tend to be feminine. This is a very important distinction to establish. What the archetype is and what it projects upon are different. The latter can be held and touched and seen, the former never can be.

When Jung speaks of the anima as the archetype of life, he is speaking of *psychic life*. Jung writes: "The anima ... is a 'factor' in the proper sense of the word. Man cannot make it; on the contrary, it is always the *a priori* element in his moods, reactions, impulses, and whatever else is spontaneous in psychic life."[46]

'The Fat Lady Sings" – Anima in a Woman's Psyche

A woman dreamed that she was in a house with her husband. There was also this enormously fat lady upstairs in the house. The woman went upstairs to the fat lady and they both sat on a big double bed. The woman said to the fat lady that she had decided that she could

---

44 ibid, page 65.
45 *C.W.* Vol. 9i, par 142.
46 ibid., par 57.

be nothing other than heterosexual and that she would stay with her husband. She knew that sometimes life was awful with him but it could also be wonderful. She said that it would be the same with the fat lady anyway if she married her, that life would be both good and bad. In the dream the woman felt good about her decision. She felt somehow relieved.

This dream is a good example of the different ways one can interpret a same gender character in a dream. Do we see the fat lady as shadow or do we see her as the anima, the archetype of life. Or as both? If we go to the dreamer, she is a person who can be animus driven and can burn out and feel totally at a loss when it comes to the sources of life within herself. It is difficult for her to let go and to be. Her associations with the fat lady are that she is creative, sensuous, an arty figure, an actress, or painter. She is someone who is content in herself, voluptuous, larger than life, dramatic. Her associations with her husband are that he is a doer who sometimes cannot stop and gets exhausted.

If we see the fat lady as shadow then she represents an underdeveloped aspect of the woman's psyche. This is fair enough. The woman is struggling between her driven-ness and a shadow aspect that would let her pull back from doing. The shadow is enormous because she is compensating for the lack in the woman's conscious attitude. Yet in the dream the woman actually chooses her husband, that is her driven-ness, over the shadow aspect. It seems to me that the interpretation of the fat lady as shadow is valid, yet it does not go far enough. The canvas of interpretation is not broad enough. If we interpret the fat lady as anima, then she not only represents the underdeveloped aspect of the woman, a compensatory element, she also represents the archetype of life. In the dream the woman chooses the husband and heterosexuality over the fat lady. This is strange in that the imbalance in the woman's conscious attitude lies with her driven-ness. Yet in the dream, after making the choice, the woman feels relief. This is a feeling that actually stays with her the following day.

The woman had already acknowledged the dilemma of her driven-ness in her conscious attitude. She was already aware of it as a problem. Thus the dream is not introducing this idea. Rather, it is introducing a new idea, the idea of choice. The woman can choose to remain with the husband or she can marry the fat lady. The dream suggests that, because of the woman's wavering between husband and fat lady, she has been losing power, or psychic energy. Once the choice is made, she feels relief. Something falls into place. It is not the obvious choice for one who is burnt out and driven, yet more subtly it is the right choice. This is confirmed by the woman's feeling of relief, both in the dream and throughout the following day.

The woman herself said that she felt freed after this dream – freed to take time out, to let things go and to ease up on herself. It was as if, because she got right her primary commitment, which was to her husband and her animus, she could then call upon the image of the fat lady, and call in her voluptuous humour and creativity, in a secondary role. When I suggested to the woman that she imagine that she had chosen differently, that she had married the fat lady, the woman responded with a shudder. "That would have suffocated me totally," was her response. For this woman, the relationship with the life-giving fat lady or anima was healthy only when she was primarily committed to the animus. Once that dynamic was settled then the woman could work with both archetypes.

The woman's contentment with her choice only lasted for a while. About six months to a year later, the woman had a very shocking dream. In this dream she was in the passenger seat of their family car.

Her husband was driving. Her children were in the back seat. This was a car they had had before the woman had learned to drive, so it was a car she had never driven. The woman's husband was driving recklessly on a narrow, winding road that ran along the edge of a cliff. They came to a sharp curve in the road and the car did not hold to the road. They flew off the edge of the cliff and the woman woke up with shock as, in the dream, the car began sinking down into the water.

This dream, needless to say, deeply disturbed the woman. She associated it with the dream six months earlier of the Fat Lady. After a few days reflection on the dream, the woman realised that she must 'marry' the Fat Lady because her marriage to her inner husband, her animus, was about to 'go off the road' and kill herself and her children. Her children represented her projects and work in the world. She was given the message that without sourcing herself in the anima, the Fat Lady, she would be destroyed and so would her fledgling projects which she loved dearly. She had gotten it wrong. Her primary connection had to be the anima, Life, because without it the meaning, and the fruits of that meaning, would die. After her initial dream, the one with the Fat Lady, the woman had not been able or ready to make this transition. The dream of the car going off the road was a warning that it was crucial that she make the transition and that time was running out. The dream was warning her that if she did not shift in her conscious attitude disaster would follow.

Giving Back Soul to the World

A person can get caught up in the anima in the same way as one can get locked inside the mother complex. When this happens, a person is caught in the anima's power and the anima acts like an autonomous complex within which the person is a hapless victim to her whims. This can manifest as physical symptoms of illness, anxiety, or projecting it outwards and falling in love with someone who carries her projection.

It can manifest as lethargy and a lifelessness, described earlier in the story of Cú Chulainn. Basically, one is caught up and lost in the mists and twilight zone of the anima world within.

However, when one is not caught up with the anima, she can have a very powerful influence on a person's way of being in the world. Jung describes the anima as "a psychological function of an intuitive nature, akin to what the primitives mean when they say, "He has gone into the forest to talk with the spirits," or "My snake spoke with me…""[47] What Jung is pointing to is the suggestion that the anima enables a person to be in the world in a particular way. The world becomes imbued with soul, with mystery. The inner becomes the outer and vice versa.

I am speaking here of anima in its more refined understanding. It is this anima which, in the words of James Hillman "…perceives psychic life within natural life. Natural life itself becomes the vessel the moment we recognise its having an interior significance, the moment we see that it too bears and carries psyche. Anima makes vessels everywhere, anywhere, by going within."[48]

Thus anima is the capacity to see the world as magical, as full of soul and significance. It strikes me that the Irish as a race are rich in anima energy. In Irish mythology the Otherworld is hugely important and is a very real part of reality. It first appears in stories of the Tuatha de Danann, a race of people who had strong magic. When the Milesians, known later as the Celts, came to the land of Ireland they battled with the Tuatha de Danann. Some versions say that the Milesians won the battle. Other versions say that there was a stalemate. All versions agree that the resolution of the issue was that the Tuatha de Danann offered to go to the Underworld and the Milesians would take the

---

47 *C.W.* Vol. 7, par 374.
48 James Hillman. (1985). *Anima, An Anatomy of a Personified Notion*. Spring Publications, Dallas, Texas. Page 81.

Upperworld. With their powerful magic the de Danann people created the Otherworld, which is beautiful and vast and magical. The fairy forts and fairy mounds on Ireland's landscape are entrance ways or thresholds to the Otherworld. From that time until this there have been tales of mortals somehow entering the Otherworld and mixing with the fairy folk.

At the time of this division of the worlds, part of the contract between the two peoples was that there would be respect shown always to the Tuatha de Danann. For the Tuatha de Danann were the people of the goddess Dana or Anú and she was Nature/Life. As a result, the Milesians at certain times of the year put out offerings to the Tuatha de Danann and acknowledged the role the Otherworld played in their lives. When they failed to do this properly, the crops would fail and the people would suffer. To fail in one's respectful relationship with nature had dire consequences.[49]

Scratch the surface of the most sophisticated Irish people today and you will still find a respect for the Otherworld people, for the fairy folk. Many Irish people have a strong belief in them. In psychological terms, it is another way of dealing with anima reality. The Otherworld is the Collective Unconscious. What is within is also outside. The deep psyche, the unconscious, that one experiences within oneself is, at one and the same time, that which one experiences in the world. The archetype of anima gives expression to itself in both inner and outer vessels, and in this way allows itself to be perceived and experienced.

Hillman maintains that it is through fantasy that we can learn to live like this and perceive the world in this way. "The means of doing this is fantasy. Phenomena come alive and carry soul through our

---

49 For the story of the coming of the Milesians and the retreat of the Tuatha de Danann to the underworld see: T.W. Rolleston. (1986) *Myths and Legends of the Celtic Race*. Constable, London. Page130 - 138.

imaginative fantasies about them. When we have no fantasy about the world, then it is objective, dead… Fantasy is not merely an interior process going on in my head. It is a way of being in the world and giving back soul to the world".[50] Hillman makes the distinction between one's attempt to develop a relationship with one's own anima and Anima as a consciousness. While they are separate, one does lead into the other. When one develops a relationship with one's anima, one can feel special and important and different. The anima is inside of 'me'. Ironically Jung says that this is the moment when, "we are in fact most estranged from ourselves and most like the average type of *Homo sapiens*".[51] We are being inflated by an archetype, as opposed to being personally differentiated or individuated.

However, albeit that an undefined relationship to the anima lends this illusion of specialness, it is this same personal anima which is the beginning of the encounter with soul. Hillman writes:

> The reality of psyche as an all-too-convincing experience begins in the subjectivised moods and follies of the highly personalised anima. Nowhere do we more stubbornly encounter the reality of soul – in itself such a dim and wispy idea – than in the crosspatch nastiness of bad tempers, the insights that slip away, the sensitive vanities that will not be mollified. […] My conviction that psyche and its fantasies are as real as matter and nature, as real as spirit, depends on how convincing anima has made herself to me. Thus on her depends the psychological calling.[52]

---

50 James Hillman. (1985). *Anima, An Anatomy of a Personified Notion*. Spring Publications, Dallas, Texas. Page 81.
51 *C.W.* Vol. 16, par 469.
52 James Hillman. (1985) *Anima, An Anatomy of a Personified Notion*. Spring Publications, Dallas, Texas. Page 84 and 85.

We begin with the personal anima. It is because of her that what is experienced is experienced as personal in one's own soul. The more realised the anima is for a person, the more psychic existence is real to a person. To move then to an anima-consciousness is to acknowledge the connectedness of that which is inner to that which is outer. It is to experience the world as soulful, mystical, mystery-filled. To say that there is such a thing as anima-consciousness comes from the notion that "…every archetype, by forming a pattern of behavior and a cluster of imagery, informs consciousness and has a kind of consciousness".[53] Thus, anima-consciousness is rich and fecund with unconscious material and perceives the world as being the same.

Integration of the Anima

From Hillman's point of view, it is the archetype of the anima that makes it possible to experience things as personal. For Jung anima is the basis of consciousness. It is in this context that he defines anima as the archetype of life. Jung defines her as "… the personification which unconsciously involves us with larger collectives of both inner and outer worlds".[54] On the one hand, in relation to integration, Jung claims that one must depersonalise anima and use her like a function making her work for us.[55] On the other, he claims that she is the basis of consciousness and cannot possibly be fully integrated: "It is something that lives of itself, that makes us live, it is a life behind consciousness that cannot be completely integrated with it, but from which, on the contrary, consciousness arises".[56]

To depersonalise the anima would be, in anthropological terms, like a "loss of soul". A person suffering from this loss of soul experiences the world in merely materialistic, sensate terms. There are no

---

53 ibid., page 91.
54 ibid., page 105.
55 *C.W.* Vol. 7, par 339.
56 *C.W.* Vol. 9i, par 57.

invisible forces, no mystery or magic. There are no spirits, ancestors, supernatural agents. This is how the loss of soul effects one's perception of the outer world. Loss of soul is a terrible phenomenon. Sadly, western civilisation is suffering from this very thing.

Loss of soul also means the loss of one's personal genius or daimon.[57] On the inner level this loss of soul means one is deaf to the promptings of one's inner guiding force. One experiences a dryness, monotony, apathy, a sense of weariness. It means that the mythology is missing that enables one to see that one's life has unique meaning and purpose and that everything in life conspires to manifest that inner uniqueness. Jung could hardly have intended this when he spoke of depersonalising the anima.

Hillman writes: "Loss of anima means both the loss of internal animation and external animism".[58] Without the anima the world becomes a 'soulless flatland'[59] while the inner psyche is a vast and unmeasurable abyss. "Not only is the guide and the bridge gone, but so too is the possibility of a personal connection through personified representations. For it is through anima that the autonomous systems of the psyche are experienced in personified form."[60] The anima animates not only the personal psyche, it also animates the world. It facilitates the creation of a mythology wherein the world is alive, magical. Jung refers to this as the *anima mundi*[61]; "The work on one's own person aims to open the senses and the heart to the life and beauty of an animated world".[62] Image and imagination are the way

---

57 For a stimulating book on the genius or daimon see: James Hillman. (1997) *The Soul's Code, In Search of Character and Calling*. Bantam Books.
58 James Hillman. (1985) *Anima, An Anatomy of a Personified Notion*. Spring Publications, Dallas, Texas. Page 109.
59 Ibid.
60 Jung mentions this in C.W. Vol. 13, par 61.
61 *C.W.* Vol. 8, par 393
62 James Hillman. (1985) *Anima, An Anatomy of a Personified Notion*. Spring Publications, Dallas, Texas. Page 109.

to reanimate both the *anima mundi,* and the inner, personal anima. Fantasy and active imagination are the tools to use. However, one must believe in the imaginings, one must place value in the fantasies.

The question now arises: is it possible to integrate the anima? The anima is an archetype. Jung describes her eloquently when he writes: "The unconscious anima is a creature without relationships, an autoerotic being whose one aim is to take total possession of the individual".[63] She does not lend to easy integration! Like Cúchulainn who followed Fand into the Otherworld, like the Norwegian woodcutters who follow the siren deep into the forest, to follow the anima onto her own territory is to get lost in the mists of the unknown. However, to depersonalise her, to reduce her to a function of the psyche, also has disastrous effects, as Jung describes: "Depersonalising the anima can produce unnecessary damage in human affairs when this idea is taken literally, leading to brutal dejection (presented as noble renunciations) and a subsequent diminution of vitality, of flexibility, and of human kindness".[64]

The potential of integrating the anima lies somewhere between these two possibilities: being entrapped by her and losing your life, or depersonalising her and losing your soul. We can begin by recognising the tendency of the archetype to become personalised and not be fooled by the form it takes. One must realise that these personal contents spring from an impersonal archetype. The answer is not to depersonalise it, but to recognise the dynamic and therefore not be trapped, tricked, or captivated by it so totally.

We must therefore ask if it is possible to integrate the contents of the personalisation, yet leave the archetype where it belongs, in the

---

63 *C.W.* Vol. 16, par 504.
64 *C.W.* Vol. 9i, par 147.

unconscious, the unknown, the invisible, the Otherworld? According to Jung even though the anima can be made conscious she must be left in the unconscious: "Though the anima and animus can be made conscious they themselves are factors transcending consciousness and beyond the reach of perception and volition. Hence they remain autonomous despite the integration of their contents".[65] Also:

> For the archetypes are universal and belong to the collective psyche over which the ego has no control. Thus animus and anima are images representing archetypal figures which mediate between conscious and the unconscious. Though they can be made conscious they cannot be integrated into the ego-personality, since as archetypes they are also autonomous.[66]

To strip the anima of her magic and reduce her to a function is to 'slay the angel' as Hillman writes.[67] It is an attempt to allow the ego consciousness to be dominant. However, Hillman believes that: "Integrating the anima ... could only take place by our remembrance that we are already in her. Human being-in-soul (*esse* in anima) from the beginning. Integration is thus a shift of viewpoint from her in me to me in her..."[68]

Experience of the Anima

Experience of the anima is ironically an awareness of the unconscious. She is the archetype of the psychological calling. Hillman claims that this is why soul-making precedes self-individuating.[69] "For, before we can become conscious we must be able to know that we are

---

65 *C.W.* Vol. 9ii, par 40.
66 Jung, 2 Jan. 1957, *Letter to anonymous.*
67 James Hillman. (1985) Anima, *An Anatomy of a Personified Notion.* Spring Publications, Dallas, Texas. Page 117
68 ibid., page 127.
69 ibid., page 137.

unconscious, and where, when and to what extent".[70] Basically the anima takes what is solid and known away from any solid footing and brings it into deeper waters. This is soul-making in one of its forms. She leads a person away from knowing and towards imagining.

Once again we are brought to the place of imagination and of fantasy. For a modern Western person to calmly speak about spirits or fairies or angels is one thing. For this same person to actually believe in them is quite another, and yet that is the anima consciousness. This is the belief that the inner and the outer world are rich with invisible energies and forces, in whatever shape or form one wishes to imagine them. This is anima consciousness.

I walk my dog each day off the road and through the fields. We pass by an ancient monastic ruin, up through a passage in a rocky cliff face and across a flat, limestone overhang. We have to climb over three walls. Over the third wall, we step down into a copse of whitethorn bush and we have to push our way through. The whitethorn in Irish lore is associated with the fairies. Many farmers will not clear it away for fear of offending these Otherworld folk. Each day, as I step over this third wall, I consciously greet the fairy folk, the ancestors, and ask their leave to pass. This is anima consciousness. While the anima is about soul, the animus is about spirit. Jung spoke of The Syzygy motif which expresses their relationship to each other.

The Syzygy

Jung: "… the syzygy motif … expresses the fact that a masculine element is always paired with a feminine one".[71] The idea of the syzygy is that the archetype of the anima is intimately connected with the archetype of the animus. One cannot be involved with one

70 ibid.
71 *C.W.* Vol. 9i, par 134.

without somehow being involved with the other. They go hand in hand. They balance each other, compensate for each other. "The notion of the syzygy demands that an exhaustive exploration of anima examine animus to the same extent. To do her full justice one has to give him equal time. But this has been happening indirectly. All our observations have come from a contrasting position, and each of these other positions can be conceived as representing the other, the animus, in one of his perspectives".[72]

If the anima is about soul and the animus is about spirit, then the syzygy suggests that one needs access to both in order to live fully. The animus and anima are the guardians of choice. Each of us must find our right relationship to them. There can be no false dichotomy. It cannot be a matter of either/or but must be a both/and situation. Men and women need both meaning and lifeforce in their lives – Sun and Earth, Meaning and Life, Spirit and Soul.

In traditional Jungian thought the anima is the counter-sexual element in the psyche of a man. She is the woman within. Her role in the psyche is to bring the unconscious to a man. She will do this, not as the animus does for a woman, as a light-bearer, but rather in a hazy way. She creates moods and fantasies. As with all the archetypes, one way that the anima becomes known is by being projected out onto the world. This can lead a man to his future partner or can create havoc by attracting a married man to a mistress. The value of being aware of the anima is that a man may have choices in how he deals with her in the world. He can play it all out in his life and relationships or he can reclaim what the anima represents within his own psyche and work with her there, in the inner realm. While the anima is a contra-sexual element in a man's psyche, she is more than this. She is an archetype

---

72 James Hillman. (1985) *Anima, An Anatomy of a Personified Notion.* Spring Publications, Dallas, Texas. Page 173.

that is available to women also. She is an archetype of life and with her we can breathe soul back into our perception and experience of the world.

CHAPTER TEN

Reflections on Self

That Which Has No Opposite

Wild Place

There is a wild place
at the heart
of every single thing.

It is here
we know,
that
despite appearances,
all is well.

According to Jung it takes the first half of life to establish oneself in the world, to adapt to life. During the second half of life one has the opportunity to deal with issues of meaning. The ego begins to develop an attitude of humility. In the course of our lives we individuate the shadow, we become familiar with the animus and anima in their many guises. In time we may catch initial glimpses of something that feels benevolent, a kind of integrative energy – the Self. For Jung, the Self is an archetype. It is at the centre of the psyche, both conscious and unconscious and is the organising principle of the entire psyche. In the Self and therefore at the heart of the psyche there is a drive towards wholeness. Jung discerned that it is this drive towards wholeness that inspires our night dreams, our behaviours and even the events in our lives. Writing about the Self is another book's worth and I can do no justice to it here. I offer only the following observations.

On the 8th of July 2006 I had, what I believe to be, my first dream of the Self. At that time, I was finishing the initial draft of this book and was anticipating the possibility of doing further work looking into to the Self and the felt experience of Divinity. This was the dream:

> *I am in a building where there is preparation taking place for a major performance. There is an orchestra tuning up and a sense that a play is about to be enacted. I leave this building and walk through a beautiful garden. I have some work to do in relation to the performance. It is a very minor piece of work, something like checking through a part of one of the players. It occurs to me that my name will not appear anywhere in the programme. My part in the overall event is very minor. Yet this does not matter. I feel so appreciative to have anything at all to do with this performance. As I think this, a burst of music comes from behind me and I feel completely uplifted by the sound of it.*

This dream may sound unremarkable. What is difficult to get across is the feeling I was left with when I woke up. I feel it still years later. It was a feeling of profound wellbeing, of belonging, of worthiness. The dream, for mere seconds, opened up a crack wherein I caught a glimpse of the wonder of the connectedness of all things and my part in the middle of this connectedness. It opened up a felt connection with Self.

There is the well-known statement[1] – "The most important question you can ever ask is if the world is a friendly place." No matter how often we try to answer this question with our minds, it is the felt experience of a benevolent universe that verifies the presence of the Self. I believe that the inner reflects the outer and that the same Self that is the organizing principle of the human psyche is the Source or Self that is the organizing principle of the Universe. It is, in fact, the backdrop to everything. It has no opposite.

Imagine if one's awareness was centred upon this connection? It is what Jesus intimated, when he said "Seek first the Kingdom of heaven".[2] It is what the saying: "There is no way to happiness, happiness is the way"[3] alludes to. This is the true goal of individuation. It is not to arrive anywhere, nor to resolve anything. It is not to become perfect. Put simply, it is to come to a place in yourself where you can allow, more and more consistently, the wonder of the Self, to reach you, or more accurately, to shine through you. In doing so, you cannot but allow for that Self to be the primary guiding force in your life.

---

1 This statement is, in fact, generally mis-attributed to Einstein. In Emil Carl Wilm's 1912 book *The Problem of Religion*, he writes in a footnote on page 114 that a friend asked the late F.W.H.Myers: What is the most important question? This was the answer he received.
2 Matthew 6:33.
3 Thich Nhat Hanh uses this phrase but acknowledges that he is quoting A.J.Muste. (pg42 of *Peace is Every Step: The Path of Mindfulness in Everyday life.*)

CONCLUSION

After The Rain

After three days
of fecund persistence,
the rain
finally
stopped.
And everything
was fresh washed and vivid.

The stillness
was pierced
by the stream waters flowing
down,
to the sea tides
washing
over
stones,
and the thrill
of the birds.

The challenge
breathed
by
that wet green world
was not to respond
but simply this,
to take
one shot,
for that short time,
at
being part of
it all.

I began this work speaking about psychological hygiene. It is clear that when something is unconscious in our lives, it is the force behind our actions. Jung has said this over and over. In *Aion* he writes: "When an inner situation is not made conscious, it happens outside as Fate". In his book called *Dream Analysis*, he says: "When we are unconscious of a thing, which is constellated, we are identified with it, and it moves us or activates us as if we were marionettes. We can only escape that effect by making it conscious and objectifying it, putting it outside of ourselves, taking it out of the unconscious".[4] If people are to be psychologically hygienic, then they must strive to see what energies are behind the scenes, motivating their behaviour. They must dare to be aware of their unconscious psyche. Dealing with what comes from this realm supports the journey towards greater wholeness.

If we can understand the workings of complexes, and the archetypes at their centre, and if we can begin to grasp how psychic energy works, then we have the beginnings of a psychic toolbox. If we can begin to learn the unusual, beautiful, oftentimes humourous and bizarre language of dreams, then we have a direct link to the unconscious. Those tools can help us to chisel away at some of the patterns of behaviour that we have felt victim to, and helpless to overcome, for years.

Our personalities widen and deepen over time in an organic way. This may cause people to wonder why one should bother with this attempt at understanding, if all the time we are changing anyway. When we choose not to face issues in a conscious way, fate will trip us up and we will be forced to change. So why bother? Our development is assured, even if we remain unconscious. Jung himself said: "Even though we do not understand the dream, it is working and causing changes".[5]

---

4 C.G. Jung. (1984) *Dream Analysis*. Routledge and Kegan Paul, London. Page 217.
5 ibid., page 223.

Nonetheless, Jung goes on to say: "If we understand, however, we have the privilege of working with the timeless spirit in ourselves".[6]

It seems to me that there are, at least, two reasons to commit oneself to this work of conscious individuation. The first is this – what we do not acknowledge will be what drives us without our knowing. When this is the case, we are not true creators in our own lives. We are not consciously and actively choosing how we live, how we experience life and even what we experience. We are blindly bumbling along, unimaginatively taking what comes with a certain resignation. Robert Fritz has written a powerful book called *The Path of Least Resistance*.[7] In it, he, as a musician, observed how he composed music; how he created a piece of music. He watched the process. He realised that he could apply this process of creativity to his own life. He observed that, if left alone, the creative energy in our lives flows down the path of least resistance. This path of least resistance is like a riverbed in our psyches that has been carved out by our past experiences and our conditioning. If we merely passively take life as it comes, our energy flows along these paths. Our fate is sealed. Fritz discovered that we can carve out new paths in our unconscious and in doing so we can live creatively. I find Fritz's book exciting because it works! He provides a very simple series of exercises that allow us to name what is going on in our conscious minds and also which help us to uncover what is happening in our unconscious psyche. By doing this we are taking on to live consciously and creatively.

It is possible to become aware of our patterns and of our complexes. I do not claim that by doing so we can control what happens to us in our lives. Life is essentially mysterious. However, I believe that if we are committed to naming our complexes, and the archetypes at the

---

6 ibid.
7 Robert Fritz. (1943) *The Path of Least Resistance*. Stillpoint Pub. Walpole, N.H. USA.

centre of them, we are in a much better position to live our lives more creatively. To consciously strive to know who we are at that deeper level is to tap into a force in life that is powerful. It takes a certain humility. It requires befriending some three-headed demons and slaying some fearsome dragons. It demands that our ego recognise that it is, in fact, not in control. It must acknowledge that there are forces beyond itself which influence our lives.

Ironically, the more we acknowledge how much we are not in control, the more we have a chance to increase our control. The more we can claim to consciousness the archetypal players that inhabit our projections, the more likely the ego is able to relinquish control to a benevolent orchestrating force that flows through all of life. The fulcrum of our consciousness moves from the Ego, which is on the surface of our psyches, to the Self, which is a touchstone deep within our psyches. The Self, and the not the Ego, becomes the acknowledged organising principle of our lives. The task is to individuate the archetypes – to see their workings, recognise them and to develop a conscious relationship to them in our lives.

The second reason to commit oneself to this heroic task is this: as we have seen, the process of psychic growth continues on regardless of any effort on our part, slowly and organically. However, if we tune into this process, we can accelerate it significantly. Not only, as Jung says, do we have the privilege of working "with the timeless spirit within ourselves", but in working with that spirit we clear the way for greater progress towards wholeness.

The image of a garden comes to mind. I like a garden that is a strange mix of wildness and cultivation. I enjoy the colour, the wildness, the rampant sense of growth. But I acknowledge the value in fertilizing the soil and pulling away weeds that would suffocate the plants. So too with psychic growth. The personal psyche benefits from conscious attention, from observation, from working on dreams and noticing patterns of behaviour, just as much as it benefits from the flow of unconscious energy that flows through it as life is lived. It is worth repeating what Marie-Louise von Franz said: "We are alive when we feel alive and what makes us feel alive is the contact with that flow of the unconscious psyche. That's why dreams are so important"[8]

In the introduction, I spoke of our Western culture and how it seems now time for people to grow up psychically. It is time to step out from under the all-pervading influences of the many institutions upon which we have, up until now, relied so heavily. Erich Fromm had the insight that what we fear most is freedom.[9] We have gone beyond the time of prophets and gurus. What we need to know, for the moment, has already been said. This is why Jung's work is so important. In it, he gives us the skills and tools to find the way to freedom, ourselves. To embrace freedom, freedom from being driven by the archetypes within and freedom from being dominated by the institutions and dominant values outside of ourselves. Freedom to consciously pursue our own unique path of individuation.

---

8   Marie-Louise von Franz in conversation with Fraser Boa. (1988). *The Way of the Dream*. Windrose Films Ltd., Toronto, Canada. Page192

9   This is the basic premise of his book *The Fear of Freedom* (1941) Farrar & Rinehart.

Appendix 1

Marie-Louise von Franz was born on January 4th, 1916 and died on February 16th, 1998. She was a Swiss Jungian psychologist and scholar. She worked with Carl Jung whom she met in 1933 when she was 17 years of age. She worked with him until his death in 1961. She founded the C.G. Jung Institute in Zurich. As a psychotherapist she is said to have interpreted over 65,000 dreams, primarily practicing in Kusnacht, Switzerland. She wrote over 20 volumes on Analytical Psychology.

James Hillman was born on April 12th, 1926 and died October 27th, 2011. He trained at the Jung Institute in Zurich and developed Archetypal psychology which involved an independent departure from Jung in some of his ideas. In 1970, Hillman became editor of *Spring Publications,* a publishing company that promoted Archetypal Psychology. Hillman was a prolific writer and international lecturer as well as a private practitioner.

Appendix 2

Paul Rebillot born May 19th, 1931 and died February 11th, 2010, was an actor, director and teacher in classical and contemporary drama. He brought this experience to his practice of Gestalt therapy. He created ritual structures in his workshops which enabled people to heal personal biography and wake up to the transpersonal dimensions of their lives. For twenty-five years he led groups at Esalen Institute in California and in centres throughout Europe. His first book, *The Call to Adventure: Bringing the Hero's Journey to Daily Life,* was published by Harper San Francisco, in 1993.

Psychodrama is a form of drama therapy which explores, through action, the problems of people. It is a group working method, in which each person becomes a therapeutic agent for others in the psychodrama group. Developed by Jacob L. Moreno, psychodrama has strong elements of theatre, often conducted on a stage with props.

Gestalt Therapy is a psychotherapy that focuses on experiences in the now, the therapist-client relationship, and personal responsibility. It was co-founded by Fritz Perls and Paul Goodman in the 1940's –1950's.

BIBLIOGRAPHY

A Course in Miracles. (2007) Foundation for Inner Peace, CA

Alexander, Christopher. (1979) *The Timeless Way of Building*, Oxford University Press, N.Y.

Borysenko, Joan. (1999) *A Woman's Journey to God, Finding the Feminine Path*. Riverhead Books, NY.

Bodo, Murray. (1972) *Francis, The Journey and The Dream*. St. Anthony Messenger Press, Cincinnati, Ohio, U.S.A.

Bolen, Jean Shinoda. (1985) *Goddesses in Everywoman, A New Psychology of Women*. Harper Colophon Books, N.Y.

Bolen, Jean Shinoda. (2003) *Crone's Don't Whine, Concentrated Wisdom for Juicy Women*. Conari Press, San Francisco, U.S.A.

Bradshaw, John. (1990) *Bradshaw on the Family*. Health Communications Inc., Florida, U.S.A. Revised ed.

Bronte, Emily. (First published 1847). *Wuthering Heights*. Penguin Books, Edinburgh. 1946

Campbell, Joseph. (1949/1968) *The Hero with a Thousand Faces*. Bollingen Series XVII, Princeton University Press, New Jersey, U.S.A.

Campbell, Joseph. (1988/2001) *The Power of Myth*. Broadway Books, Random House, N.Y.

Carlson, Kathie. (1989) *In Her Image, The Unhealed Daughter's Search for Her Mother*. Shambhala Publications, Inc., Boston, Massachusetts, U.S.A.

Cayley, David. (1992) *Ivan Illich In Conversation*. House of Anansi Press Limited, Ontario, Canada.

Chopra, Deepak. (2006) *The Seven Spiritual Laws of Success, A Practical Guide to the Fulfilment of Your Dreams*. Bantam Press, London.

Condren, Mary. (1989) *The Serpent and the Goddess, Women, Religion, and Power in Celtic Ireland*. Harper & Row, N.Y.

de Beauvoir, Simone. (1972) *The Second Sex*. Penguin Books, England.

de Chardin, Teilhard. (1965) *Hymn of the Universe.* Harper & Row, N.Y.

de Castillejo, Irene Claremont. (1973) *Knowing Woman, A Feminine Psychology.* Harper and Row, N.Y.

Dowling, Colette. (1982) *The Cinderella Complex, Women's Hidden Fear of Independence.* Fontana

Eliot, T.S. *Collected Poems.* (1925) Faber and Faber, London.

Estés, Clarissa Pinkola. (1992) *Women who Run with the Wolves, Contacting the Power of the Wild Woman.* Rider, U.K.

Fordham, Frieda. (1953) *An Introduction to Jung's Psychology.* Penguin, England.

Frazer, J.G. (First published by The Macmillan Press Ltd. 1922) *The Golden Bough, A Study in Magic and Religion.* Papermac, London. 1995.

Frankl, Viktor E. (First published 1946) *Man's Search for Meaning.* Beacon Press, Boston, M.A., U.S.A. (2006)

Fritz, Robert. (1943) *The Path of Least Resistance.* Stillpoint Publications Company, Massachusetts, U.S.A.

Friel, John and Friel, Linda D. (1991) *Adult Children; The Secrets of Dysfunctional Families.* Health Communications Inc., Florida, U.S.A.

Friel, John and Friel, Linda D. (1999) *The 7 Worst Things Parents Do.* Health Communications Inc. Florida, U.S.A.

Fromm Erich, (1941) *The Fear of Freedom*, Farrar & Rinehart.

Hillman, James. (1997) *The Soul's Code, In Search of Character and Calling.* Bantam Press, London.

Hillman, James. (1985) *Anima: An Anatomy of a Personified Notion.* Spring Publications., Dallas, Texas, U.S.A.

Illich, Ivan. (1982) *Gender.* Pantheon Books, N.Y.

Jaffe, Anela. (Edited by) (1979) *C.G. Jung, Work and Image.* (Bollingen Series XCVII: 2) Princeton University Press, New Jersey, U.S.A.

Jaxon-Bear, Eli. (2001) *The Enneagram of Liberation, From Fixation to*

Freedom. Leela Foundation, Oregon, U.S.A.

Jerusalem Bible. (1968) Eyre and Spottis Woode Ltd., London.

Johnson, Robert A. (First published in 1974 by Religious Publishing Co. P.A. U.S.A.) *He, Understanding Masculine Psychology.* Harper and Row. 1977.

Johnson, Robert A.. (First published in 1976 by Religious Publishing Co. P.A. U.S.A) *She, Understanding Feminine Psychology.* Harper and Row. 1977.

Jung, C.G. (1983) *The Zofingia Lectures.* (Bollingen Series XX). Published by Princeton University Press, New Jersey, U.S.A.

Jung, C.G. (1957) *Psychiatric Studies.* Volume 1 of *The Collected Works.* (Bollingen Series XX). Published by Princeton University Press, New Jersey, U.S.A.

Jung, C.G. (1973) *Experimental Researches, Including the Studies in Word Association.* Volume 2 of *The Collected Works.* (Bollingen Series XX). Published by Princeton University Press, New Jersey, U.S.A.

Jung, C.G. (1960) *The Psychogenesis of Mental Disease.* Volume 3 of *The Collected Works.* (Bollingen Series XX). Published by Princeton University Press, New Jersey, U.S.A.

Jung, C.G. (1961) *Freud and Psychoanalysis.* Volume 4 of *The Collected Works.* (Bollingen Series XX). Published by Princeton University Press, New Jersey, U.S.A.

Jung, C.G. (1956) *Symbols of Transformation.* Volume 5 of *The Collected Works.* (Bollingen Series XX). Published by Princeton University Press, New Jersey, U.S.A.

Jung, C.G. (1971) *Psychological Types.* Volume 6 of *The Collected Works.* (Bollingen Series XX). Published by Princeton University Press, New Jersey, U.S.A.

Jung, C.G. (1953) *Two Essays on Analytical Psychology.* Volume 7 of *The Collected Works.* (Bollingen Series XX). Published by Princeton University Press, New Jersey, U.S.A.

Jung, C.G. (1960) *The Structure and Dynamics of the Psyche, Including*

'*Synchronicity: An Acausal connecting Principle*'. Volume 7 of *The Collected Works*. (Bollingen Series XX). Published by Princeton University Press, New Jersey, U.S.A.

Jung, C.G. (1959) *The Archetypes and The Collective Unconscious*. Volume 9(i) of *The Collected Works*. (Bollingen Series XX). Published by Princeton University Press, New Jersey, U.S.A.

Jung, C.G. (1959) *Aion*. Volume 9(ii) of *The Collected Works*. (Bollingen Series XX). Published by Princeton University Press, New Jersey, U.S.A.

Jung, C.G. (1964) *Civilisation in Transition, Including 'Flying Saucers' and 'The Undiscovered Self'*. Volume 10 of *The Collected Works*. (Bollingen Series XX). Published by Princeton University Press, New Jersey, U.S.A.

Jung, C.G. (1958) *Psychology and Religion: West and East*. Volume 11 of *The Collected Works*. (Bollingen Series XX). Published by Princeton University Press, New Jersey, U.S.A.

Jung, C.G. (1953) *Psychology and Alchemy*. Volume 12 of *The Collected Works*. (Bollingen Series XX). Published by Princeton University Press, New Jersey, U.S.A.

Jung, C.G. (1967) *Alchemical Studies*. Volume 13 of *The Collected Works*. (Bollingen Series XX). Published by Princeton University Press, New Jersey, U.S.A.

Jung, C.G. (1963) *Mysterium Coniunctionis*. Volume 14 of *The Collected Works*. (Bollingen Series XX). Published by Princeton University Press, New Jersey, U.S.A.

Jung, C.G. (1954) *The Practice of Psychotherapy*. Volume 16 of *The Collected Works*. (Bollingen Series XX). Published by Princeton University Press, New Jersey, U.S.A.

Jung, C.G. (1954) *The Development of Personality, Papers on Child Psychology, Education, and Related Subjects*. Volume 17 of *The Collected Works*. (Bollingen Series XX). Published by Princeton University Press, New Jersey, U.S.A.

Jung, C.G. (1950) *The Symbolic Life*. Volume 18 of *The Collected Works*. (Bollingen Series XX). Published by Princeton University Press, New Jersey, U.S.A.

C.G. Jung. (1984) *Dream Analysis.* Routledge and Kegan Paul, London.

C.G. Jung. (First published 1963 by Collins and Routledge & Kegan Paul, England.) *Memories, Dreams, Reflections.* Flamingo, Fontana Paperbacks, 1983.

C.G. Jung. (First published 1964 by Aldus Books Ltd. London) (Edited and conceived by Jung). *Man and His Symbols.* Picador: Pan Books, London.

C.G. Jung. (1972) (Edited by G. Adler and A. Jaffe). *C.G. Jung Letters.* (Bollingen Series XCV). 2 Vols. Princeton: Princeton University Press, New Jersey, U.S.A.

C.G. Jung. (1976) *The Visions Seminars: Notes of the Seminary, 1930-1934.* Spring Publications, Zurich.

Jung, Emma. (1985) *Animus and Anima.* Spring Publications. Dallas, Texas.

Kavanagh, Patrick. *Collected Poems.* 2005. Penguin Books.

Monk Kidd, Sue. (1996) *The Dance of the Dissident Daughter.* HarperCollins, N.Y.

Molloy, Dara. (2009) *The Globalisation of God, Celtic Christianity's Nemesis.* Aisling Publications.

McLynn, Frank. (1996) *Carl Gustav Jung, A Biography.* St. Martin's Press, N.Y.

McNeely, Deldon Anne. (1991) *Animus Aeternus, Exploring the Inner Masculine.* Inner City Books, Toronto, Canada.

Neumann, E. (1971) *The Origins and History of Consciousness.* (Bollingen Series XLII). Princeton: Princeton University Press, New Jersey, U.S.A.

O'Connor, Peter. (1985) *Understanding Jung, Understanding Yourself.* Paulist Press, New Jersey, U.S.A.

O'Faolain, Eileen. (First published 1954 by Oxford university Press,

London) *Irish Sagas and Folk Tales*. Poolbeg Press Ltd. Dublin, Ireland. 1986/89

O'hOgain, Daithi. (1991) *Myth and Legend and Romance: An Encyclopaedia of the Irish Folk Tradition*. Prentice Hall Press, N.Y.

Palmer, Helen. (1988) *The Enneagram, The Definitive Guide to the Ancient System for Understanding Yourself and the Others in Your Life*. Harper & Row, N.Y.

Reilly, Patricia Lynn, (1995) *A God Who Looks Like Me, Discovering a Woman-Affirming Spirituality*. Ballantine Books, Random House, N.Y.

Riso, Don Richard. (1987) *Personality Types, Using the Enneagram for Self-Discovery*. Houghton Mifflin Company, Boston, Massachusetts, U.S.A.

Roberts, Richard. (1983) *Tales for Jung Folk, Original Fairytales for Persons of All Ages Dramatizing C.G. Jung's Archetypes of the Collective Unconscious*. Vernal Equinom Press, C.A.

Rolleston, T.W. (1986) *Myths and Legends of the Celtic Race*. Constable and Company Ltd., London.

Rowling, J.K. (1997 ff.) *The Harry Potter Series, Books 1 - 6*. Bloomsbury, London. U.S.A.

Rubenfeld, Jed. (2006) *The Interpretation of Murder*. Headline Review, Great Britain.

Schierse Leonard, Linda. (1982) *The Wounded Woman*. Shambhala Publications, Boston, Massachusetts, U.S.A.

Scott, Michael. (1992) *Irish Myths and Legends*. Warner Books, London.

Scott, Michael, (Vols. I & II, 1983, Vol. III, 1984) *Irish Folk & Fairy Tales Omnibus*. Warner Books, London.

Schneider, Pat. (1997) *Wake Up Laughing, A Spiritual Autobiography*. Negative Capability Press, Alabama, U.S.A.

Shaw, George Bernard. (First Published 1916) *Pygmalion: A Romance in Five Acts*. Penguin Books Ltd., London. (2000)

Shelly, Mary. (First published 1818) *Frankenstein*. Penguin Popular

Classics, London.

Smyth, Daragh. (1988) *A Guide to Irish Mythology.* Irish Academic Press, Dublin, Ireland.

Spong, John Shelby. (1999) *Why Christianity Must Change or Die, A Bishop Speaks to Believers in Exile.* HarperCollins, N.Y.

Squire, Charles. (2001) *Celtic Myths and Legends.* Parragon, England.

Stephens, James. (First published 1924) *Irish Fairy Tales.* Gill & Macmillan, Dublin, Ireland. 1995.

Stevenson, Robert Louis. (First Published 1886) *Dr. Jekyll and Mr. Hyde.* Penguin Books, London. 1994.

Steward, R.J. (1990) *Celtic Gods Celtic Goddesses.* Blandford, An imprint of Cassell Villiers House, London.

Stoker, Bram. (First published 1897 by Constable, England) *Dracula.* Wordsworth Editions Limited, Hertfordshire, England.

J.R.R. Tolkien. (1968/1978/1983) *The Lord of the Rings.* Unwin Hyman Ltd., London.

von Franz, Marie Louise. (1974) *Shadow and Evil in Fairytales.* Spring Publications Inc., Dallas, Texas.

von Franz, Marie Louise and James Hillman. (1986) *Lectures on Jung's Typology.* A series of lectures presented at the C.G. Jung Institute, Zurich, in the Winter Semester, January, 1961. Spring Publications, Putnam, CT. USA.

von Franz, Marie Louise. (1988) *The Way of the Dream, Dr.Marie-Louise in conversation with Fraser Boa.* Windrose Films Ltd., Toronto, Canada.

Whitmont, Edward C. (1982) *Return of the Goddess.* Routledge and Kegan Paul plc., London.

Wilde, Oscar. (2006) *A Selection of Stories and Plays.* Abbeydale Press, Leicestershire, England.

Woodman, Marion. (1982) *Addiction to Perfection.* Inner City Books, Toronto, Canada.

Marion Woodman. (1985) *The Pregnant Virgin.* Inner City Books,

Toronto, Canada.

Marion Woodman. (1990) *The Ravaged Bridegroom.* Inner City Books, Toronto, Canada.

Marion Woodman. (1993) *Leaving My Father's House.* Rider, London.

Zweig, Connie and Abrams, Jeremiah (editors). (1991) *Meeting the Shadow, The Hidden Power of the Dark Side of Human Nature.* A Jeremy P.Tarchen/Putnam Book: G.P. Putnam's Sons, N.Y.

INDEX

166, 187, 194, 198, 207, 211,
226, 228-230, 234, 235, 238,
240, 245, 248, 255, 256, 257,
263, 264, 266, 273, 285, 286,
288-290, 305, 318, 319, 333,
334, 337, 338, 347
Cú Chulainn 36, 310

D

daimon 335
Deldon Anne McNeely 264, 273,
274, 277, 283, 284
Dionysius 236
distorted type 135, 136
Divine 19, 38, 43, 237, 238, 239, 285
dominant function 118, **133-138**,
140-142, 144-148, 150-152,
155, 158, 159, 161, 169, 170,
175, 177, 185, 188, 190, 195,
260, 319
dragon 18, 110, 314, 316
dreams 5, 6, 27, 56, **74, 76, 77, 78, 80,
84-92, 94, 95, 98-100, 106, 107-
116**, 117, 146, 147, 198, 200,
201, 202, 211, 219, 231, 234,
246, 249, 253, 272, 279, 292,
294, 295, 296, 303, 316, 321,
325, 342, 348, 345

E

Edward C. Whitmont 208, 247, 265
ego 14, 17, 22, 23, 24, 29, 31, 33, 34,
35, 36, 38, 39, 94, 113, 126, 128,
129, 146, 147, 150, 152, 173,
199, 200, 202, 206-208, 211,
222, 225, 226, 245, 253, 254,
266, 268, 270, 271, 273, 276,
282, 283, 285, 287, 288, 290,
299, 302, 303, 312, 337, 342,
347
Emma Jung 181, 255, 256, 257, 263,
267, 285, 286, 288-290, 293
emotion 13, 20, 59, 93, 116, 117, 132,
140-142, 161, 166, 167, 190,

201, 220, 227, 305
enantiodromia 50, 122, 303
energy 4, 6, 10-13, 16, 17, 22, 24,
29-34, 40, 42, 45, 47, 48, 50-55,
60, 61, 62, 66, 67, 69, 70, 72, 74,
77-81, 87, 92-94, 98, 100, 107,
112, 116, 126, 127, 130, 133,
134, 141, 150, 156, 158, 175,
177, 199, 207, 208, 211, 220,
232-234, 236, 237, 243, 248,
251, 263, 271, 273, 275, 278,
283, 286, 290-293, 299, 311,
314, 331, 342, 346, 348
Eve 54, 217, 312
evil 7, 60, 142, **205**, 210, 222, 223, 225,
228, 230, **234-237, 238, 240 -
245**, 259, 281
extravert 6, 118, 119, 120, 121, **122-
126**, 128, 130, 131, 135, 138,
144, 146, **155-163**, 165, **167-
172**, 174, 175, **177-181**, 183,
185-191, 193, 299

F

fairy tales 181, 222, 231, 241, 305
Fand 36, 310, 336
father 10, 20, 21, 28, 41, 63, 64, 66,
68, 69, 72, 73, 81 - 83, 92, 93,
97, 102, 103-106, 136, 219, 236,
251, **266-279, 281-284**, 286,
293, 326, 327
Faust 221, 312
feeling 6, 13, 24, 30, 33, 50, 68, 76,
80, 87, 94, 96, 99, 106, 115, 118,
125, 127, 128, 131-134, 136,
138, 140-142, 144-147, 149,
152, 155, 156, 158-161, **164-
170, 172-174**, 176, 179, 181,
182, 187, 188, 191, 213, 218,
230, 240, 251, 256-258, 260,
261, 267, 270, 281, 283, 288,
289, 308, 310, 313, 319, 321,
329, 343
Francis of Assisi 35

Also published by Aisling Publications

THE GLOBALISATION OF GOD
CELTIC CHRISTIANITY'S NEMESIS
by Dara Molloy

LEGENDS IN THE LANDSCAPE
Pocket Guide to Árainn, Inis Mór, Aran Islands
(with translations into French, German, Italian and Spanish)
by Dara Ó Maoildhia

www.aislingpublications.com
www.aislingarann.ie
aismag@iol.ie

Aisling Publications